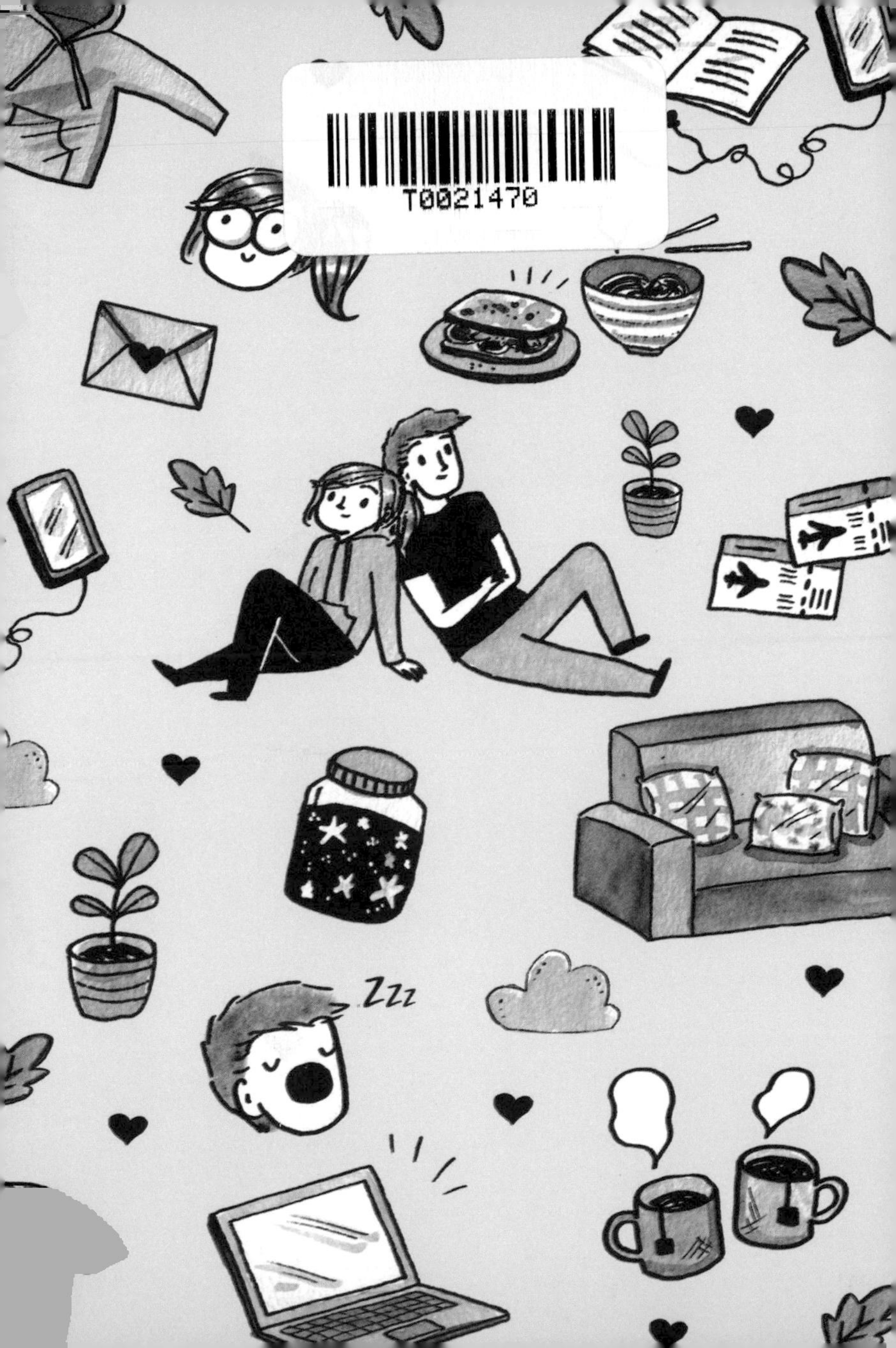
Zzz

Happily Ever After

& Everything In Between

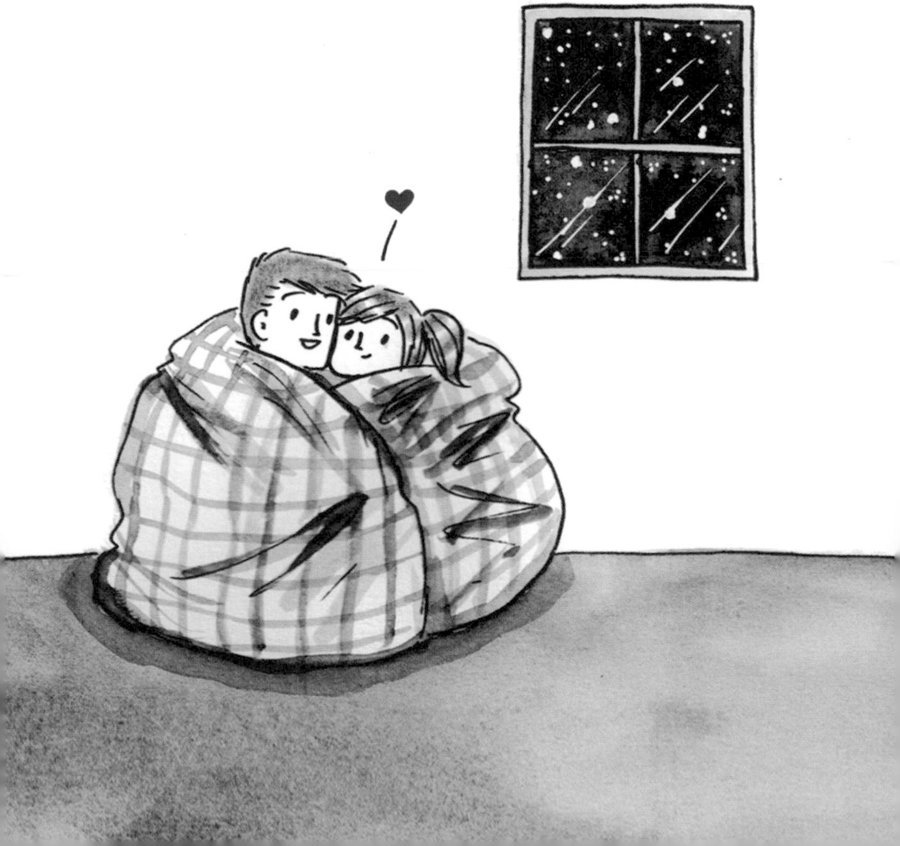

Also by Debbie Tung

Quiet Girl in a Noisy World
Book Love

Happily Ever After

& Everything In Between

Debbie Tung

Andrews McMeel
PUBLISHING®

To my husband, Jason, for your love, support, and patience, and for the many perfect cups of tea you made me.

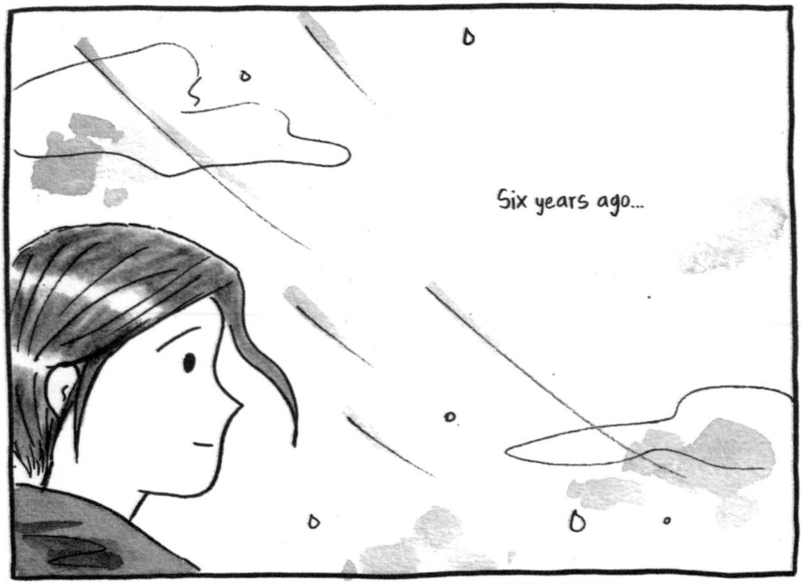
Six years ago...

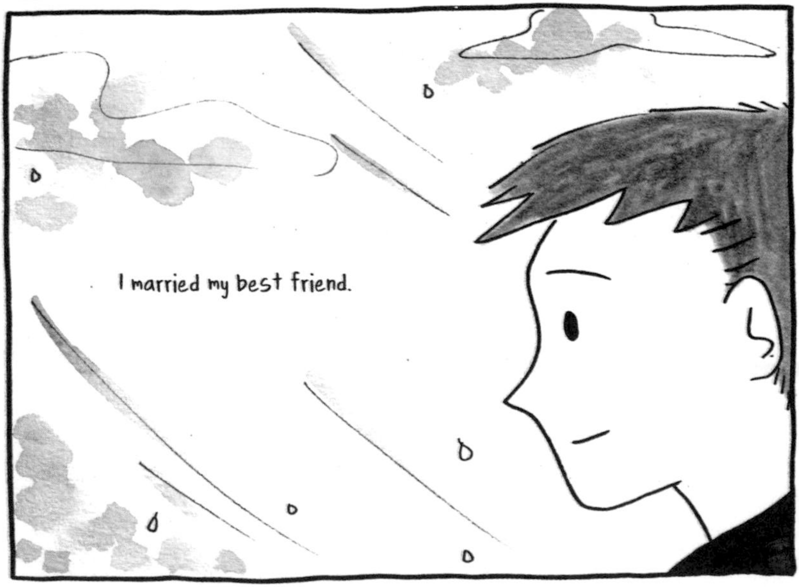
I married my best friend.

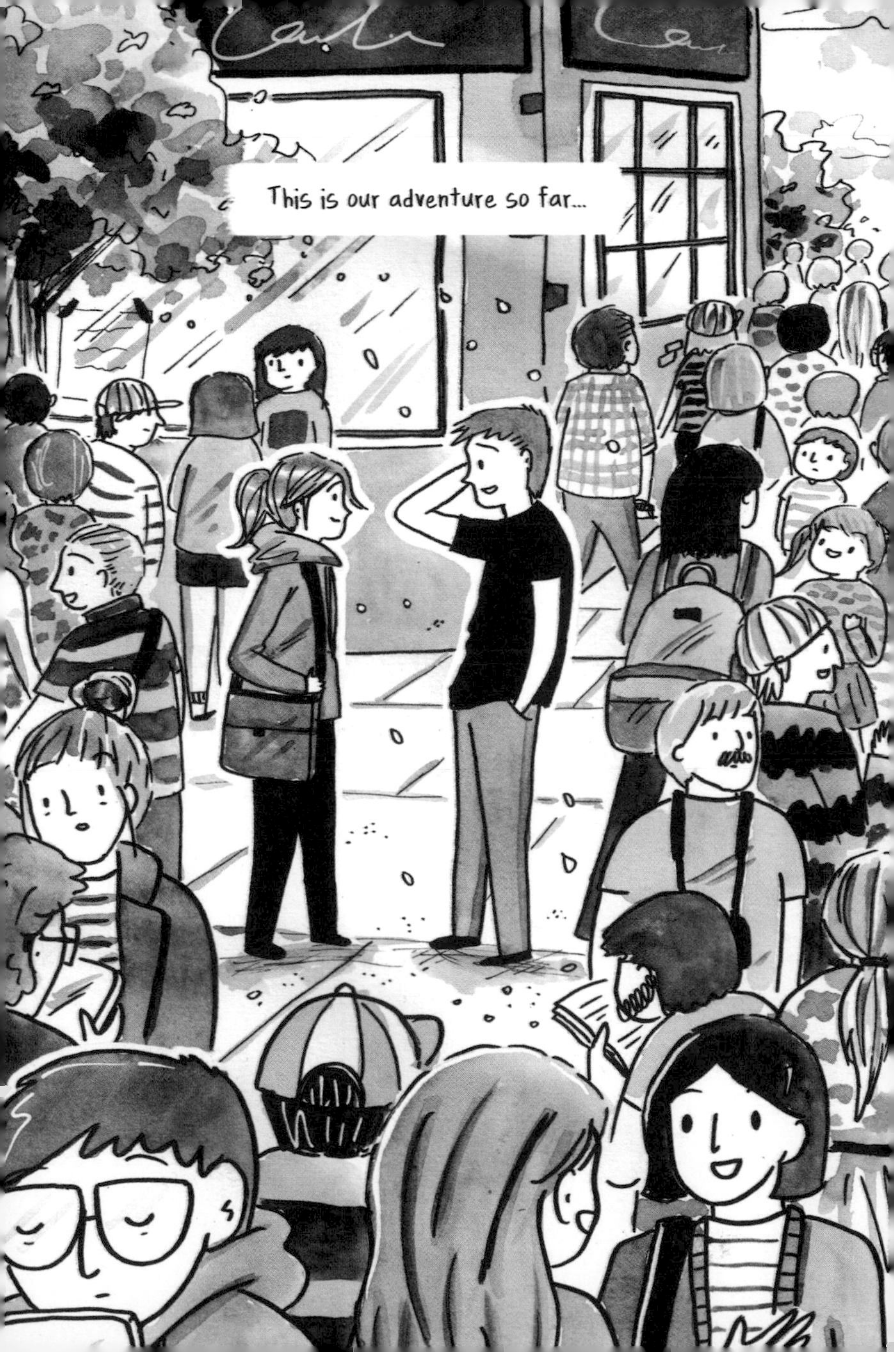
This is our adventure so far...

Being a couple

In public

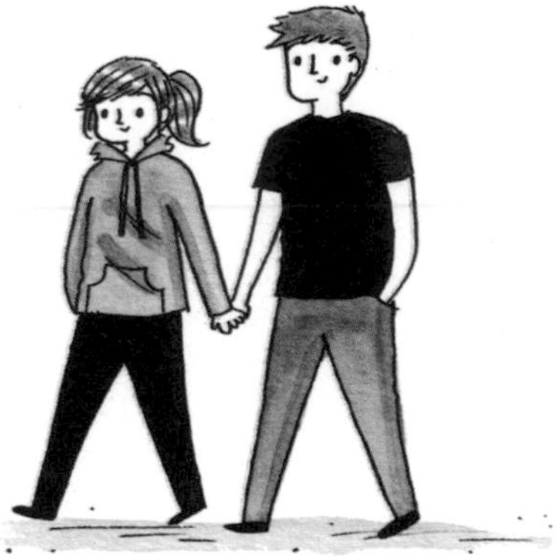

At home

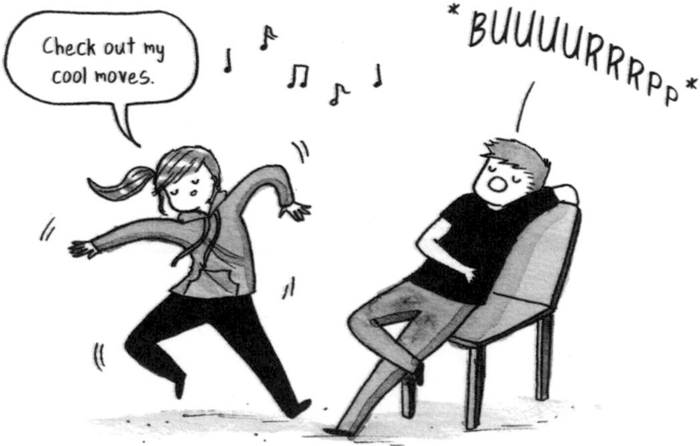
Check out my cool moves.
BUUUURRRRPP

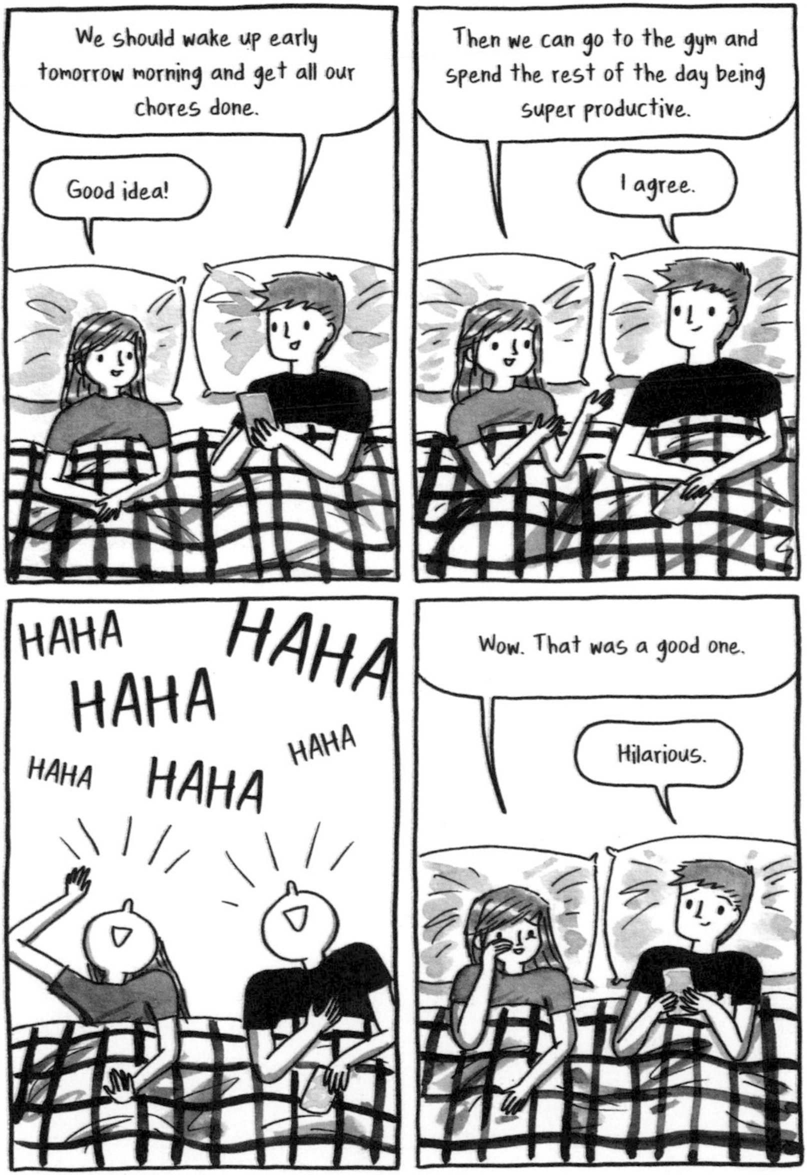
We should wake up early tomorrow morning and get all our chores done.
Good idea!
Then we can go to the gym and spend the rest of the day being super productive.
I agree.
HAHA
HAHA
HAHA
HAHA
HAHA
HAHA
Wow. That was a good one.
Hilarious.

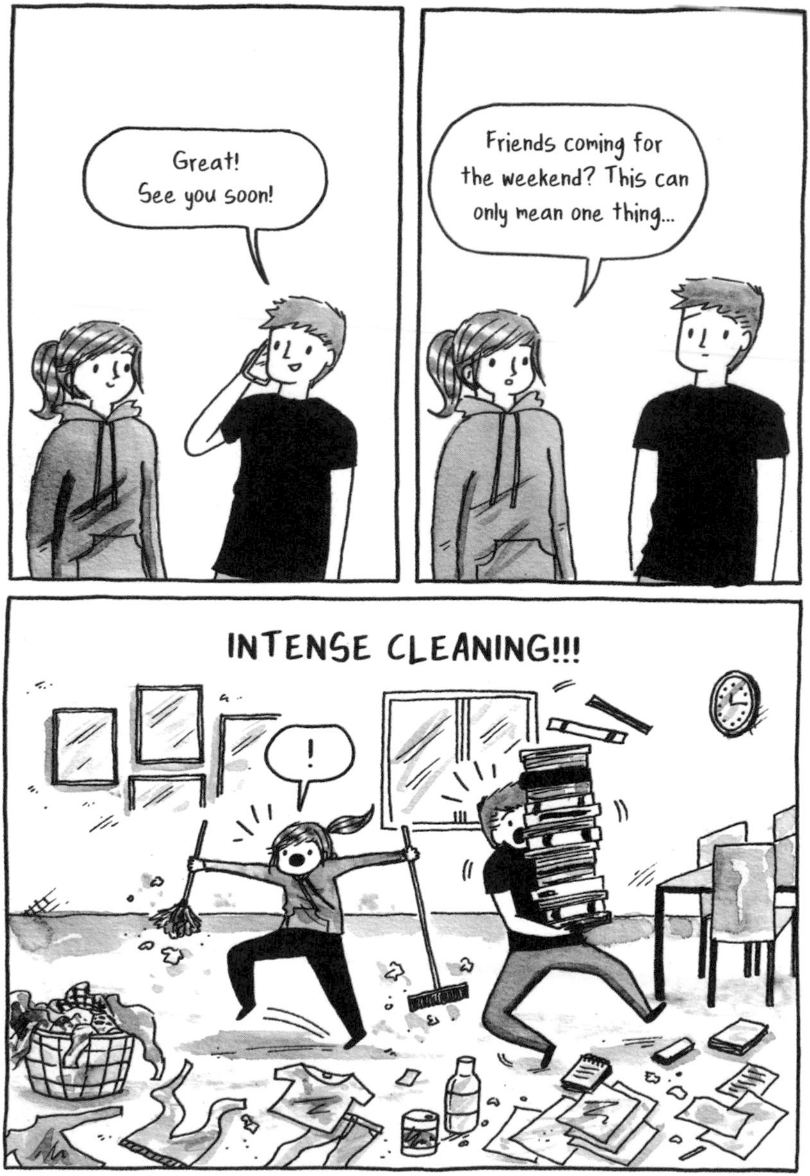
Great!
See you soon!
Friends coming for the weekend? This can only mean one thing...
INTENSE CLEANING!!!
!

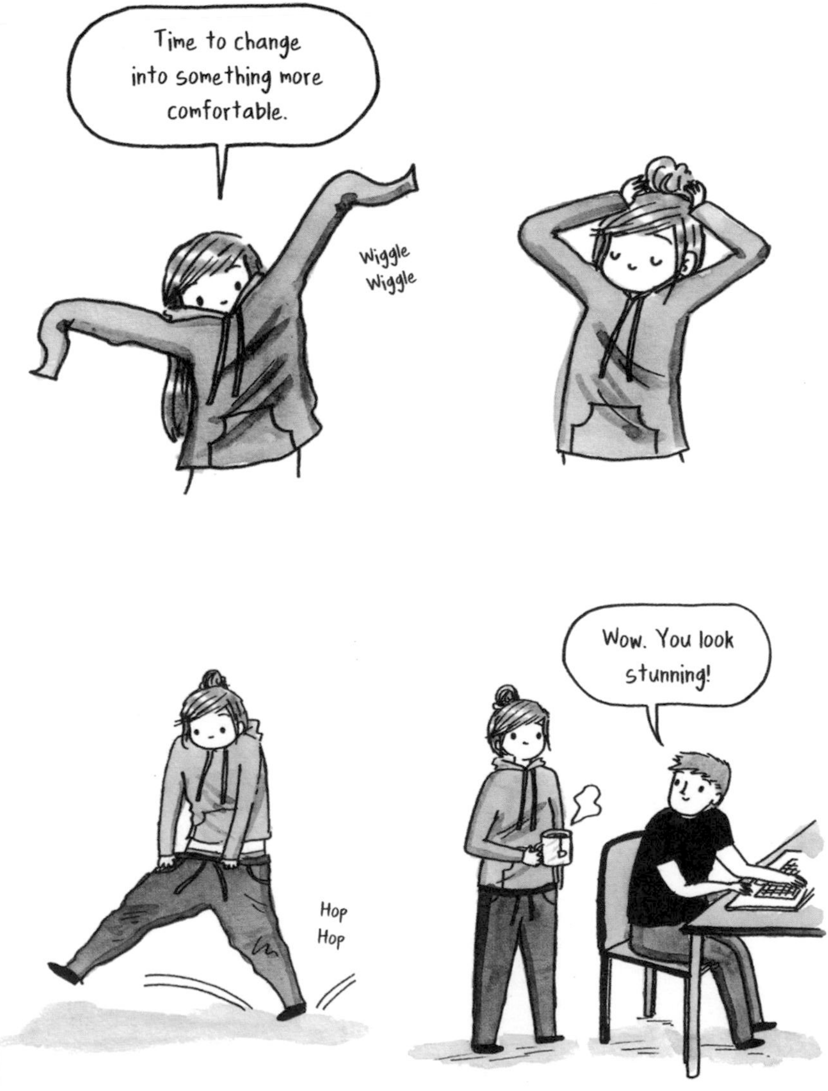
Time to change into something more comfortable.
Wiggle Wiggle
Hop Hop
Wow. You look stunning!

I love it when we have time to do our own things...

...together.

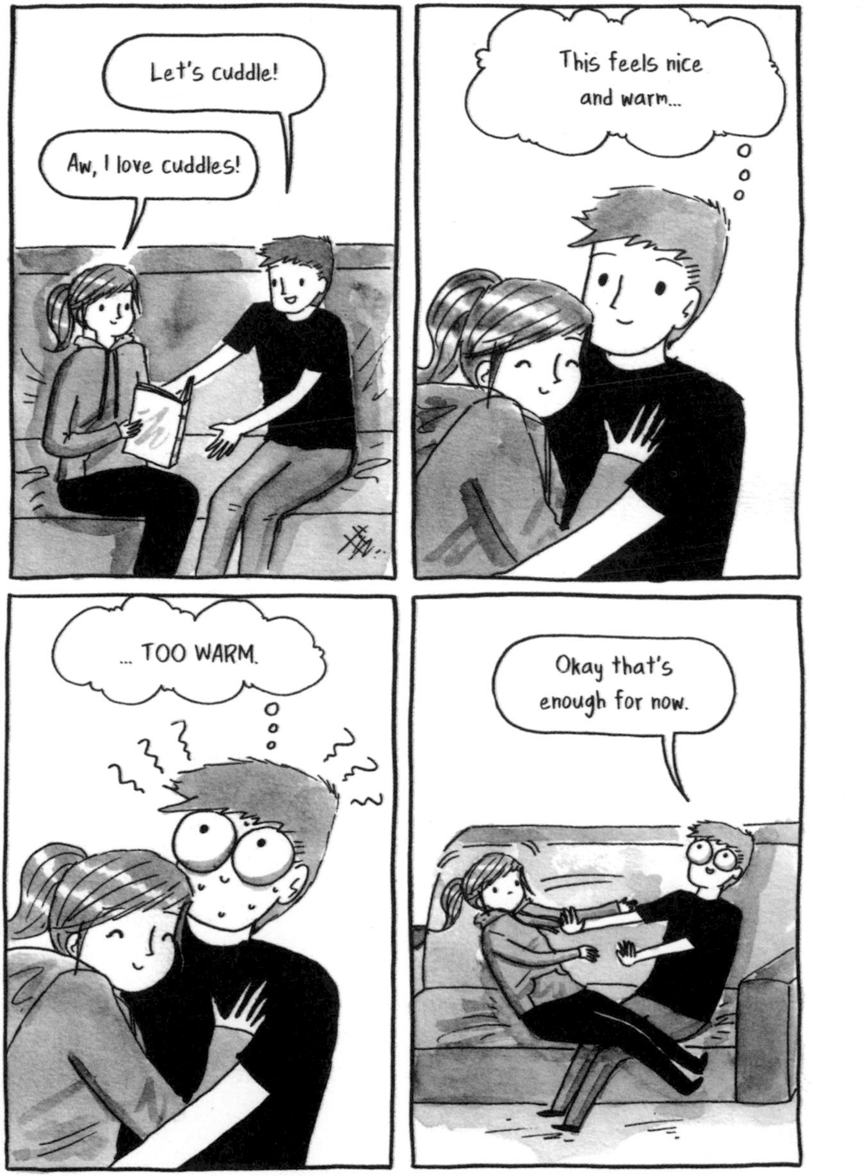
Let's cuddle!
Aw, I love cuddles!
This feels nice and warm...
... TOO WARM.
Okay that's enough for now.

Newlyweds

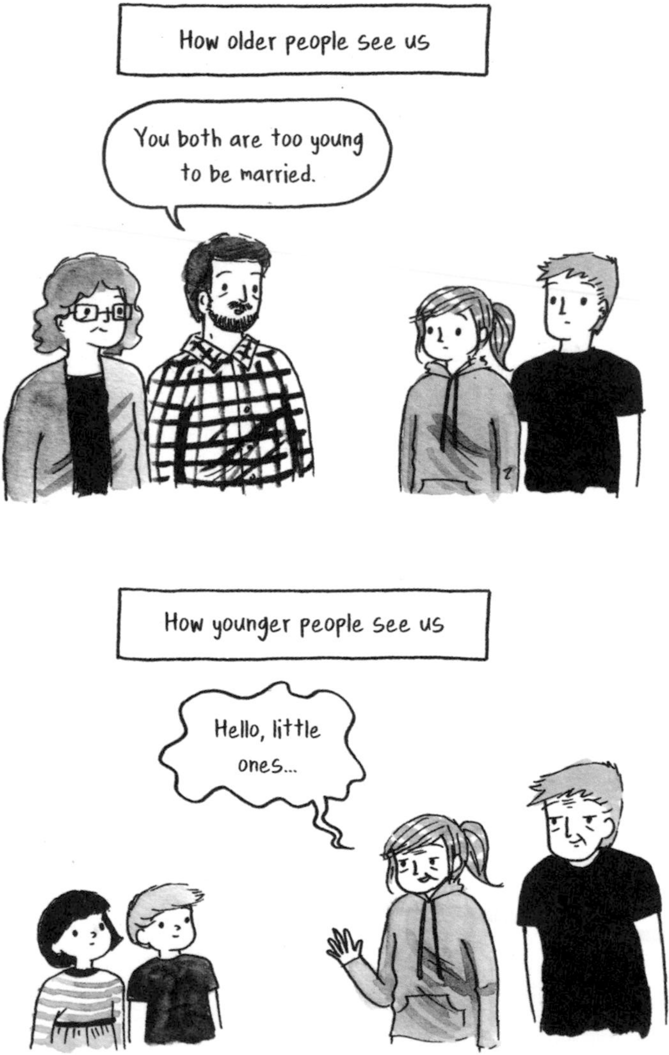
How older people see us
You both are too young to be married.
How younger people see us
Hello, little ones...

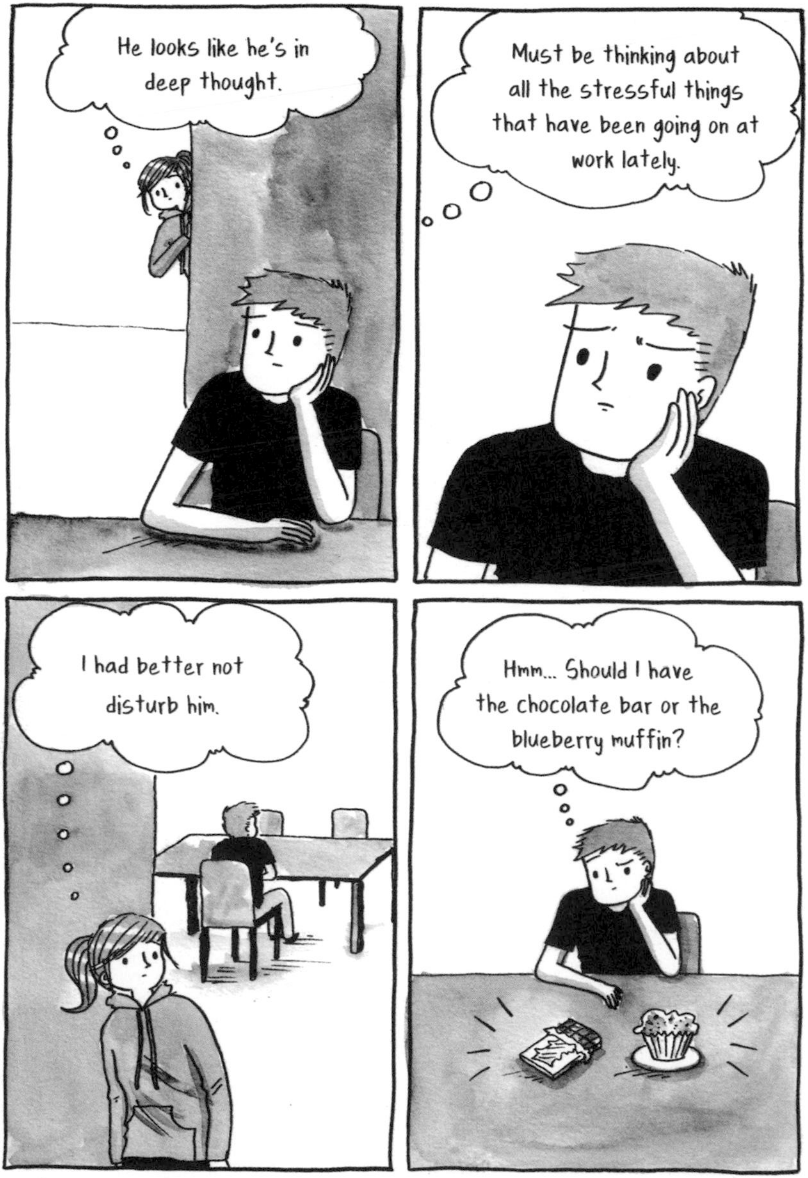
He looks like he's in deep thought.
Must be thinking about all the stressful things that have been going on at work lately.
I had better not disturb him.
Hmm... Should I have the chocolate bar or the blueberry muffin?

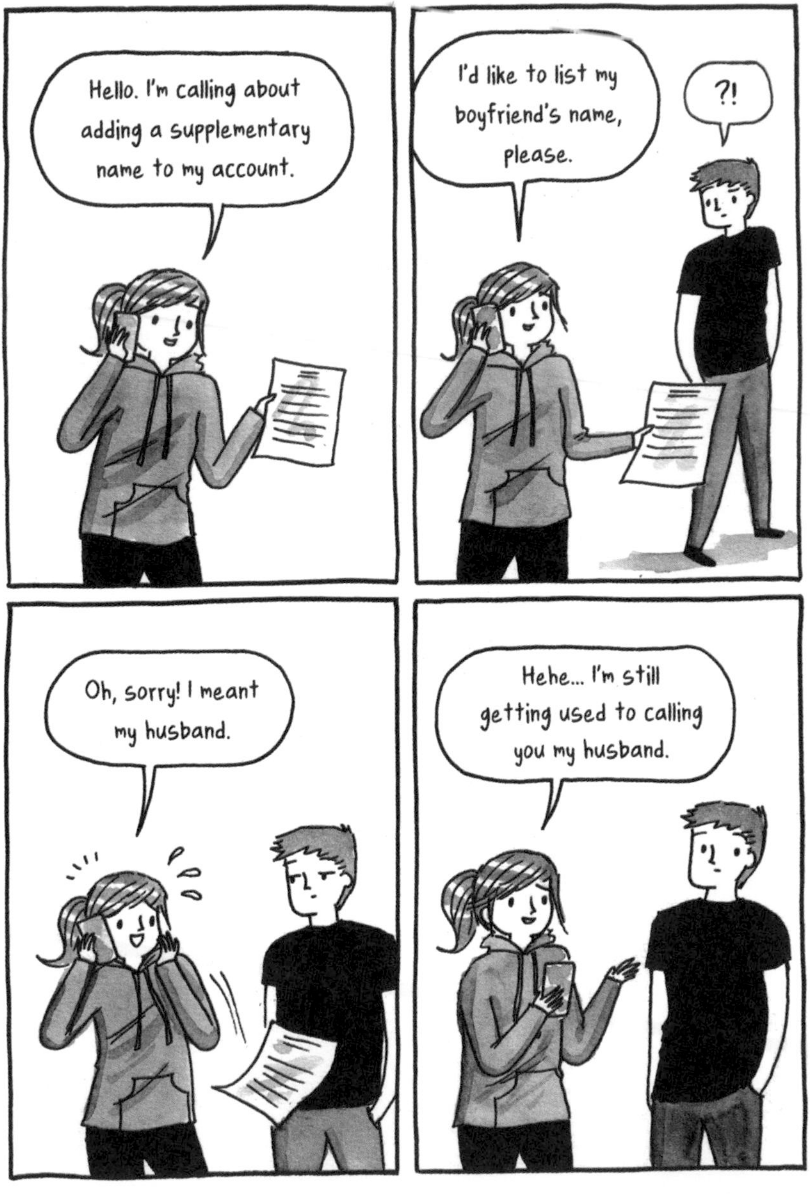
Hello. I'm calling about adding a supplementary name to my account.
I'd like to list my boyfriend's name, please.
?!
Oh, sorry! I meant my husband.
Hehe... I'm still getting used to calling you my husband.

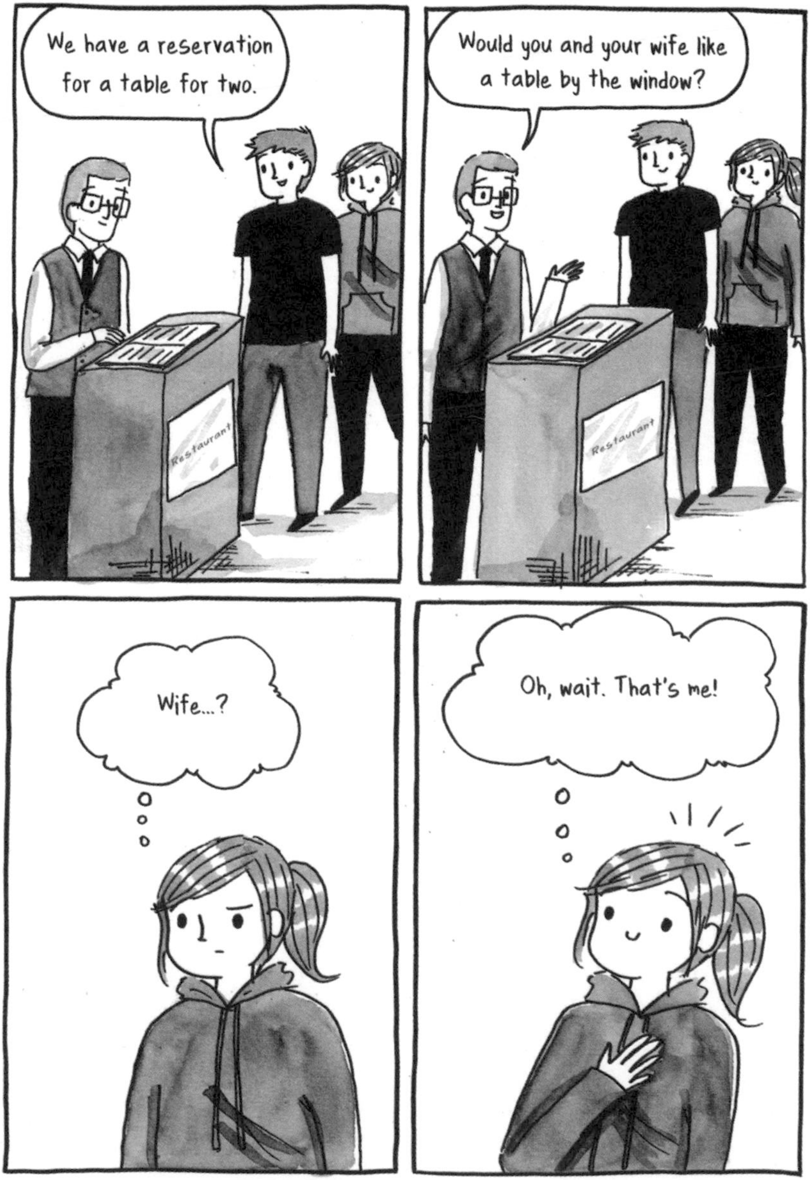
We have a reservation for a table for two.
Restaurant
Would you and your wife like a table by the window?
Restaurant
Wife...?
Oh, wait. That's me!

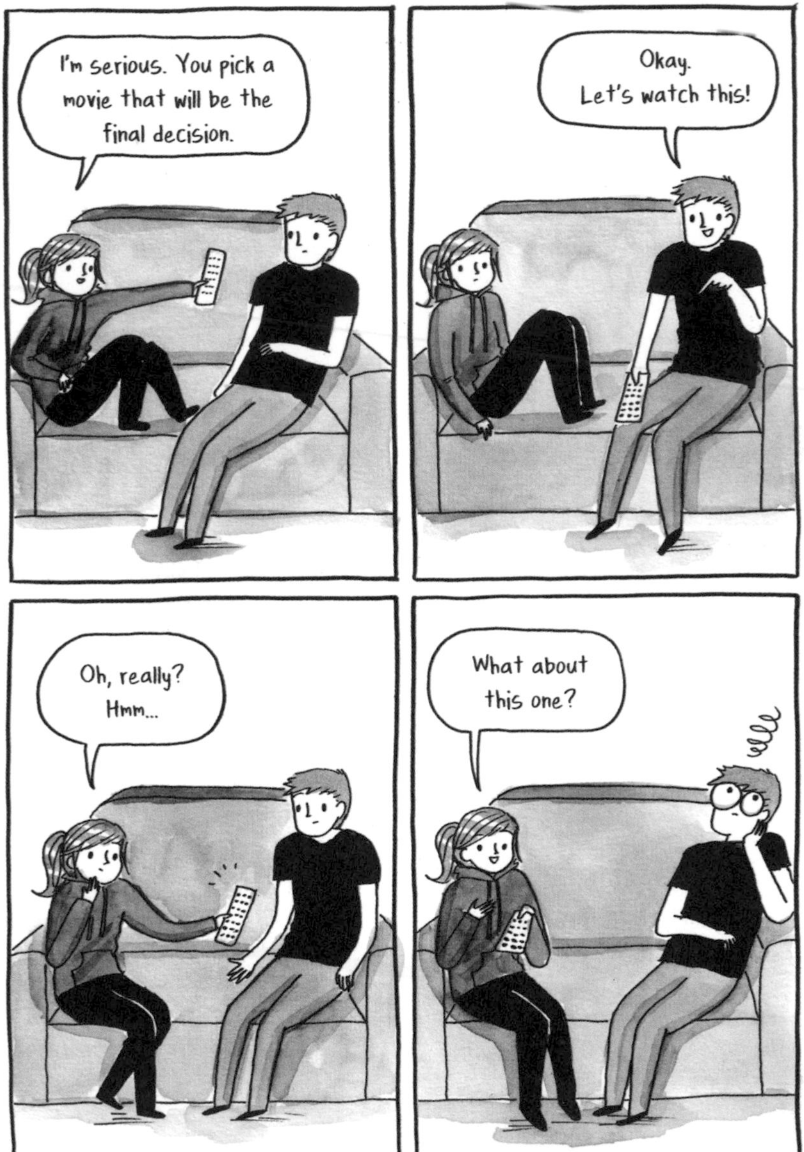
I'm serious. You pick a movie that will be the final decision.
Okay. Let's watch this!
Oh, really? Hmm...
What about this one?

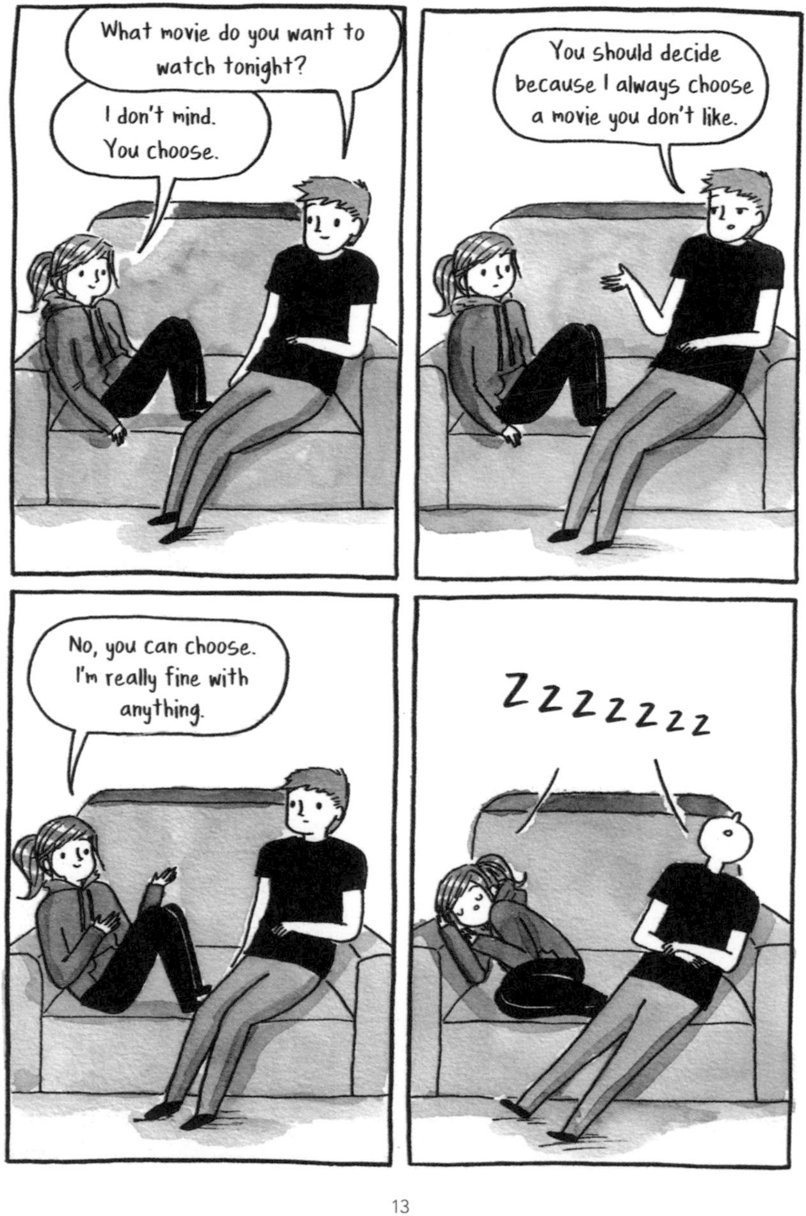
What movie do you want to watch tonight?
I don't mind. You choose.
You should decide because I always choose a movie you don't like.
No, you can choose. I'm really fine with anything.
ZZZZZZZ

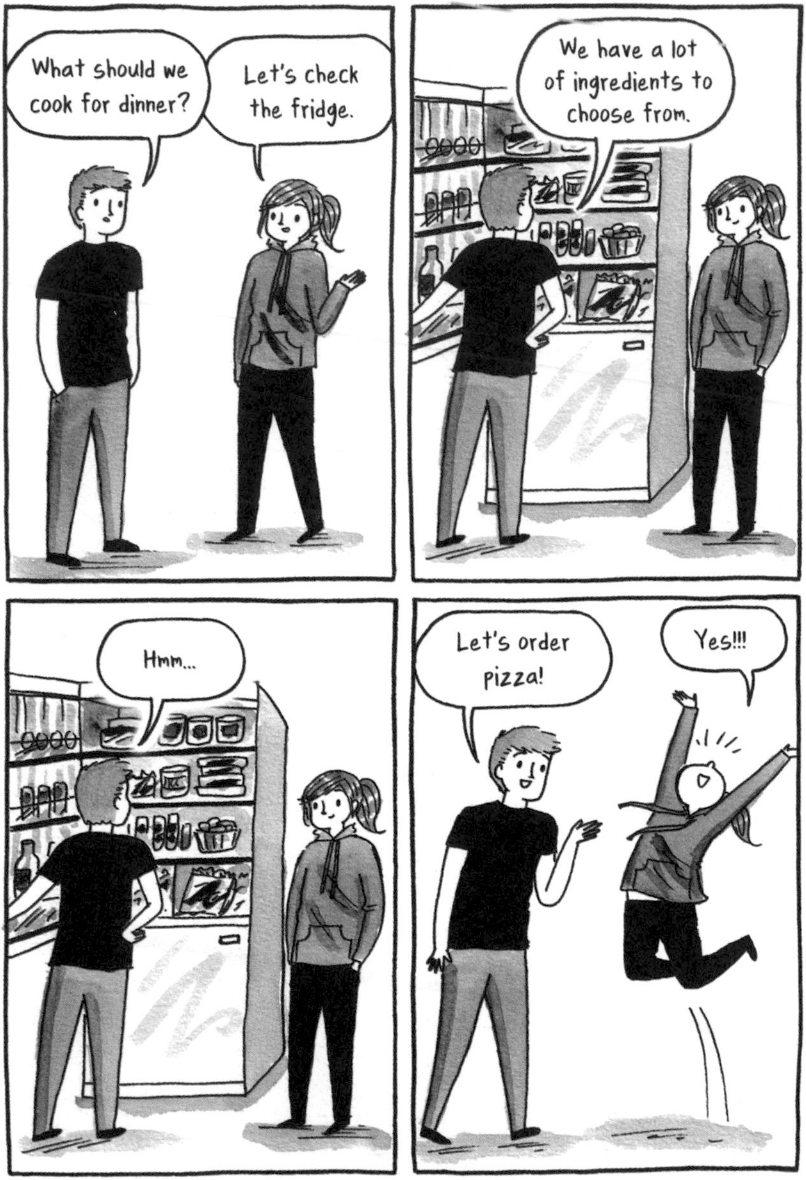
What should we cook for dinner?
Let's check the fridge.
We have a lot of ingredients to choose from.
Hmm...
Let's order pizza!
Yes!!!

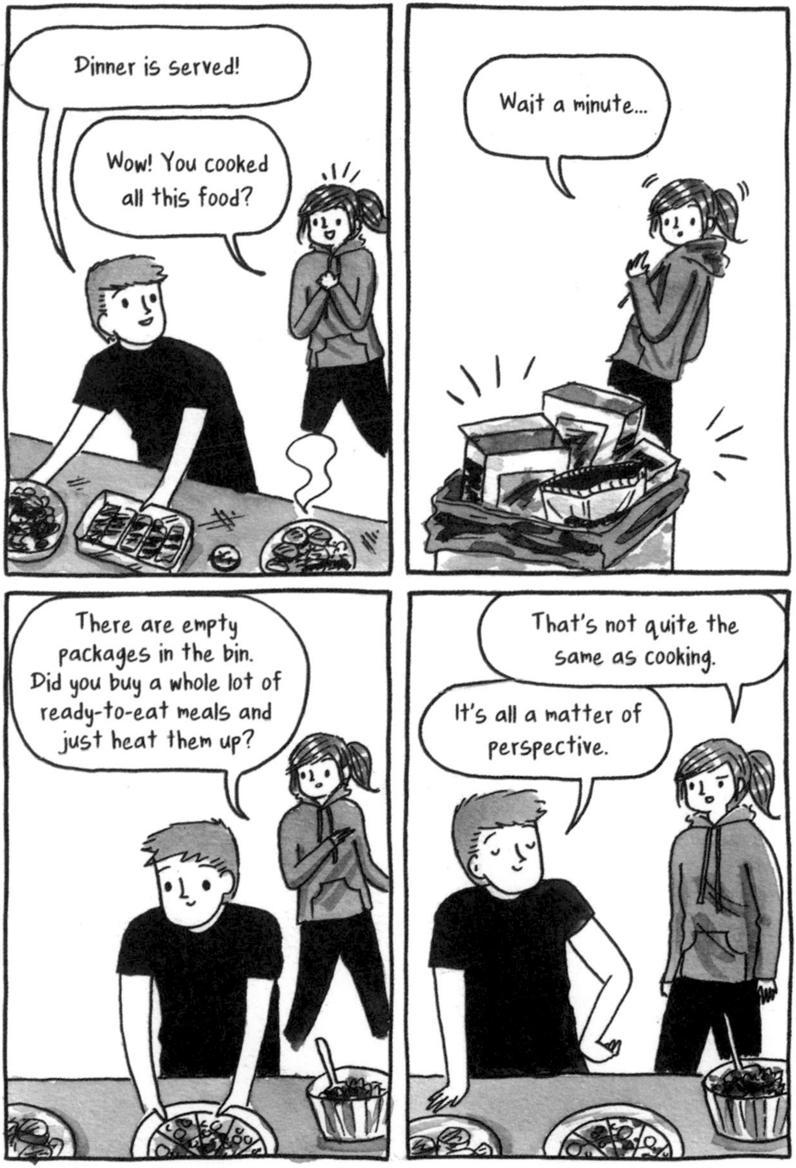
Dinner is served!
Wow! You cooked all this food?
Wait a minute...
There are empty packages in the bin. Did you buy a whole lot of ready-to-eat meals and just heat them up?
It's all a matter of perspective.
That's not quite the same as cooking.

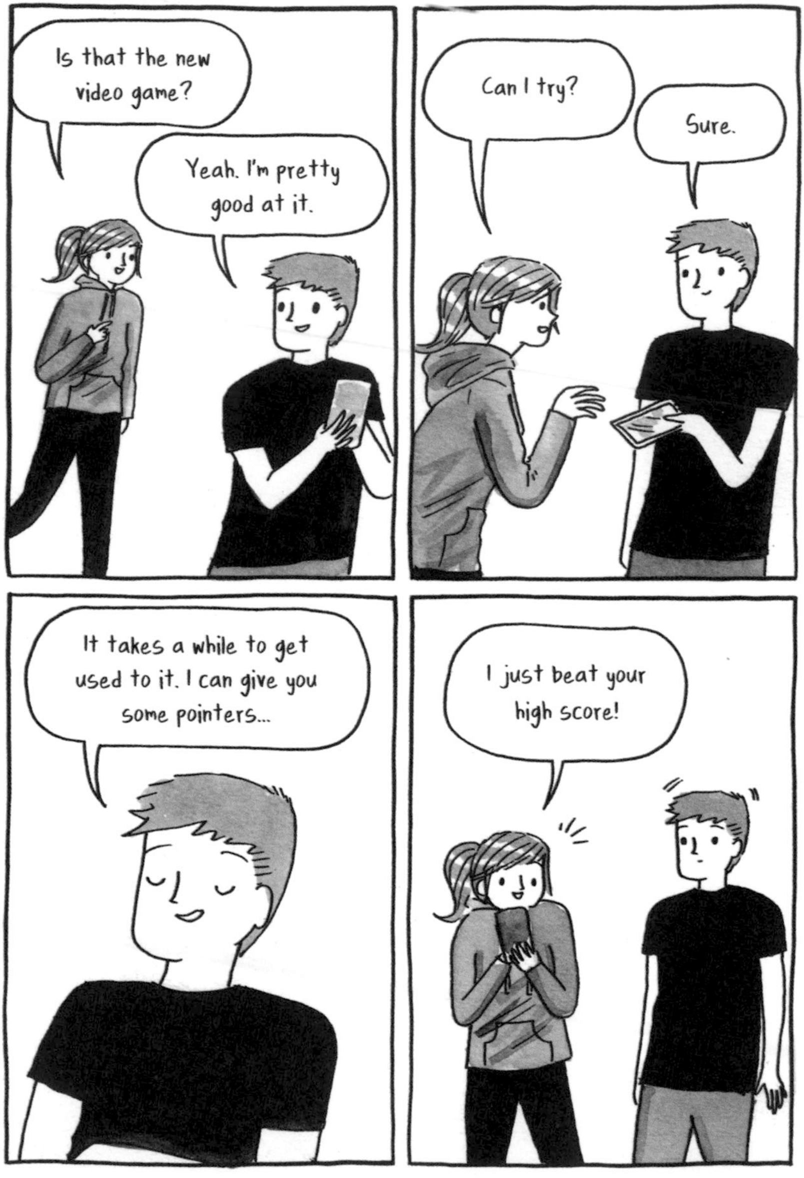
Is that the new video game?
Yeah. I'm pretty good at it.
Can I try?
Sure.
It takes a while to get used to it. I can give you some pointers...
I just beat your high score!

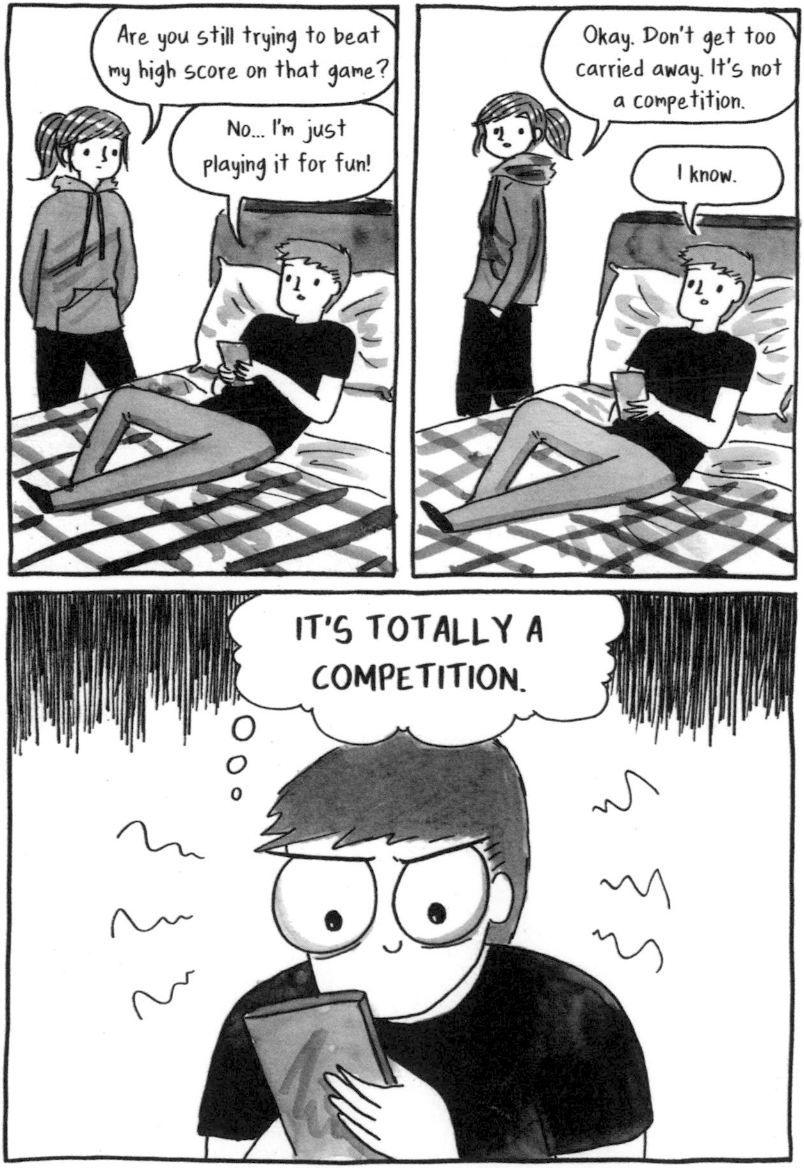
Are you still trying to beat my high score on that game?
No... I'm just playing it for fun!
Okay. Don't get too carried away. It's not a competition.
I know.
IT'S TOTALLY A COMPETITION.

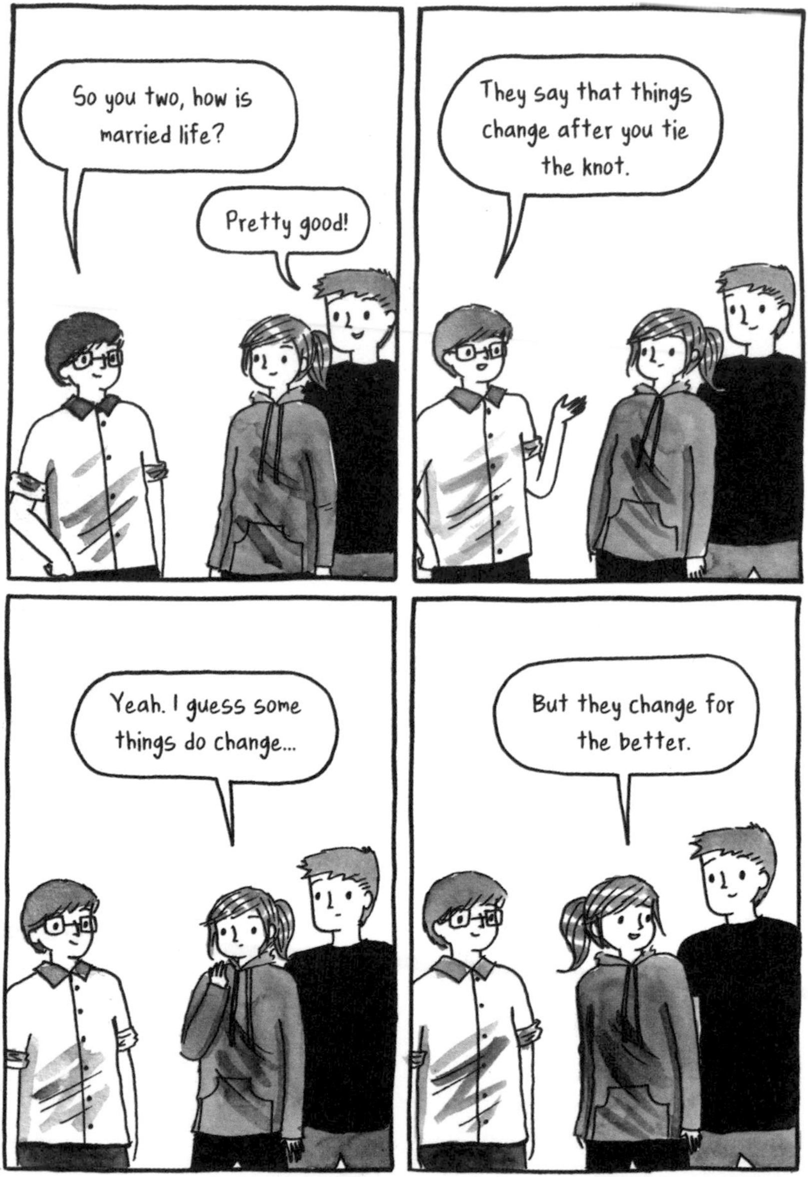
So you two, how is married life?
Pretty good!
They say that things change after you tie the knot.
Yeah. I guess some things do change...
But they change for the better.

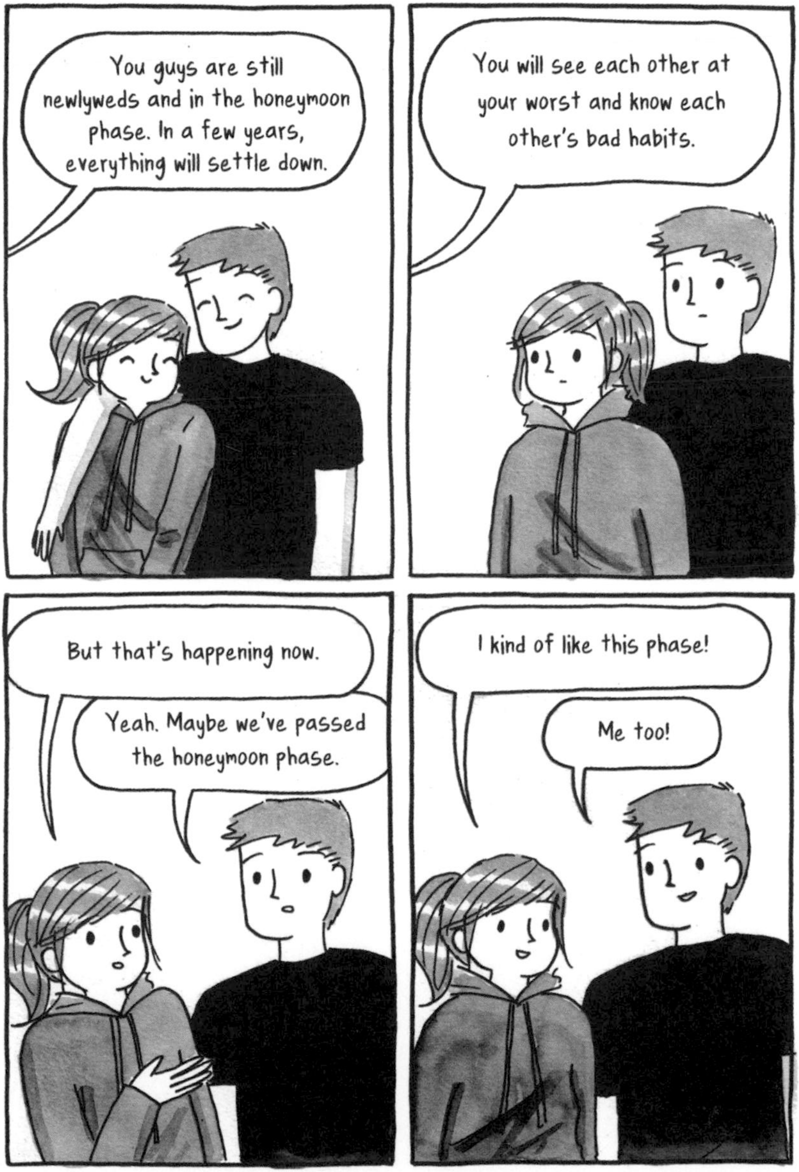
You guys are still newlyweds and in the honeymoon phase. In a few years, everything will settle down.
You will see each other at your worst and know each other's bad habits.
But that's happening now.
Yeah. Maybe we've passed the honeymoon phase.
I kind of like this phase!
Me too!

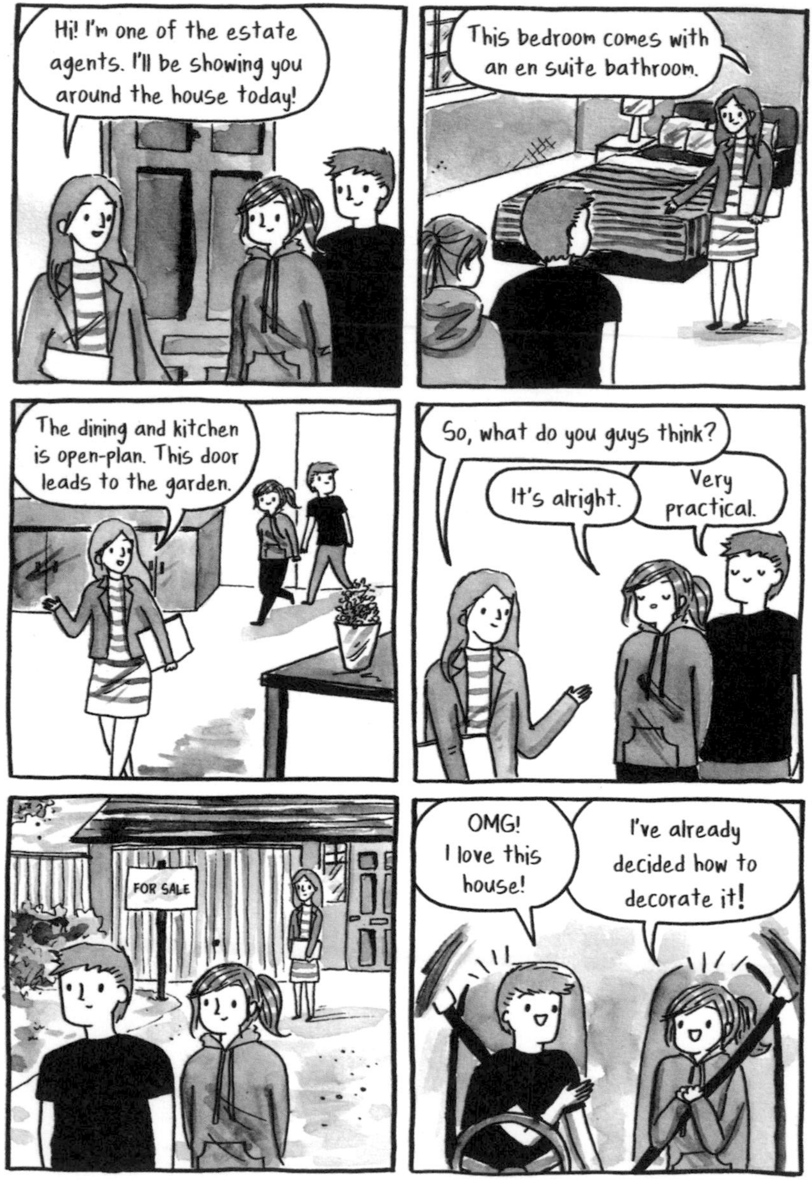
Hi! I'm one of the estate agents. I'll be showing you around the house today!
This bedroom comes with an en suite bathroom.
The dining and kitchen is open-plan. This door leads to the garden.
So, what do you guys think?
It's alright.
Very practical.
FOR SALE
OMG! I love this house!
I've already decided how to decorate it!

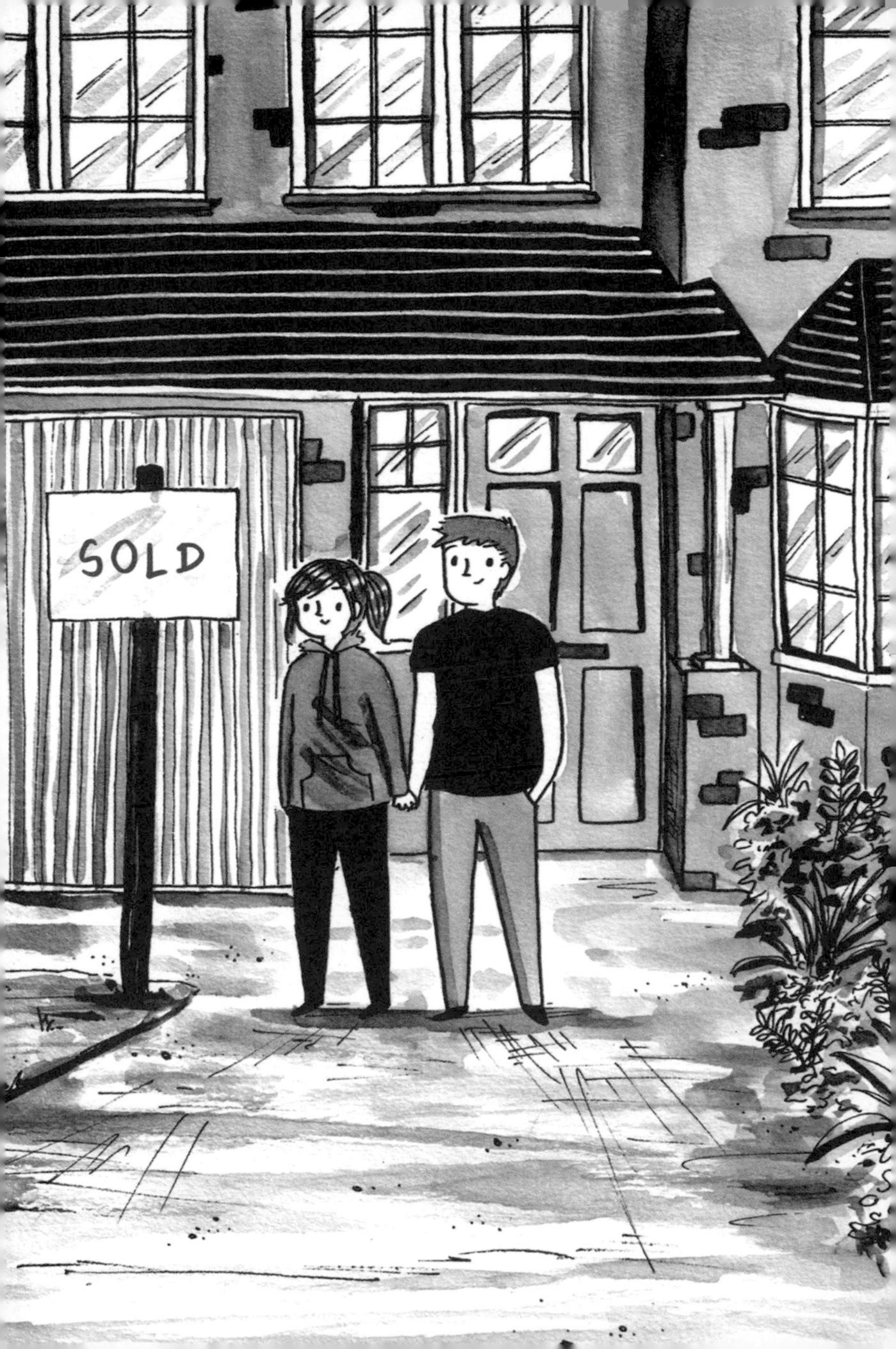
SOLD

Newlywed Adventures

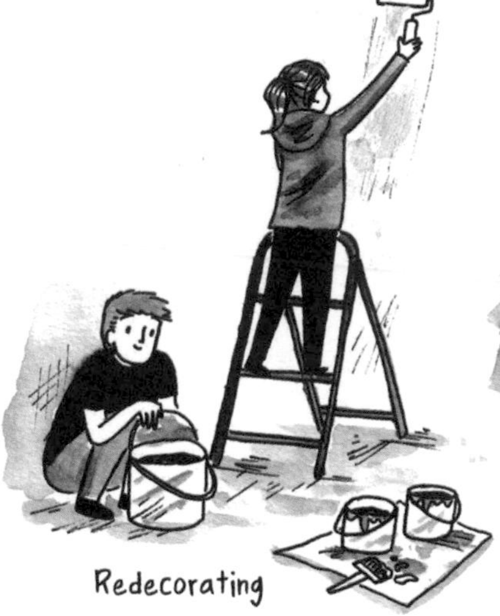

Redecorating

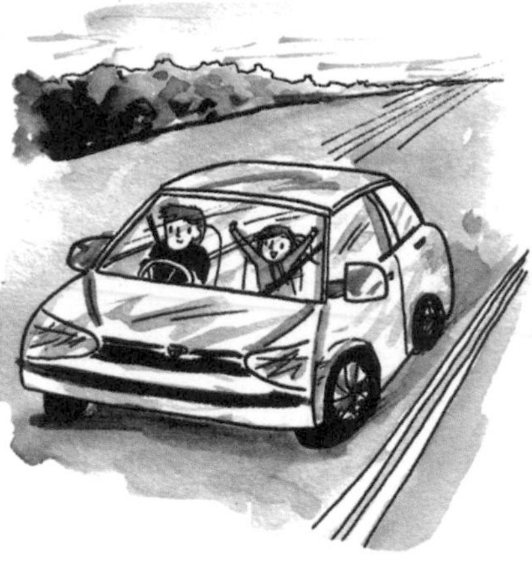

Taking a spontaneous road trip

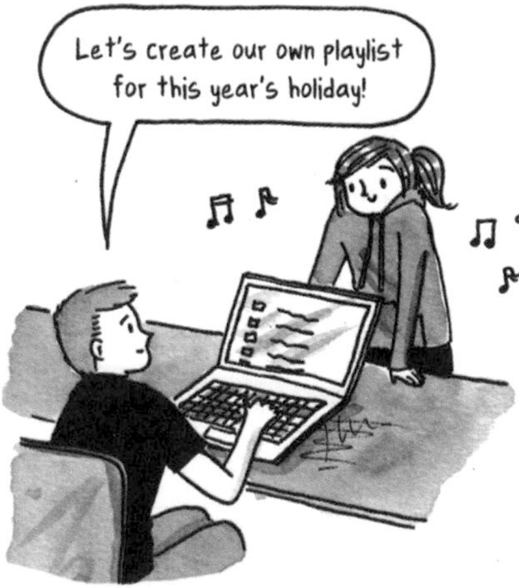
Let's create our own playlist for this year's holiday!

Starting a new holiday tradition

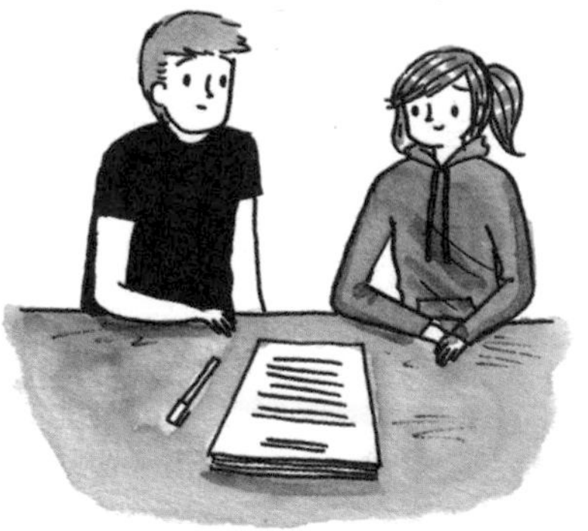

Signing a first mortgage together.

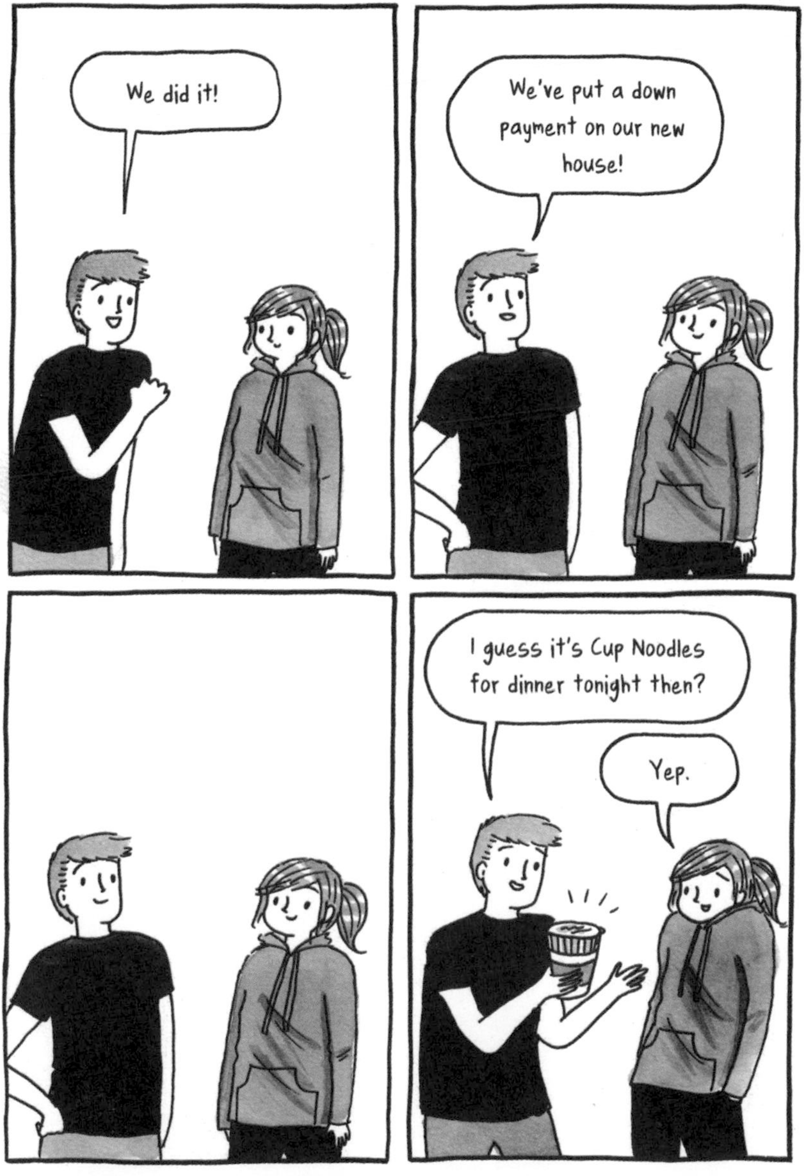
We did it!
We've put a down payment on our new house!
I guess it's Cup Noodles for dinner tonight then?
Yep.

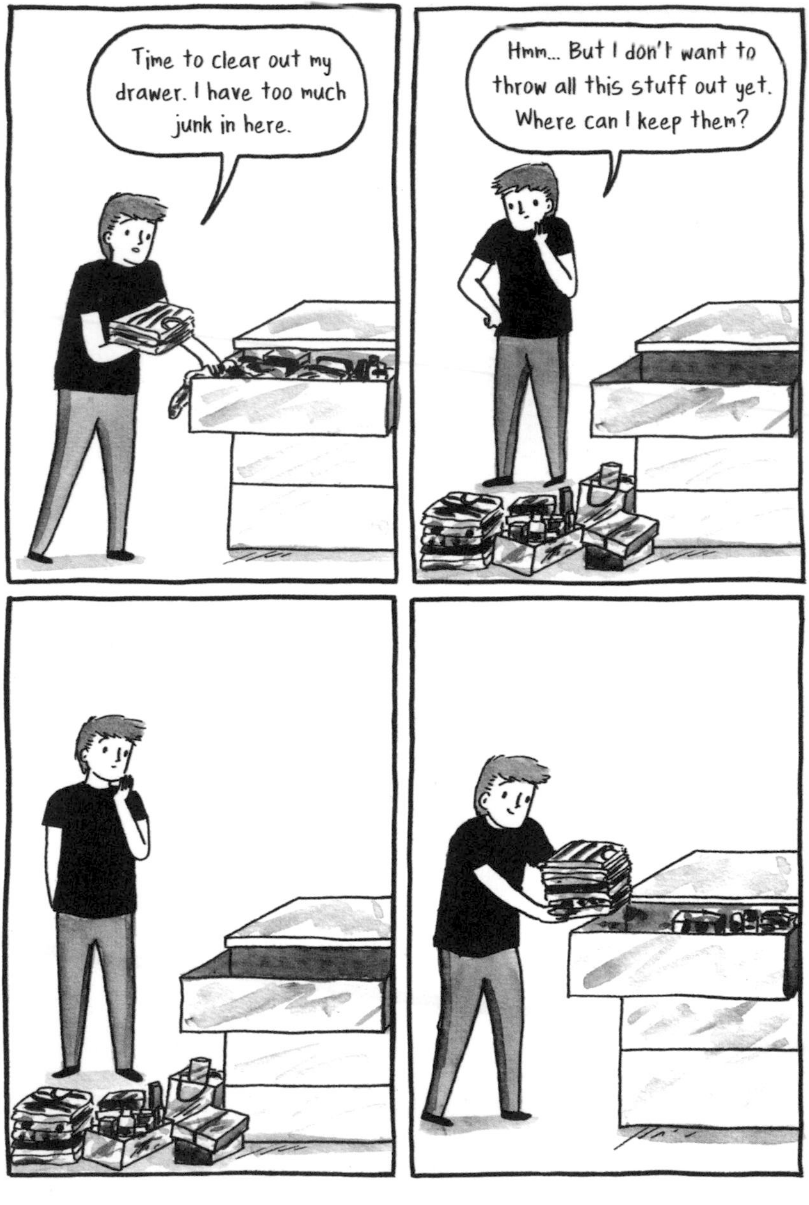
Time to clear out my drawer. I have too much junk in here.
Hmm... But I don't want to throw all this stuff out yet. Where can I keep them?

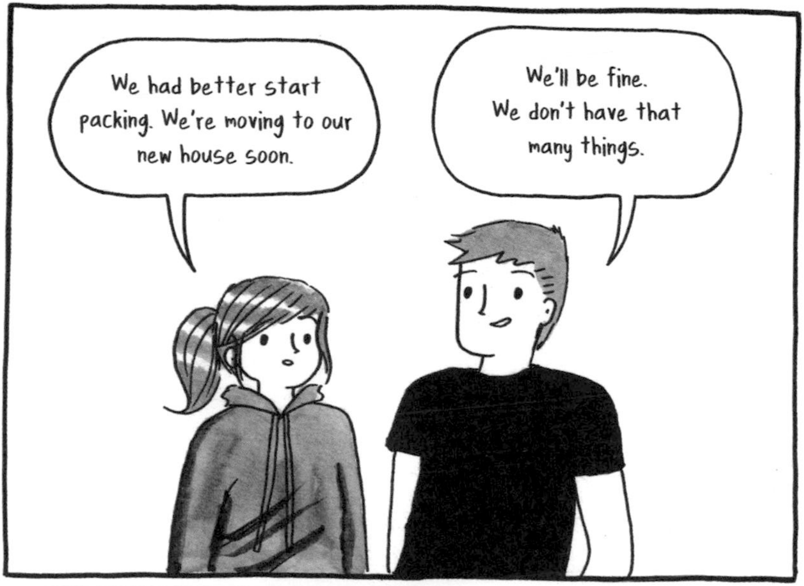
We had better start packing. We're moving to our new house soon.
We'll be fine. We don't have that many things.

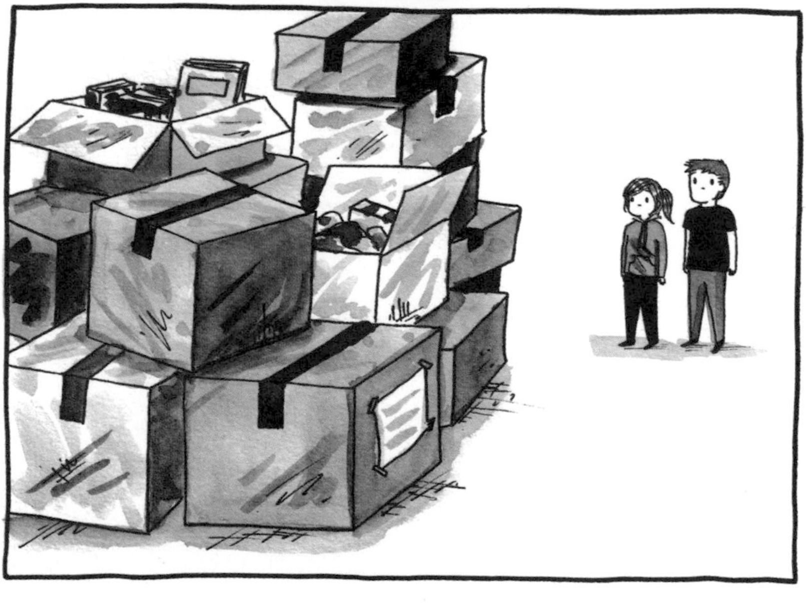

Moving to a New Home

Expectation

Reality

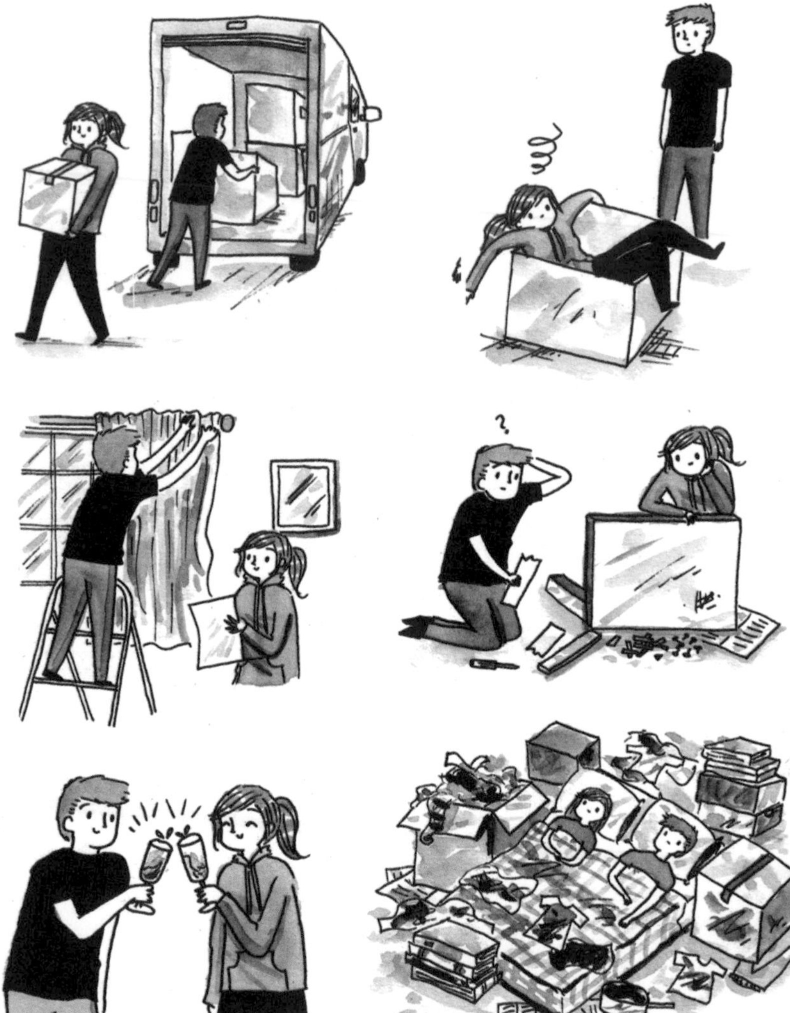

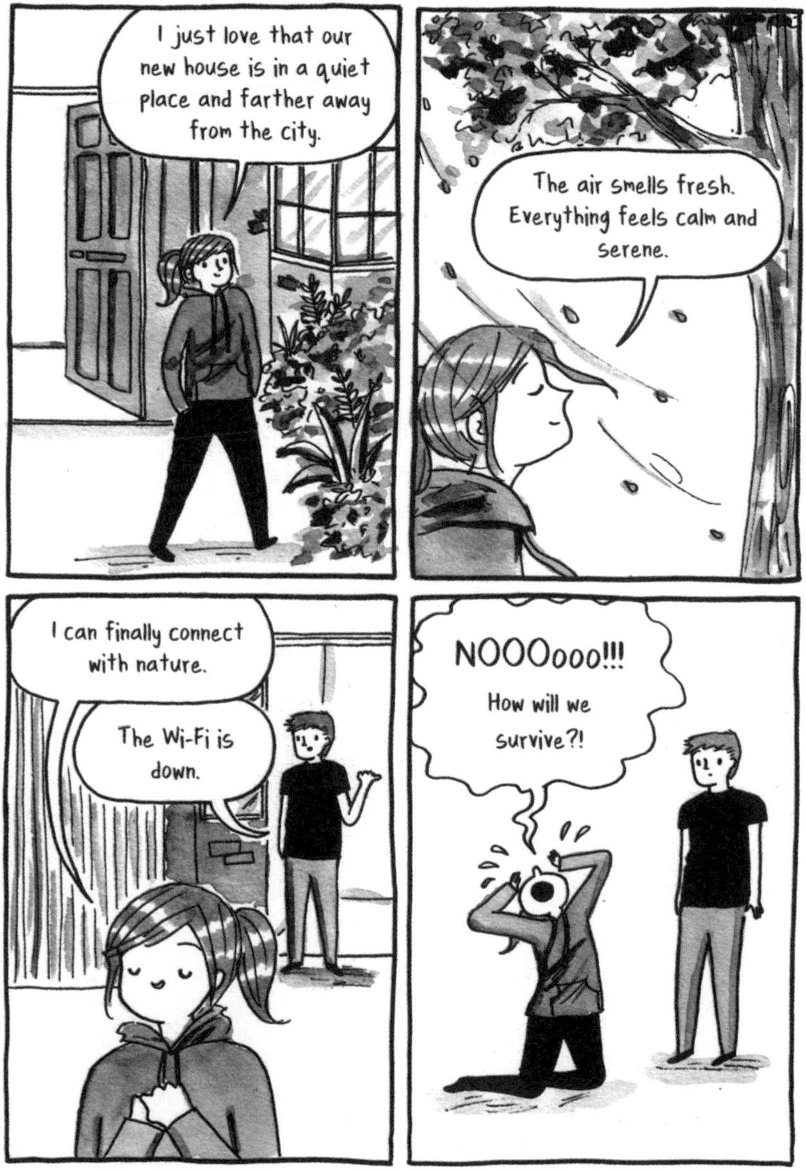
I just love that our new house is in a quiet place and farther away from the city.
The air smells fresh. Everything feels calm and serene.
I can finally connect with nature.
The Wi-Fi is down.
NOOOooo!!!
How will we survive?!

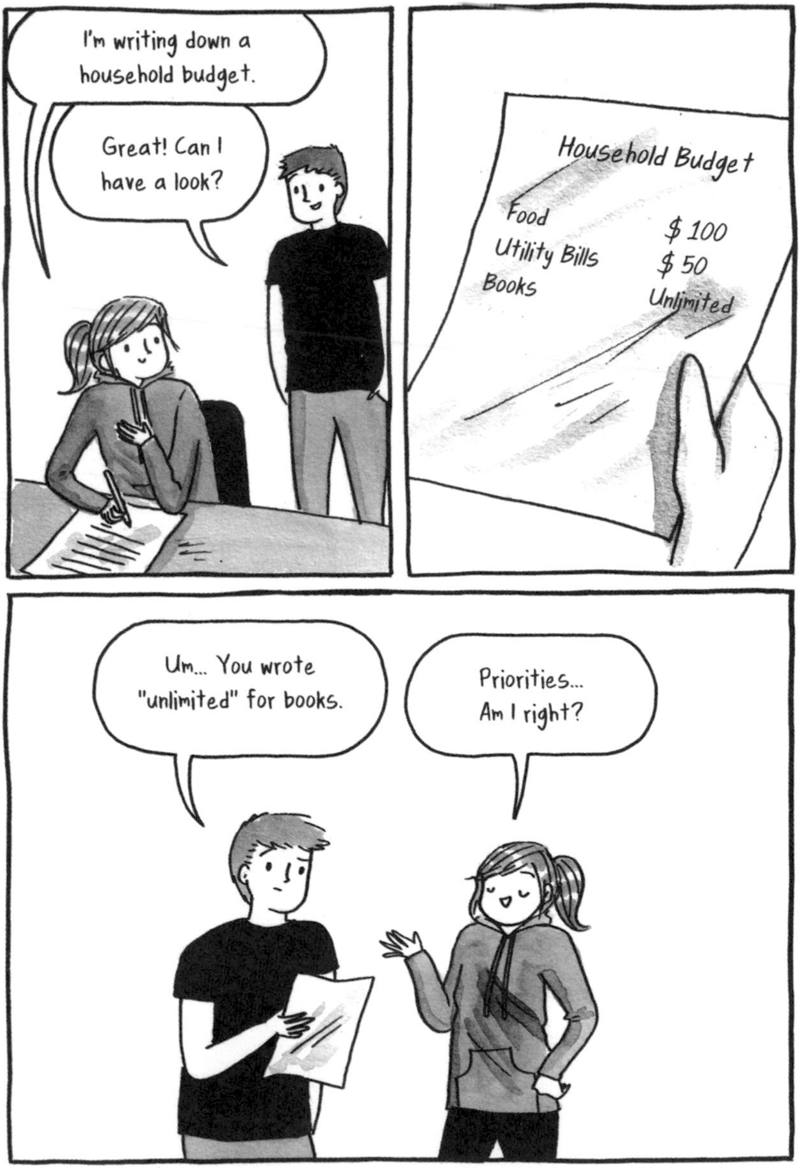
I'm writing down a household budget.
Great! Can I have a look?
Household Budget
Food $ 100
Utility Bills $ 50
Books Unlimited
Um... You wrote "unlimited" for books.
Priorities... Am I right?

Ways to Reduce Utility Bills

Layer up

Use eco-friendly appliances

Keep the thermostat at a
consistent level

Each other

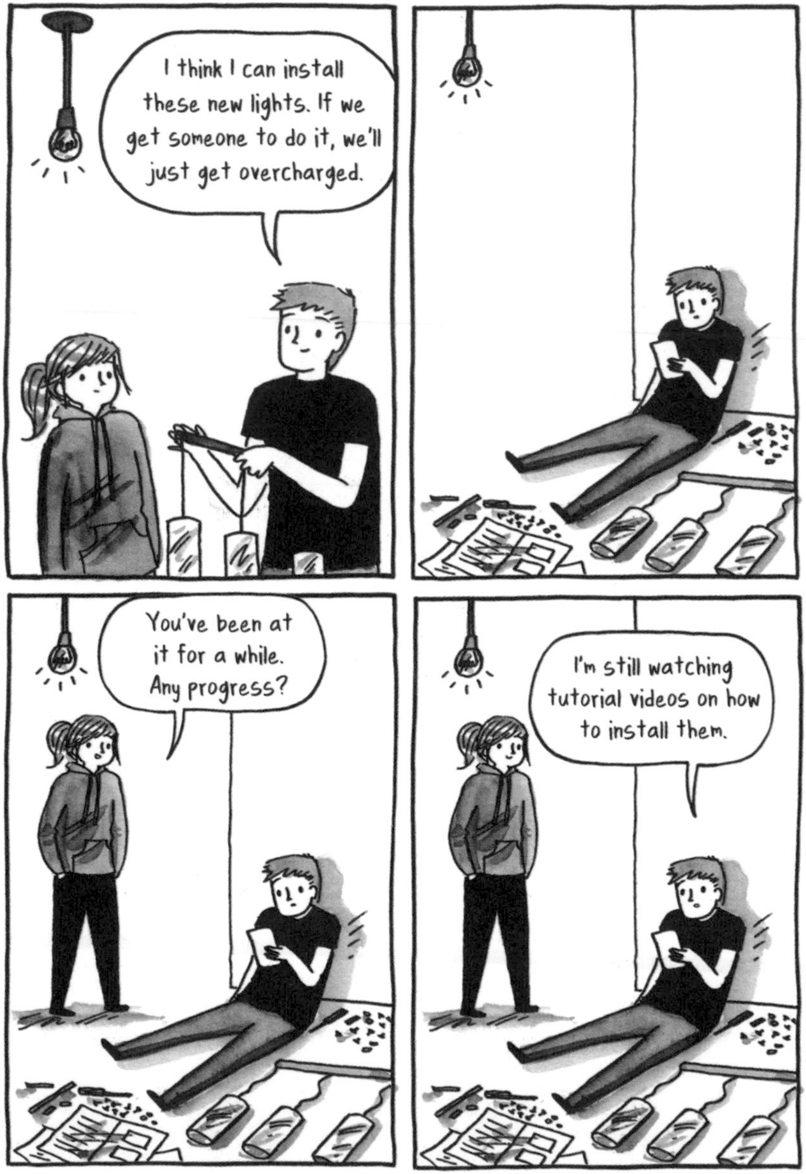
I think I can install these new lights. If we get someone to do it, we'll just get overcharged.
You've been at it for a while. Any progress?
I'm still watching tutorial videos on how to install them.

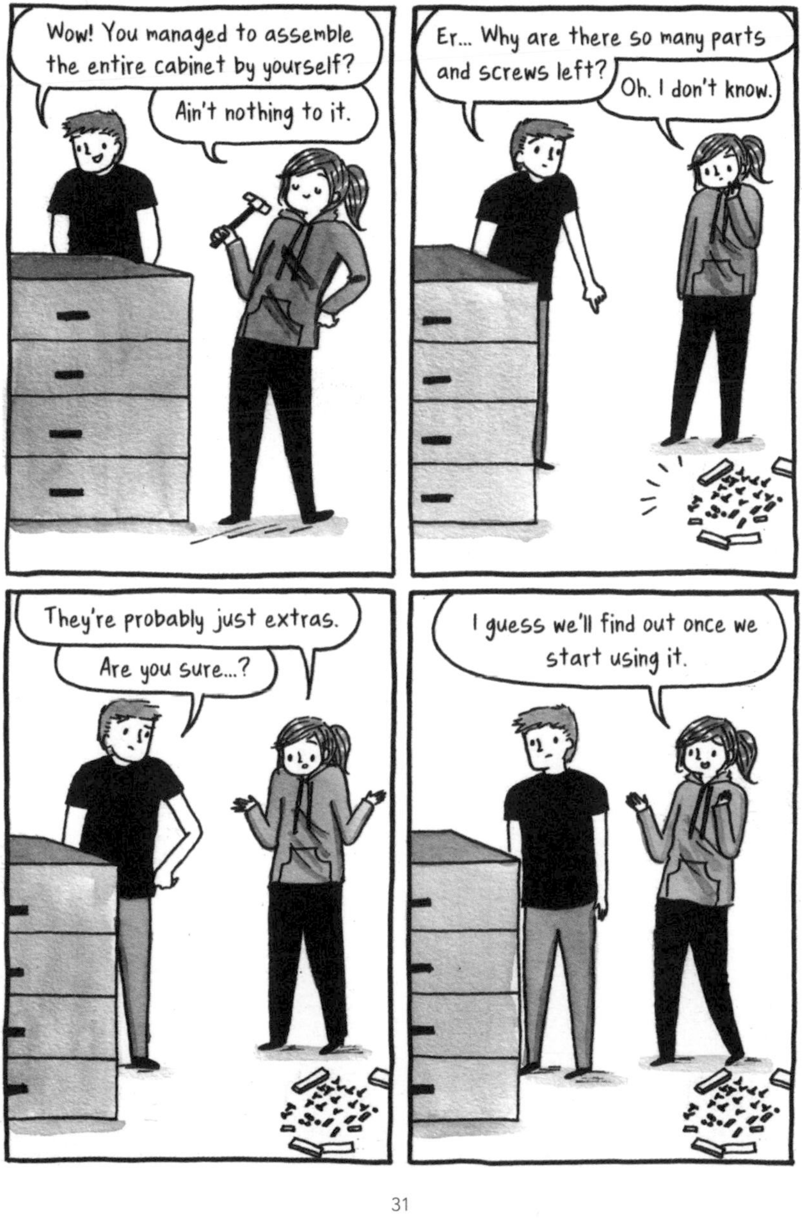

Wow! You managed to assemble the entire cabinet by yourself?
Ain't nothing to it.
Er... Why are there so many parts and screws left?
Oh. I don't know.
They're probably just extras.
Are you sure...?
I guess we'll find out once we start using it.

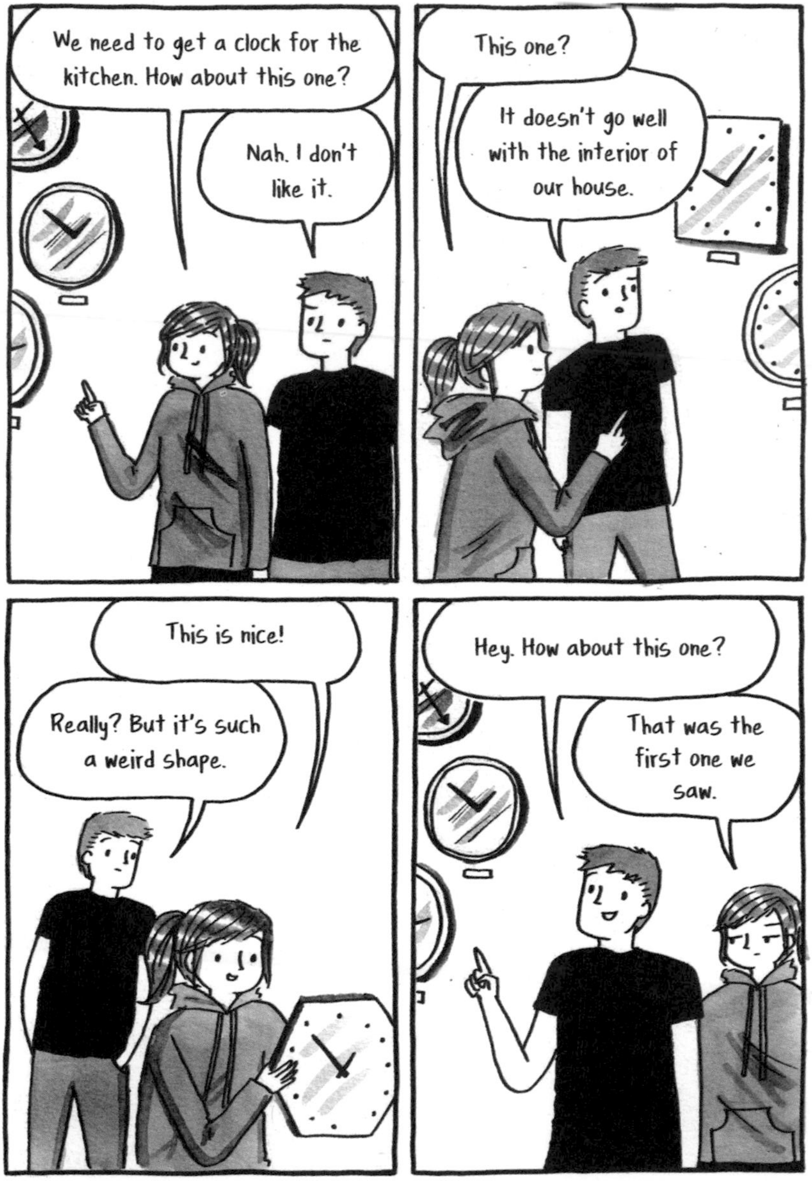
We need to get a clock for the kitchen. How about this one?
Nah. I don't like it.
This one?
It doesn't go well with the interior of our house.
This is nice!
Really? But it's such a weird shape.
Hey. How about this one?
That was the first one we saw.

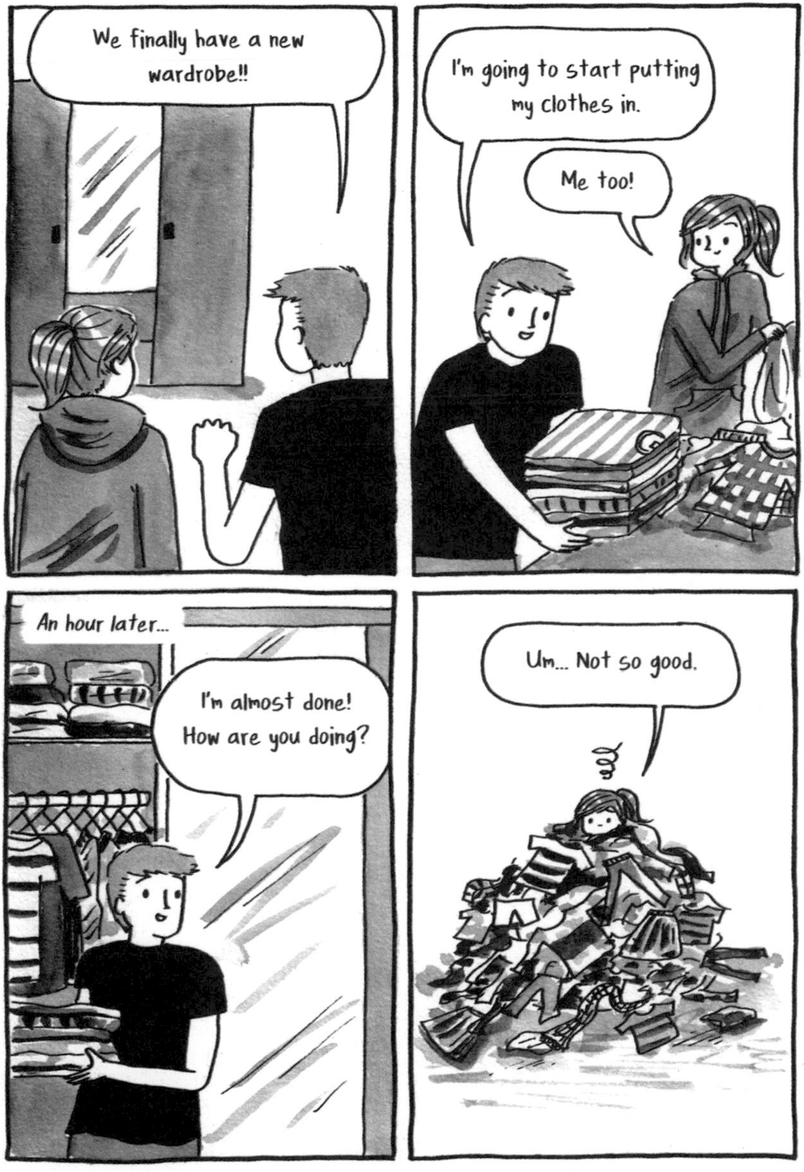
We finally have a new wardrobe!!
I'm going to start putting my clothes in.
Me too!
An hour later...
I'm almost done! How are you doing?
Um... Not so good.

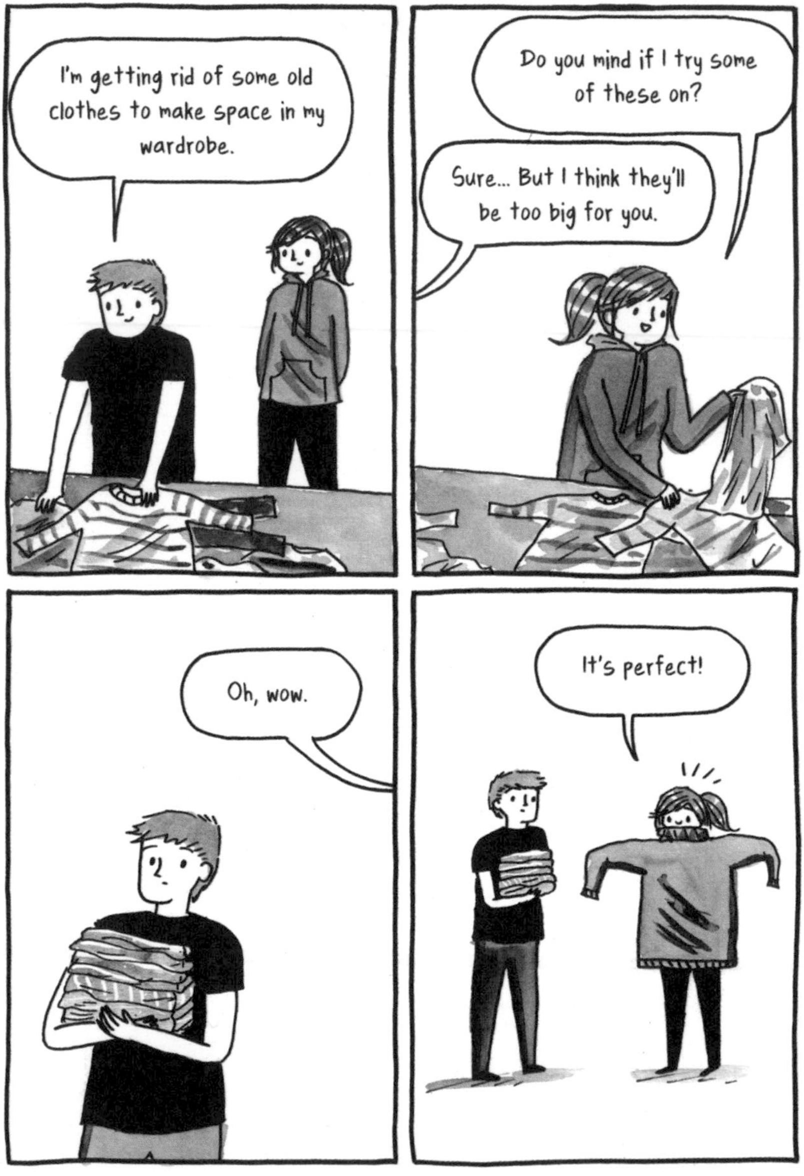
I'm getting rid of some old clothes to make space in my wardrobe.
Do you mind if I try some of these on?
Sure... But I think they'll be too big for you.
Oh, wow.
It's perfect!

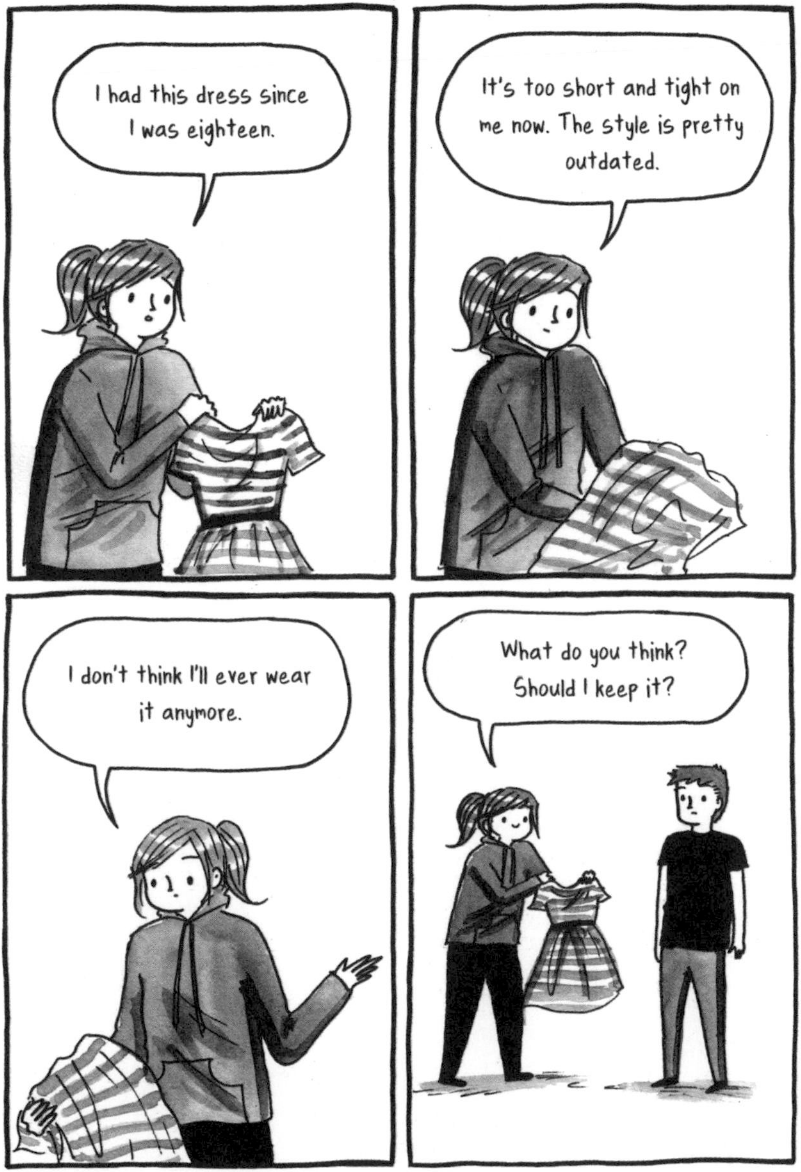
I had this dress since
I was eighteen.
It's too short and tight on
me now. The style is pretty
outdated.
I don't think I'll ever wear
it anymore.
What do you think?
Should I keep it?

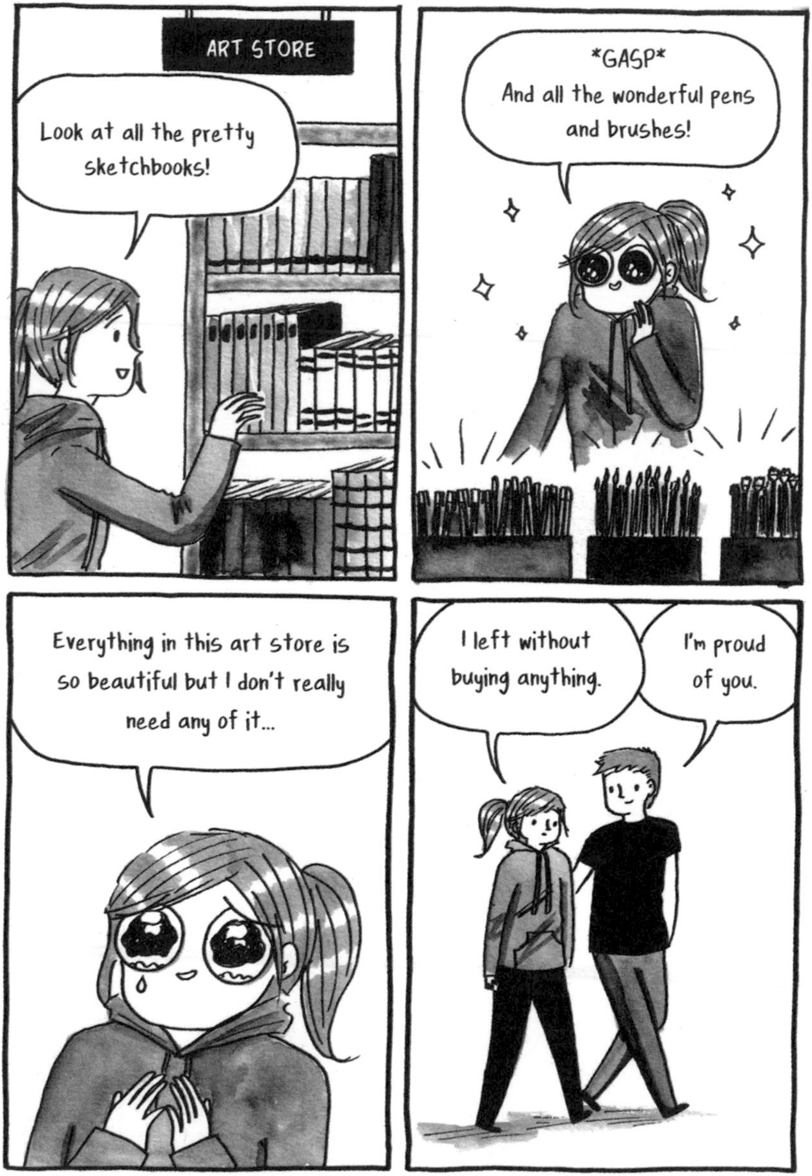
ART STORE
Look at all the pretty sketchbooks!
GASP And all the wonderful pens and brushes!
Everything in this art store is so beautiful but I don't really need any of it...
I left without buying anything.
I'm proud of you.

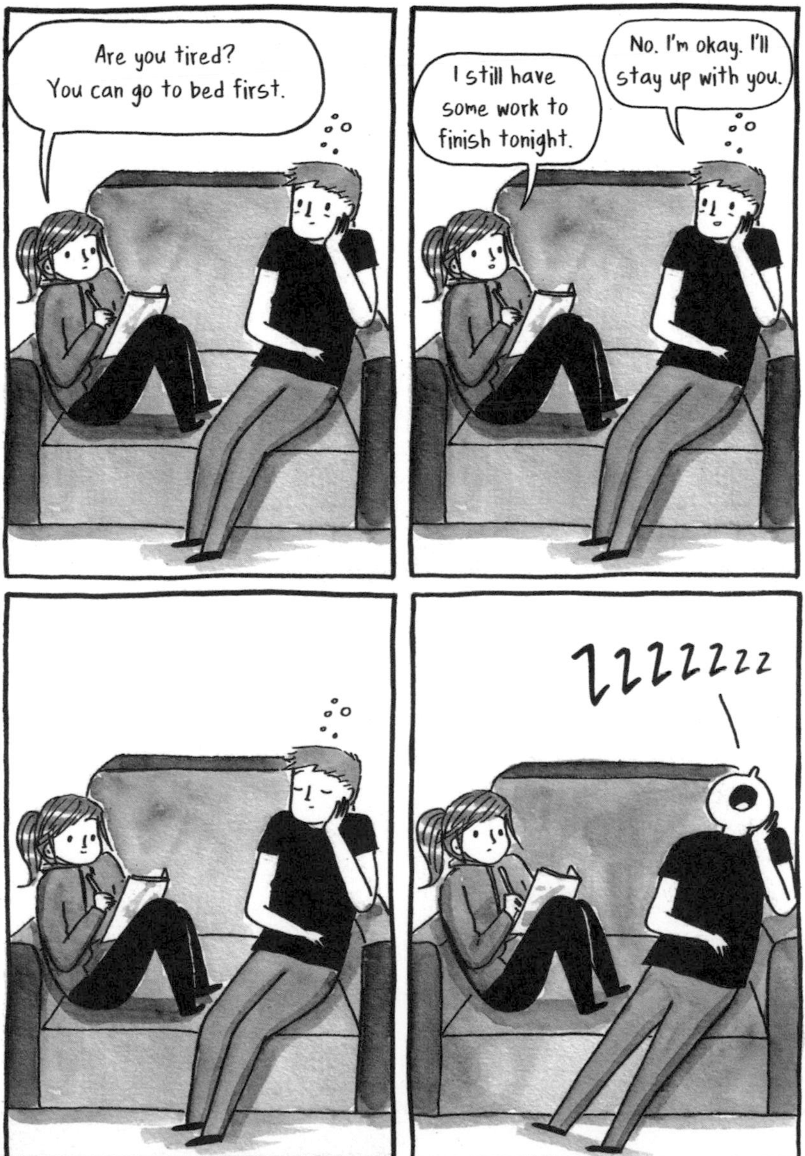
Are you tired? You can go to bed first.
I still have some work to finish tonight.
No. I'm okay. I'll stay up with you.
ZZZZZZzz

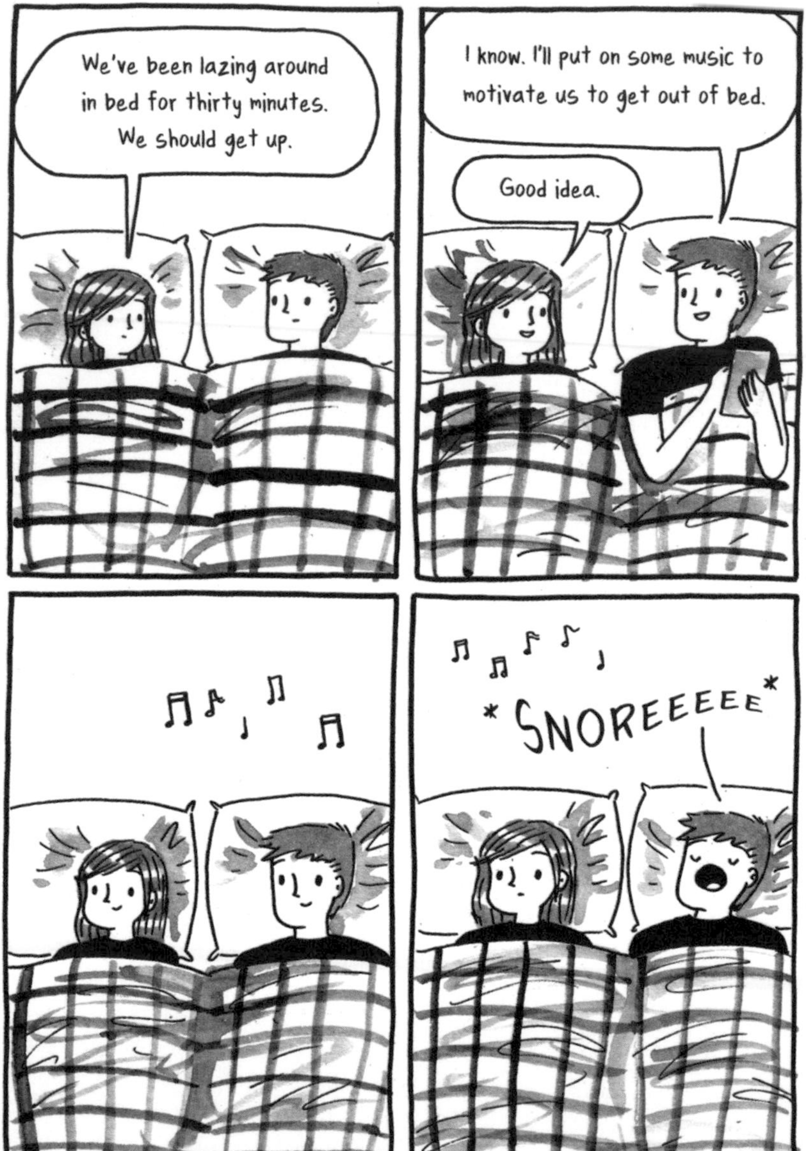
We've been lazing around in bed for thirty minutes. We should get up.
I know. I'll put on some music to motivate us to get out of bed.
Good idea.
SNOREEEEEE

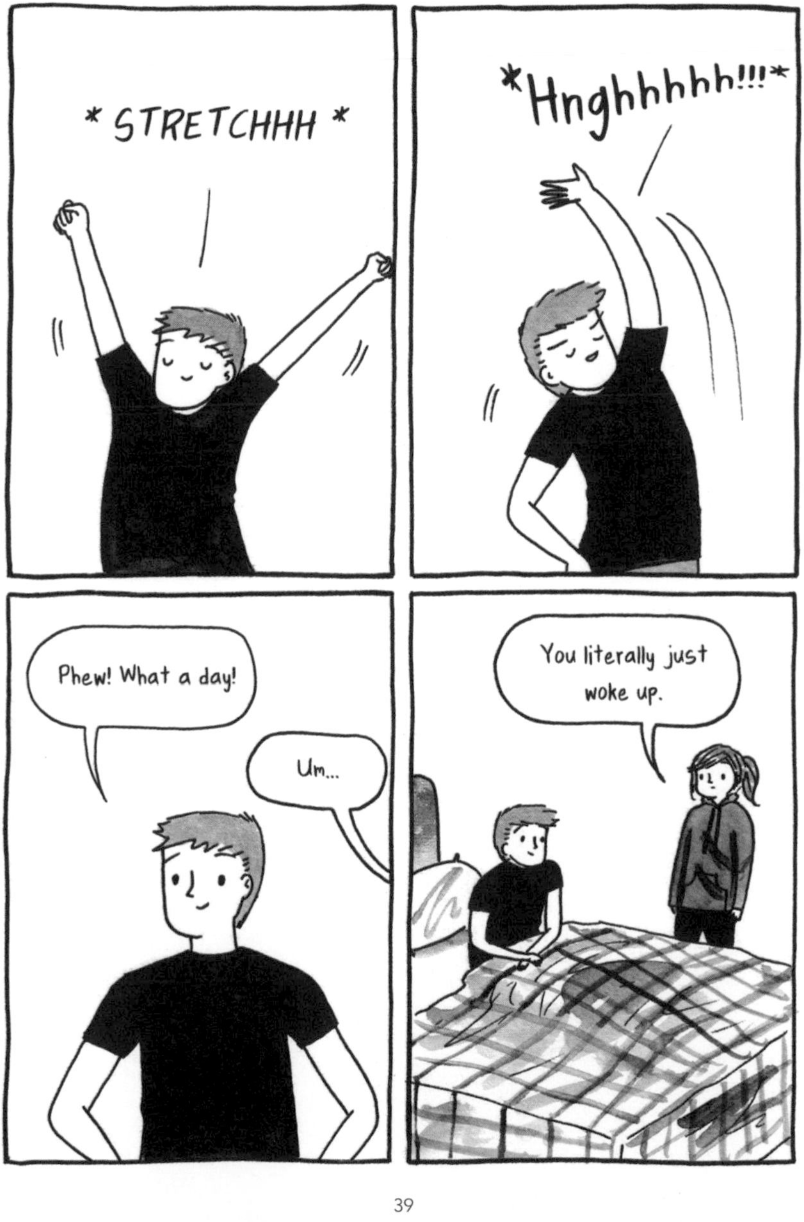
* STRETCHHH *
Hnghhhhh!!!
Phew! What a day!
Um...
You literally just woke up.

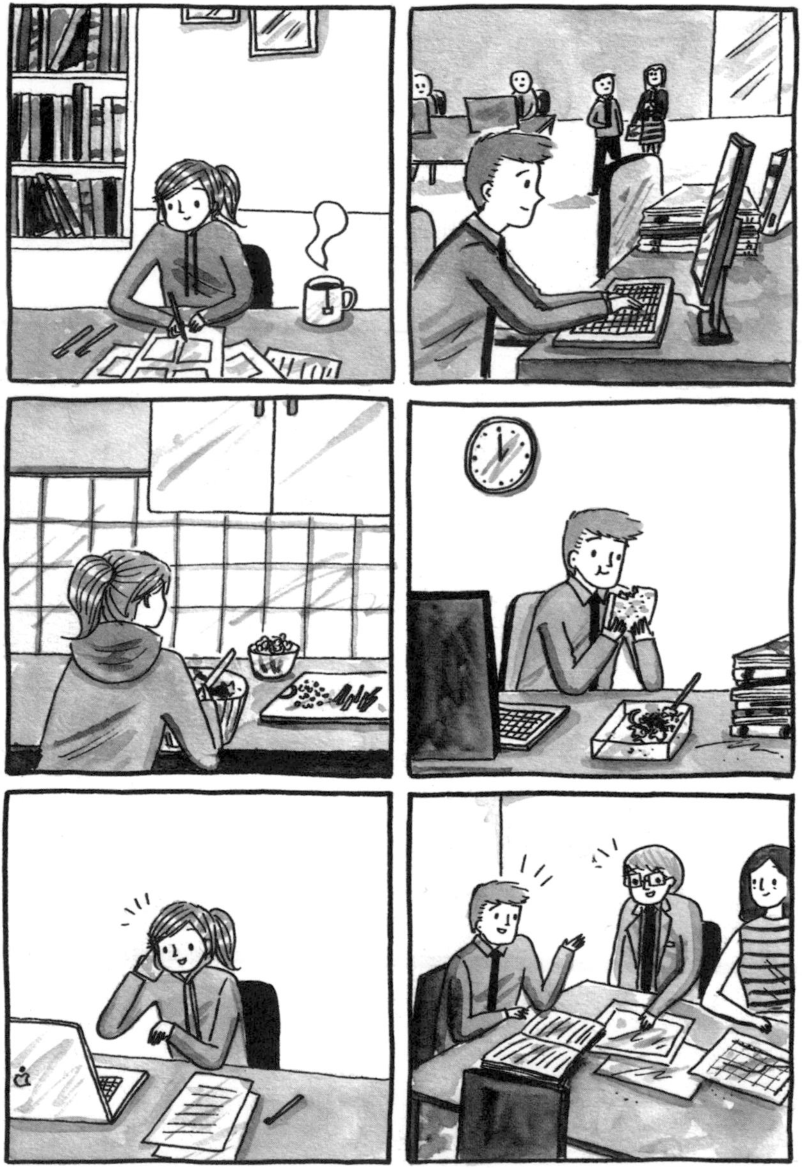

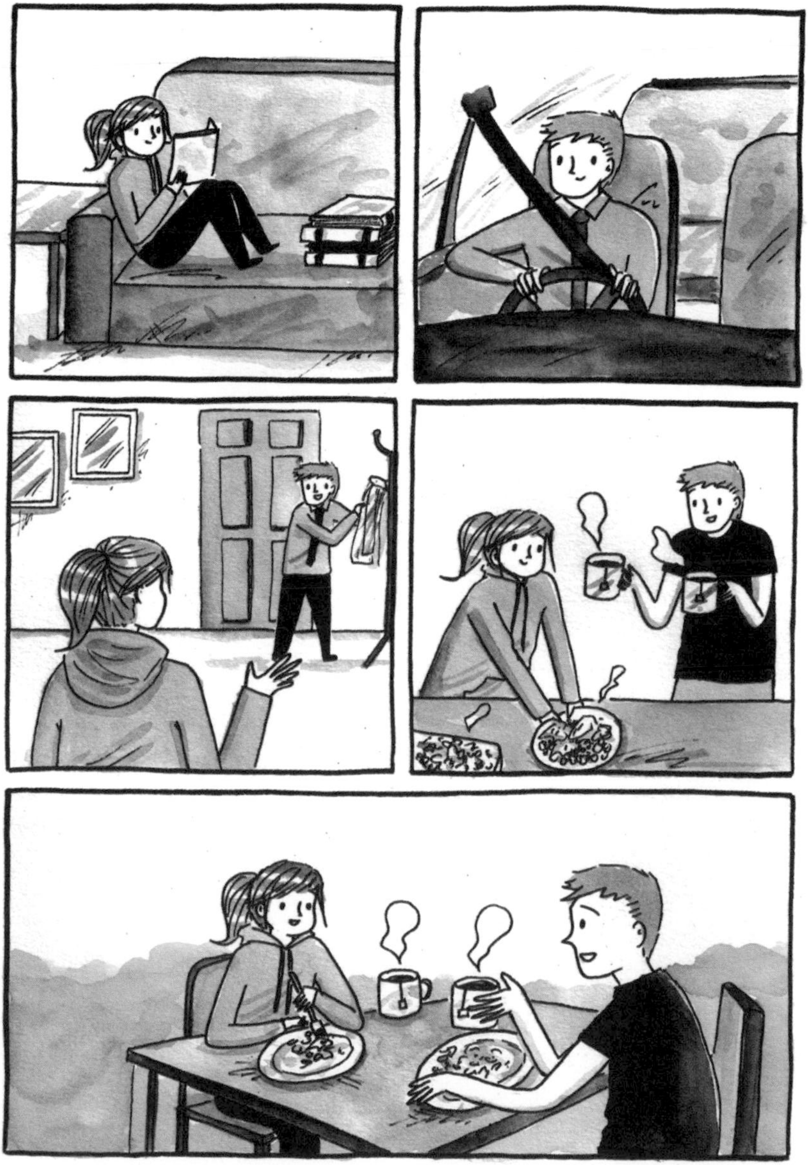

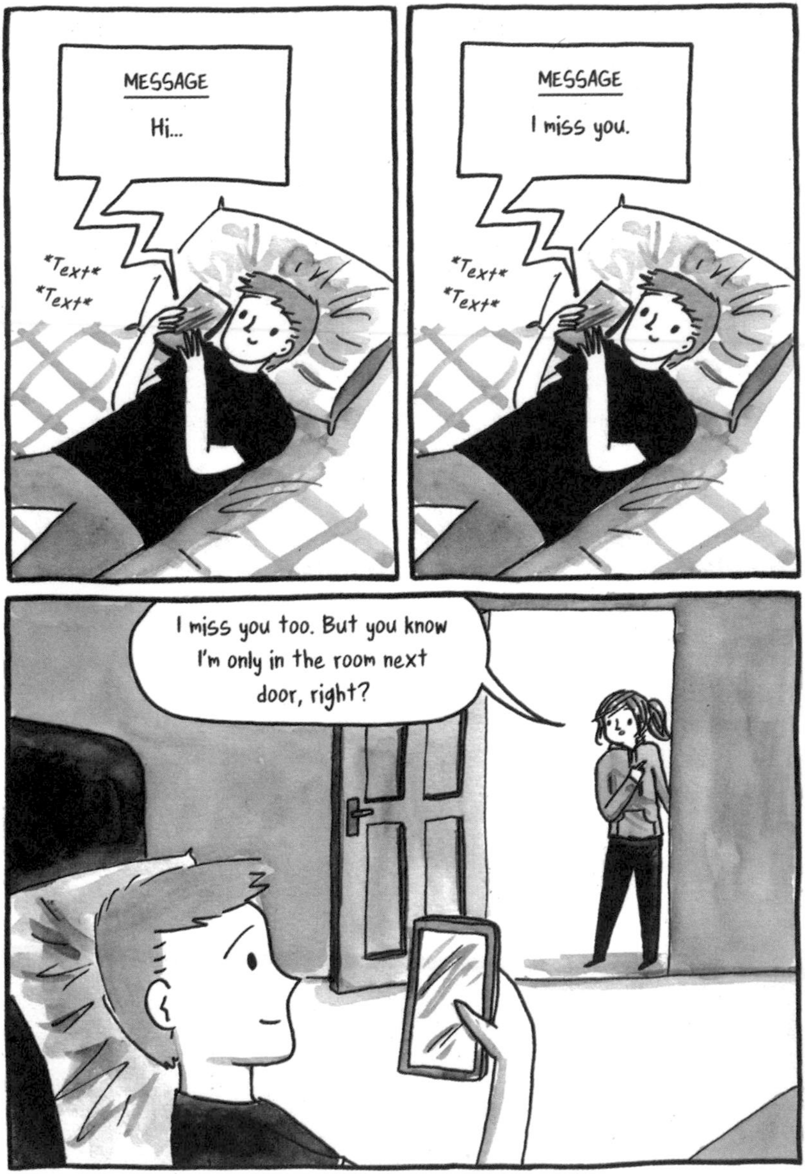
MESSAGE
Hi...
Text
Text
MESSAGE
I miss you.
Text
Text
I miss you too. But you know I'm only in the room next door, right?

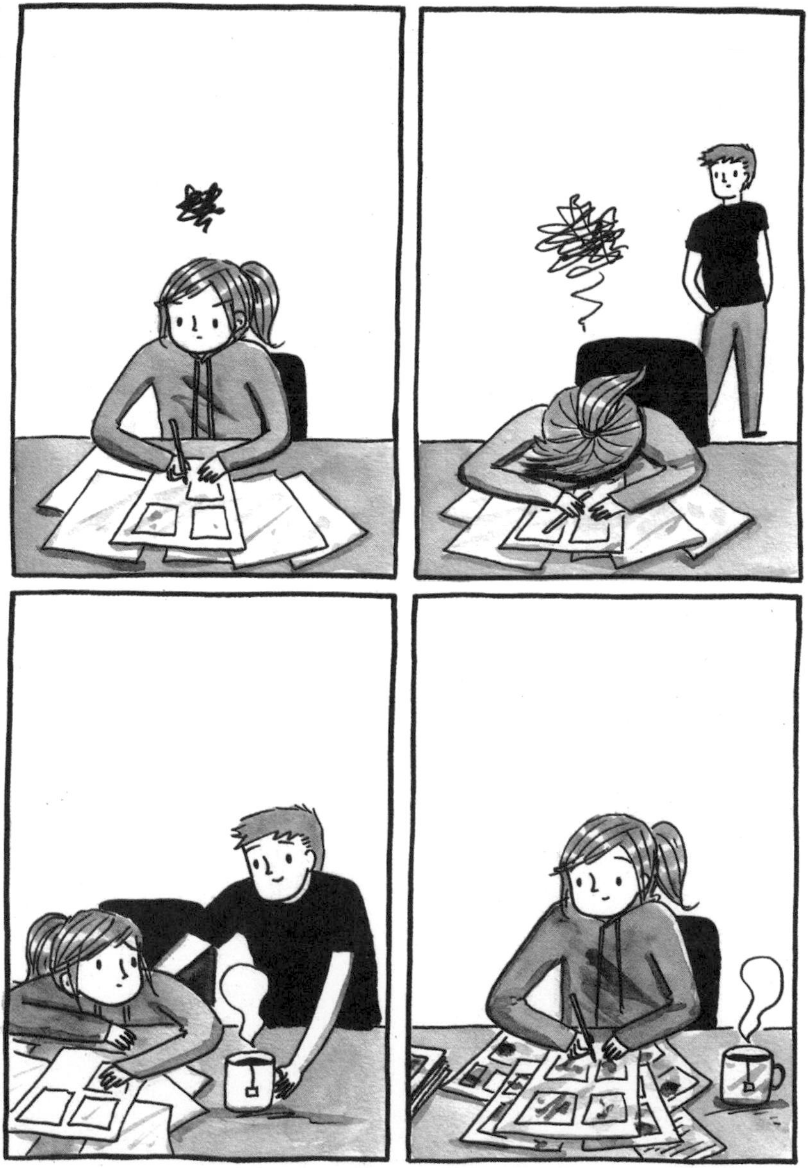

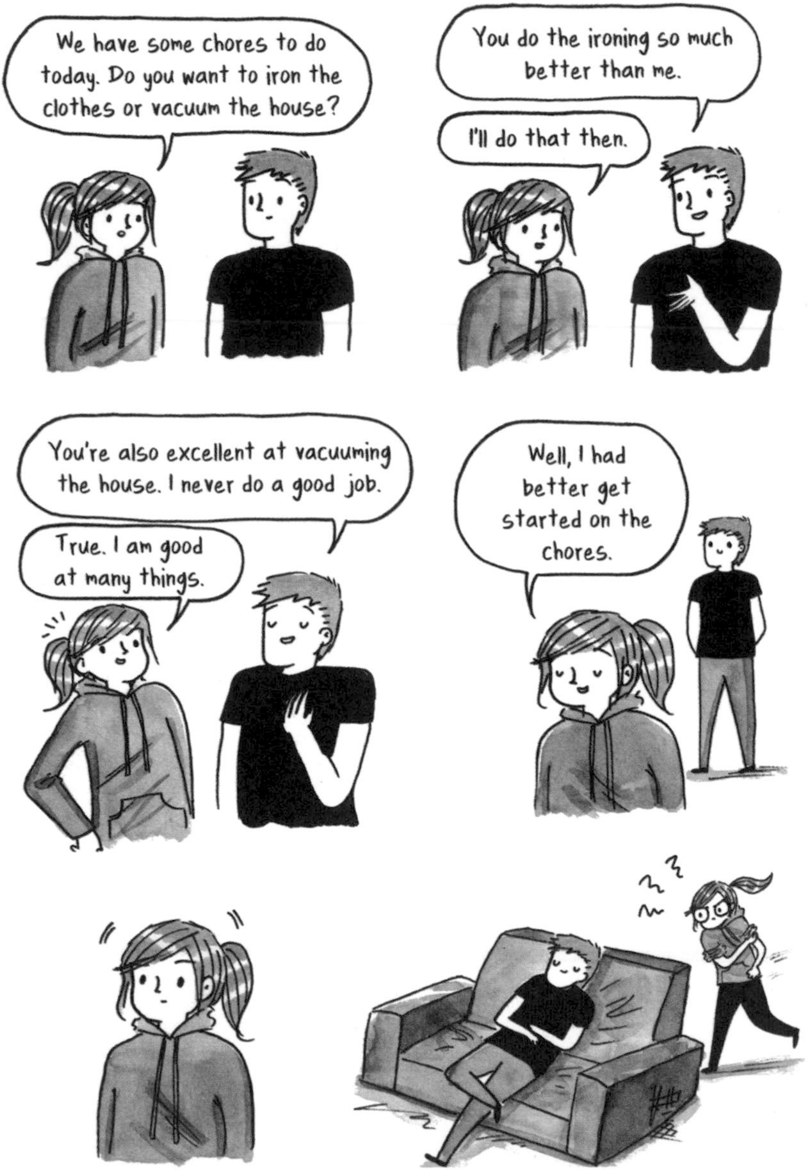
We have some chores to do today. Do you want to iron the clothes or vacuum the house?
You do the ironing so much better than me.
I'll do that then.
You're also excellent at vacuuming the house. I never do a good job.
True. I am good at many things.
Well, I had better get started on the chores.

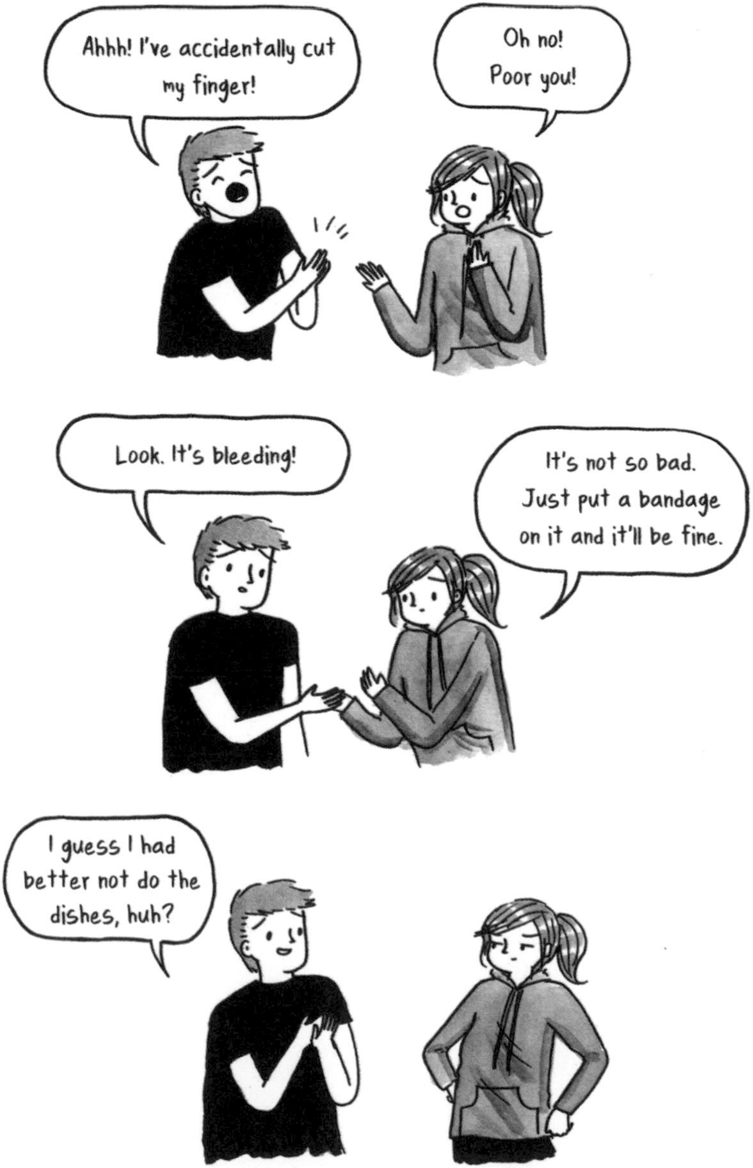
Ahhh! I've accidentally cut my finger!
Oh no! Poor you!
Look. It's bleeding!
It's not so bad. Just put a bandage on it and it'll be fine.
I guess I had better not do the dishes, huh?

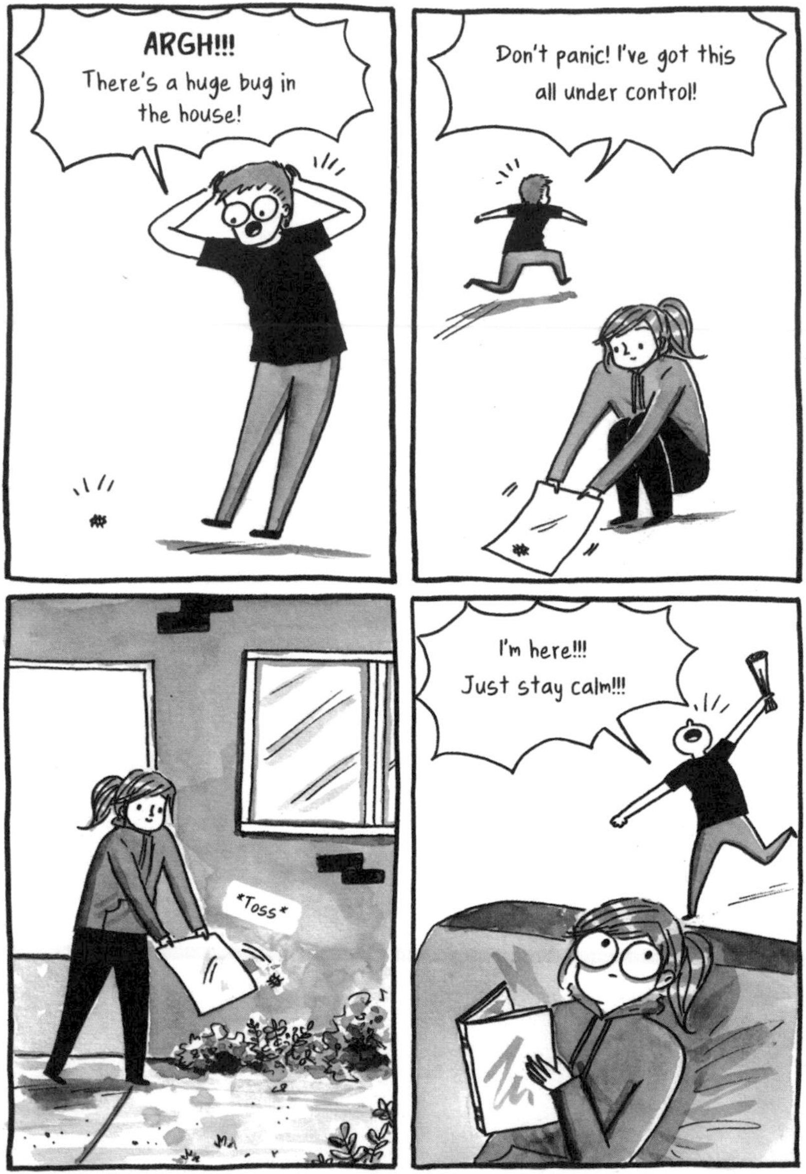
ARGH!!!
There's a huge bug in the house!
Don't panic! I've got this all under control!
Toss
I'm here!!!
Just stay calm!!!

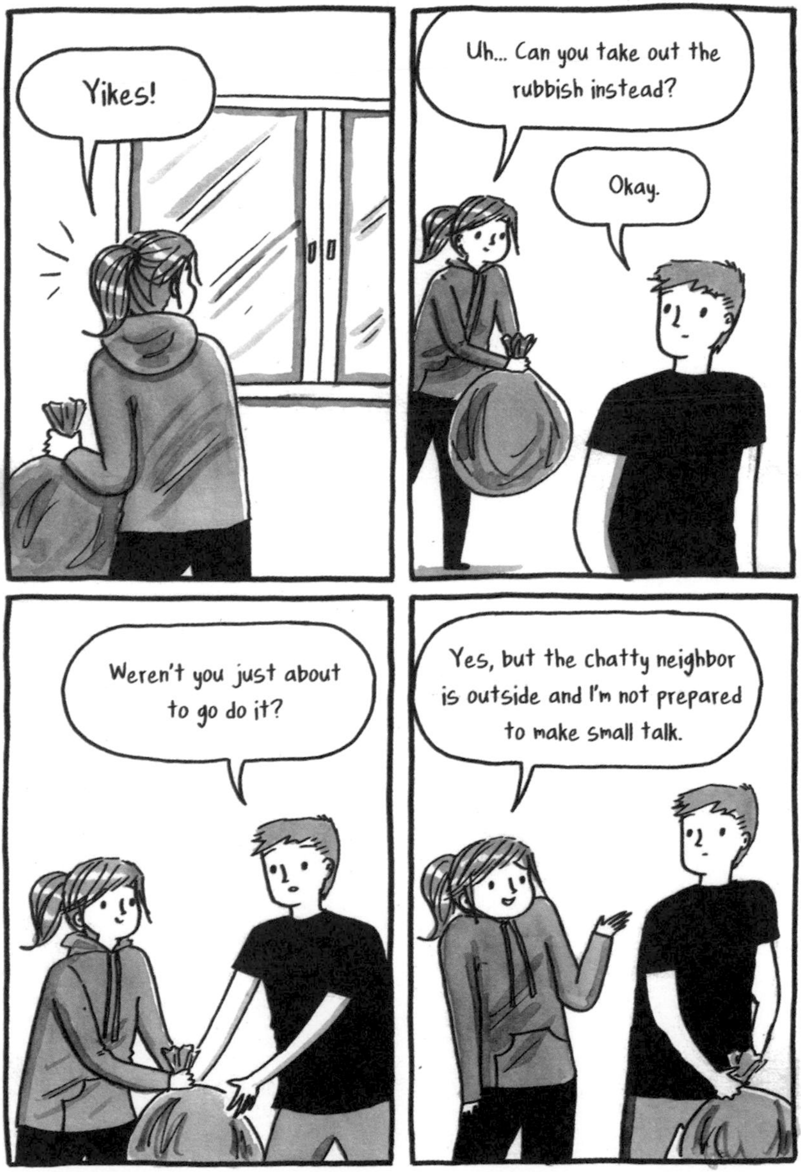
Yikes!
Uh... Can you take out the rubbish instead?
Okay.
Weren't you just about to go do it?
Yes, but the chatty neighbor is outside and I'm not prepared to make small talk.

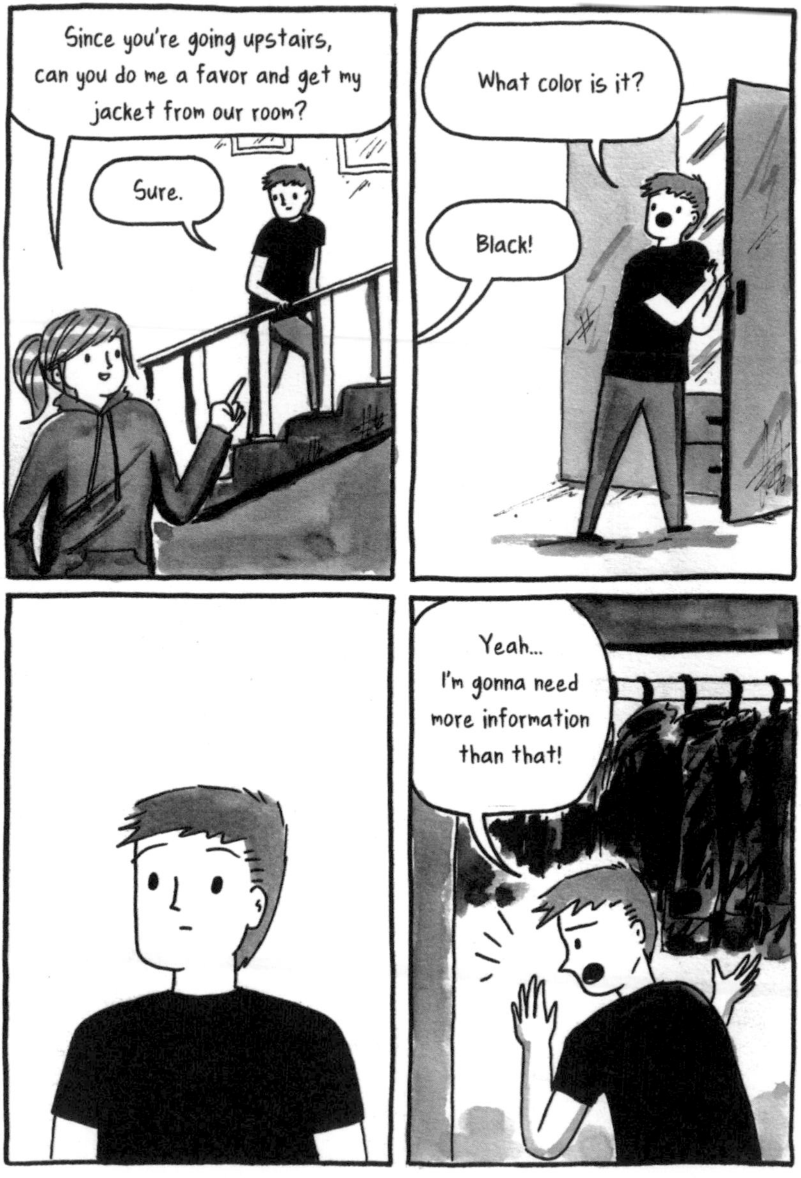
Since you're going upstairs, can you do me a favor and get my jacket from our room?
Sure.
What color is it?
Black!
Yeah... I'm gonna need more information than that!

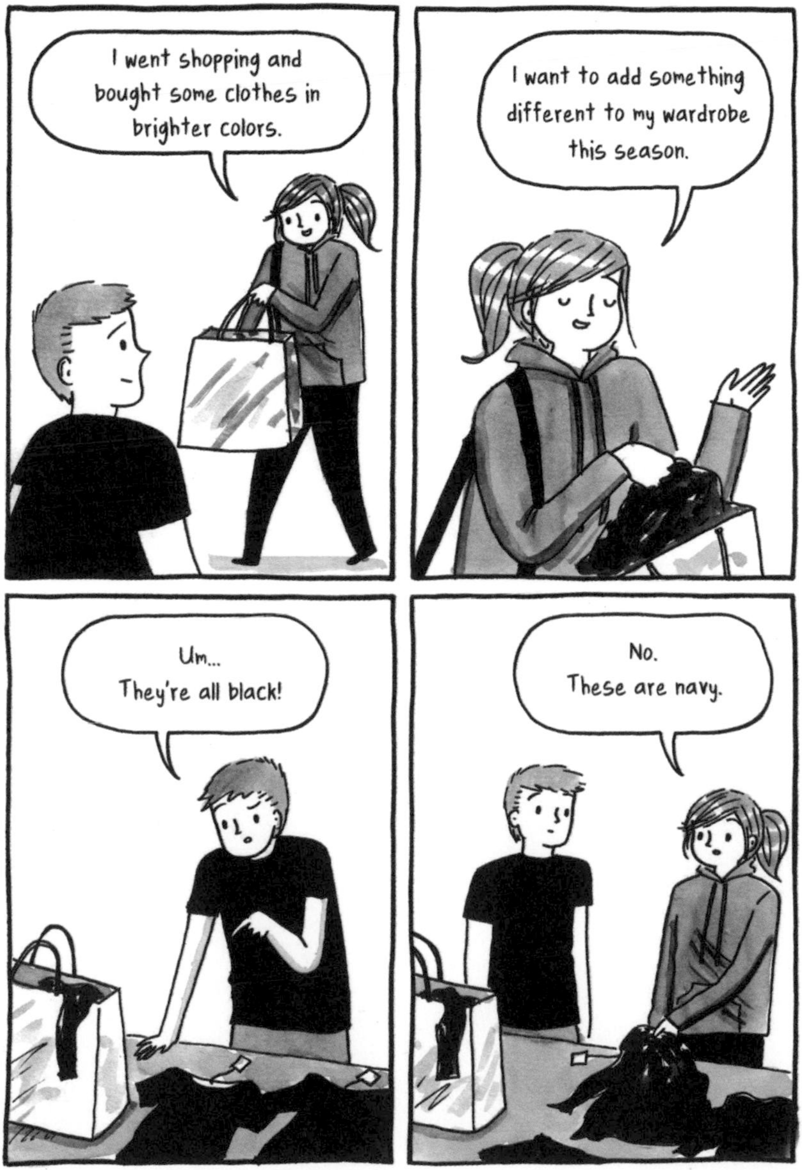
I went shopping and bought some clothes in brighter colors.
I want to add something different to my wardrobe this season.
Um...
They're all black!
No.
These are navy.

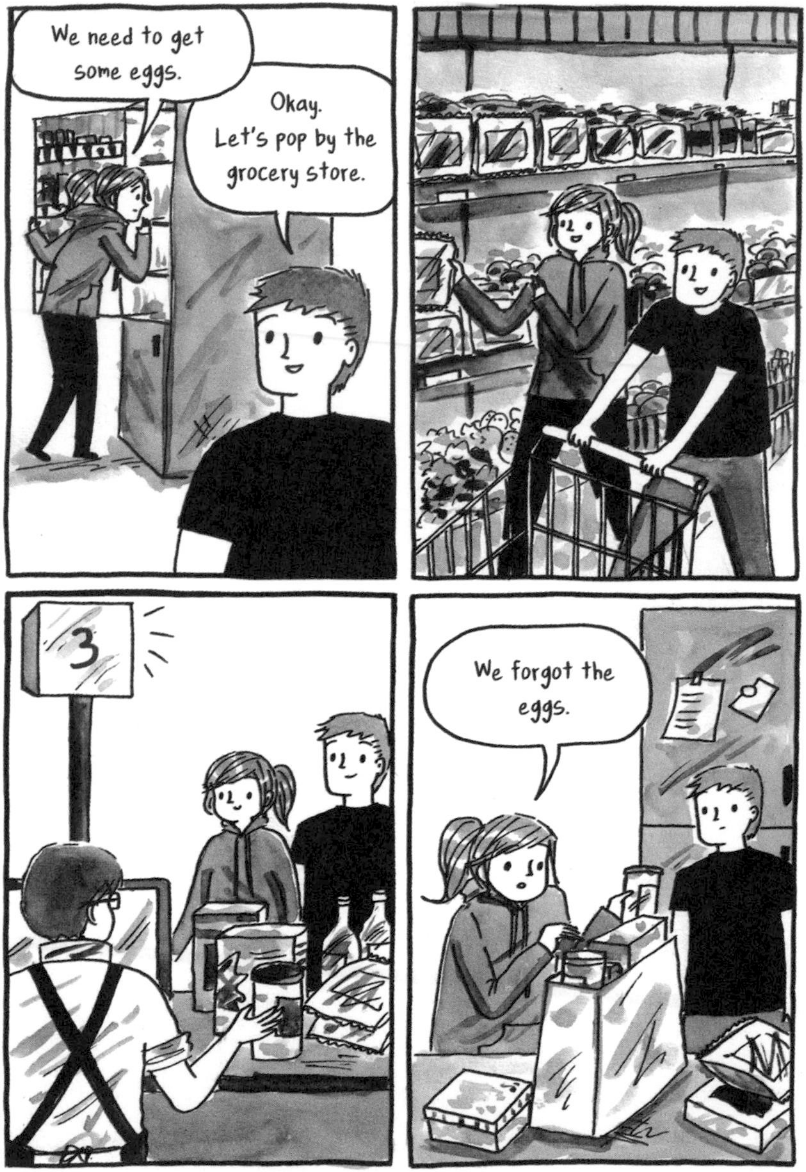
We need to get some eggs.
Okay. Let's pop by the grocery store.
3
We forgot the eggs.

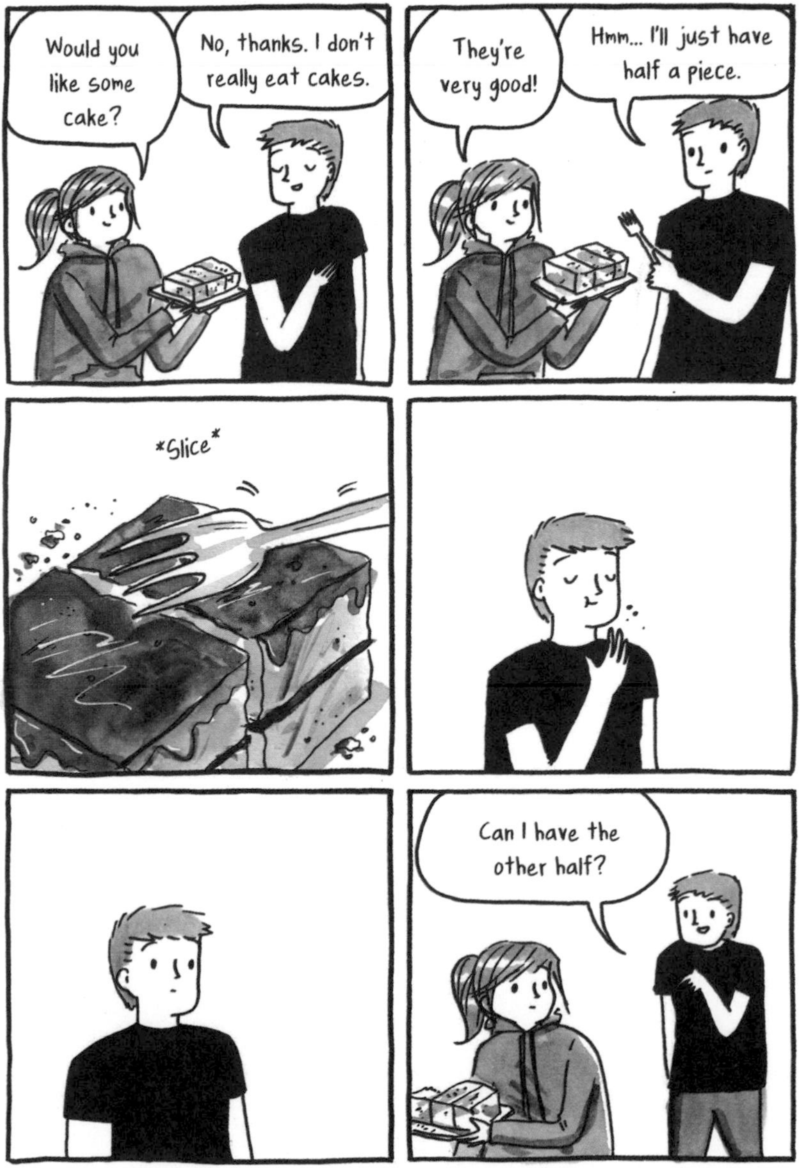
Would you like some cake?
No, thanks. I don't really eat cakes.
They're very good!
Hmm... I'll just have half a piece.
Slice
Can I have the other half?

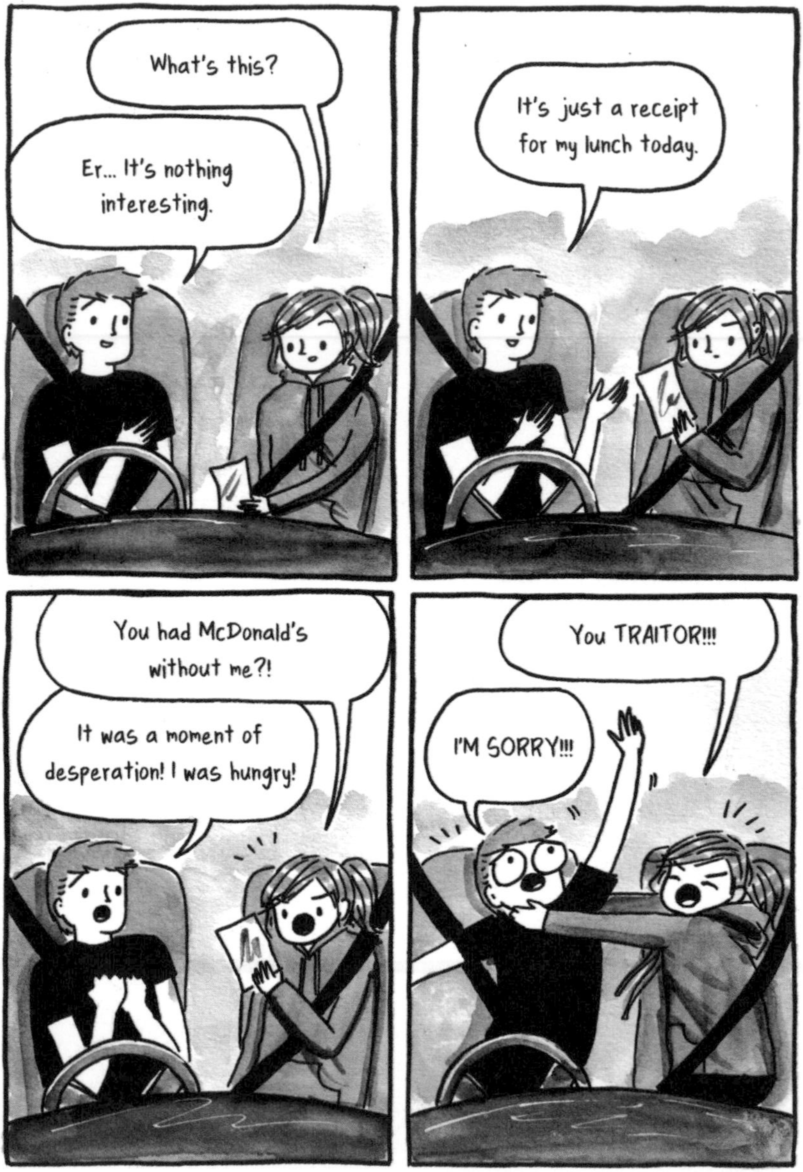
What's this?
Er... It's nothing interesting.
It's just a receipt for my lunch today.
You had McDonald's without me?!
It was a moment of desperation! I was hungry!
You TRAITOR!!!
I'M SORRY!!!

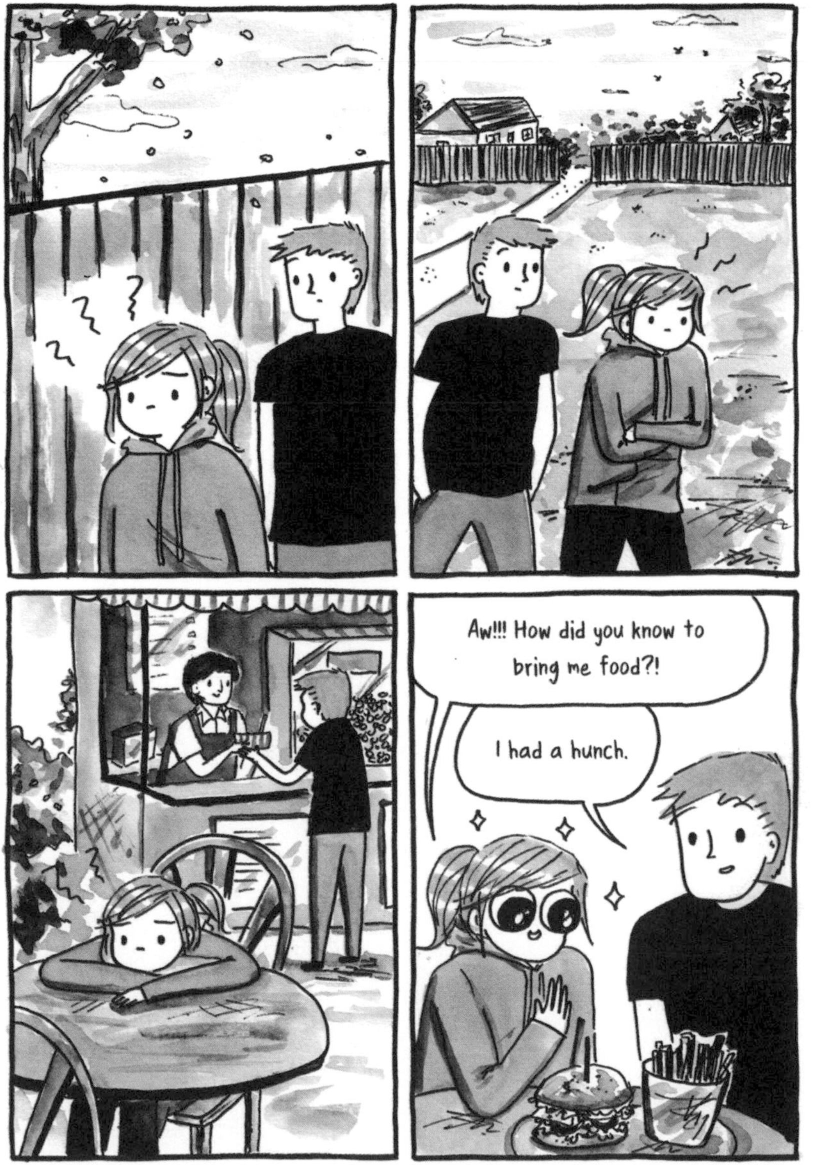
Aw!!! How did you know to bring me food?!
I had a hunch.

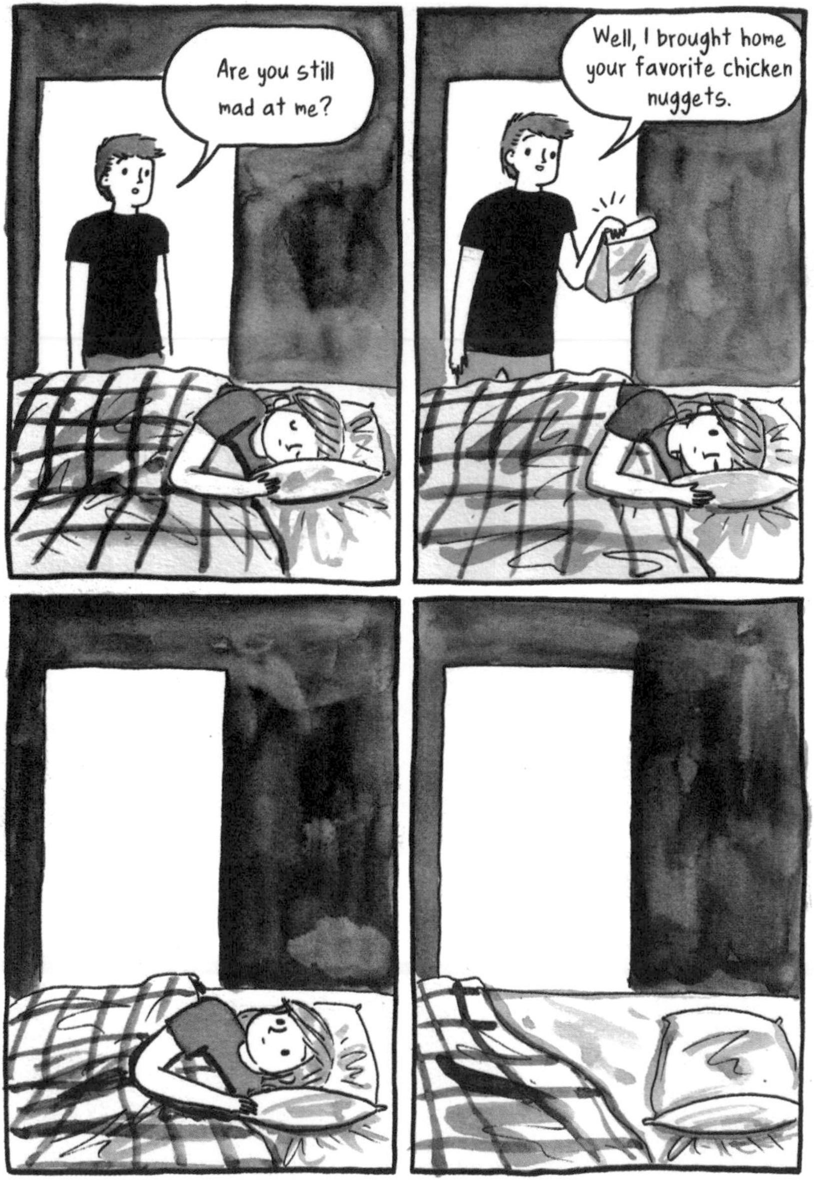
Are you still mad at me?
Well, I brought home your favorite chicken nuggets.

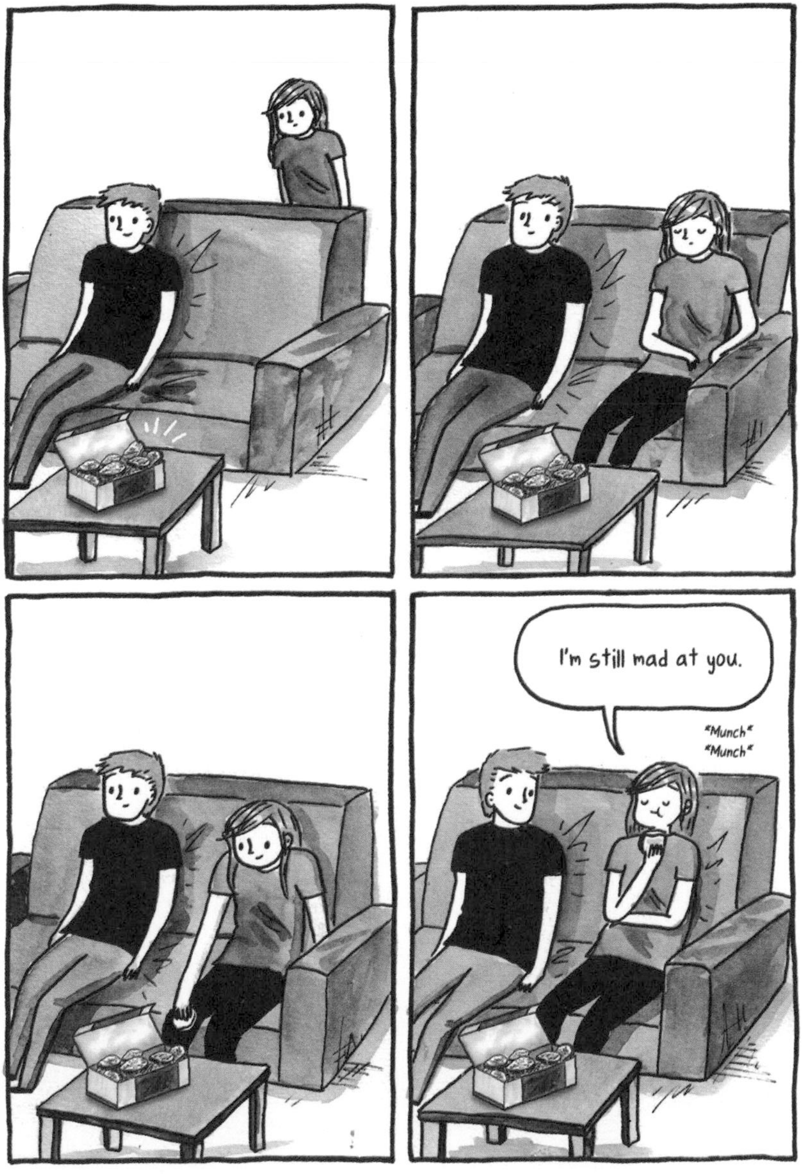
I'm still mad at you.
Munch
Munch

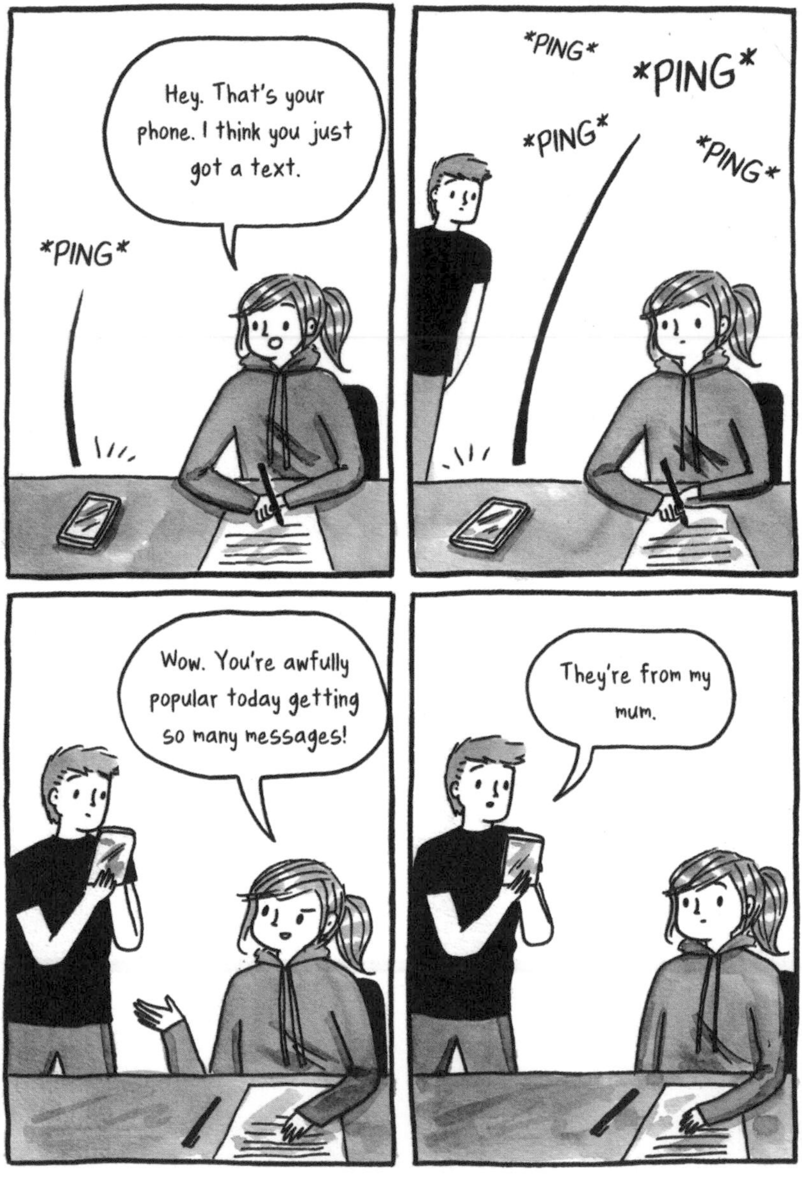

Hey. That's your phone. I think you just got a text.
PING
PING
PING
PING
PING
Wow. You're awfully popular today getting so many messages!
They're from my mum.

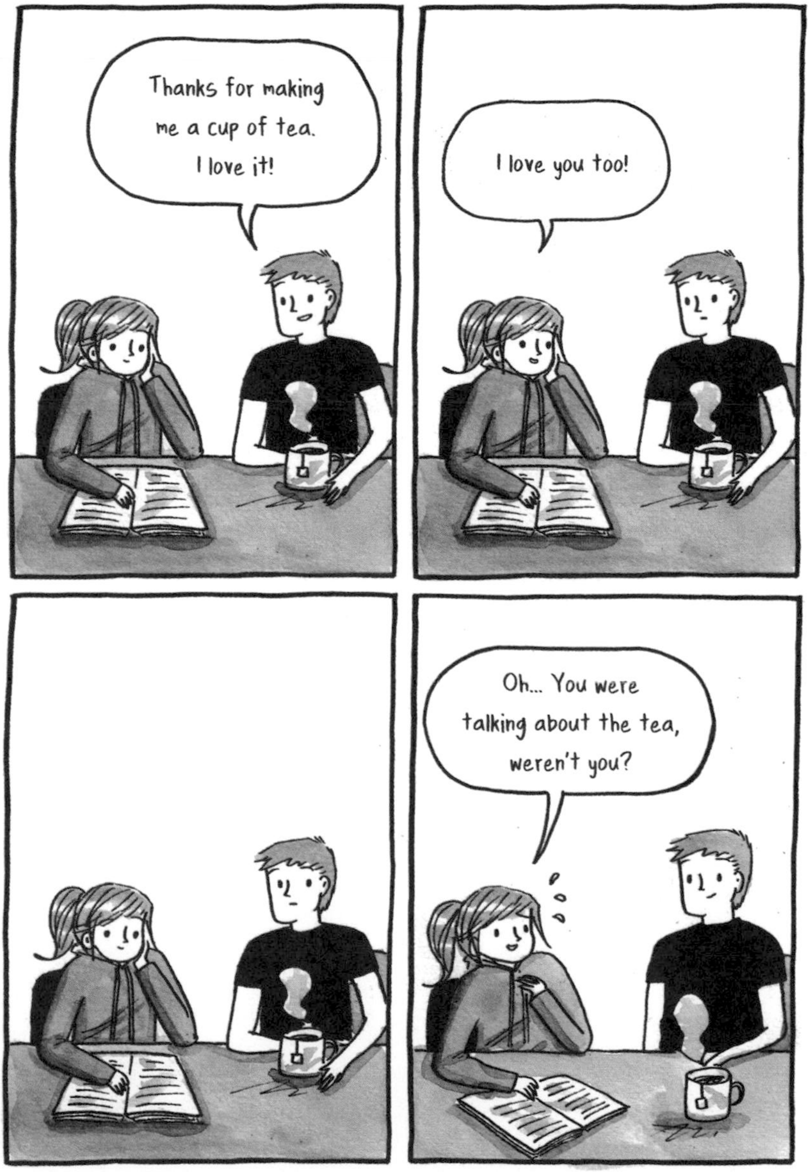
Thanks for making me a cup of tea. I love it!
I love you too!
Oh... You were talking about the tea, weren't you?

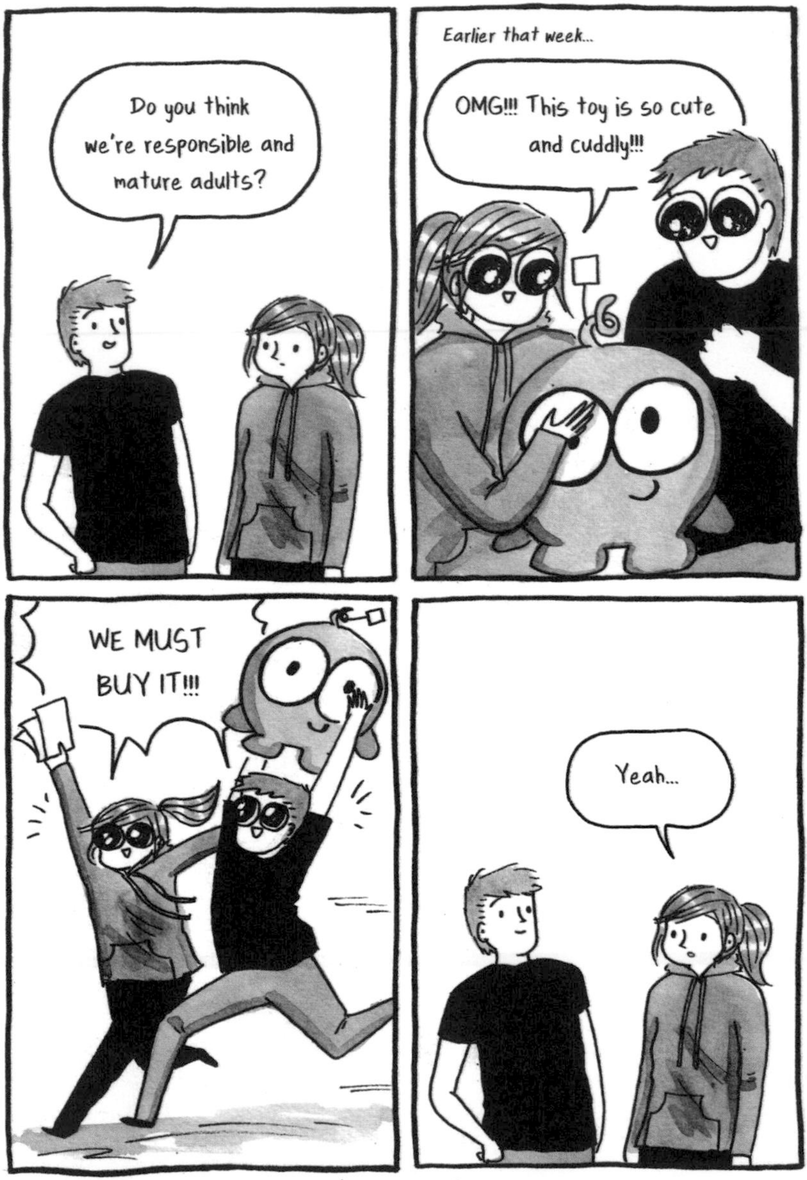
Do you think we're responsible and mature adults?
Earlier that week...
OMG!!! This toy is so cute and cuddly!!!
WE MUST BUY IT!!!
Yeah...

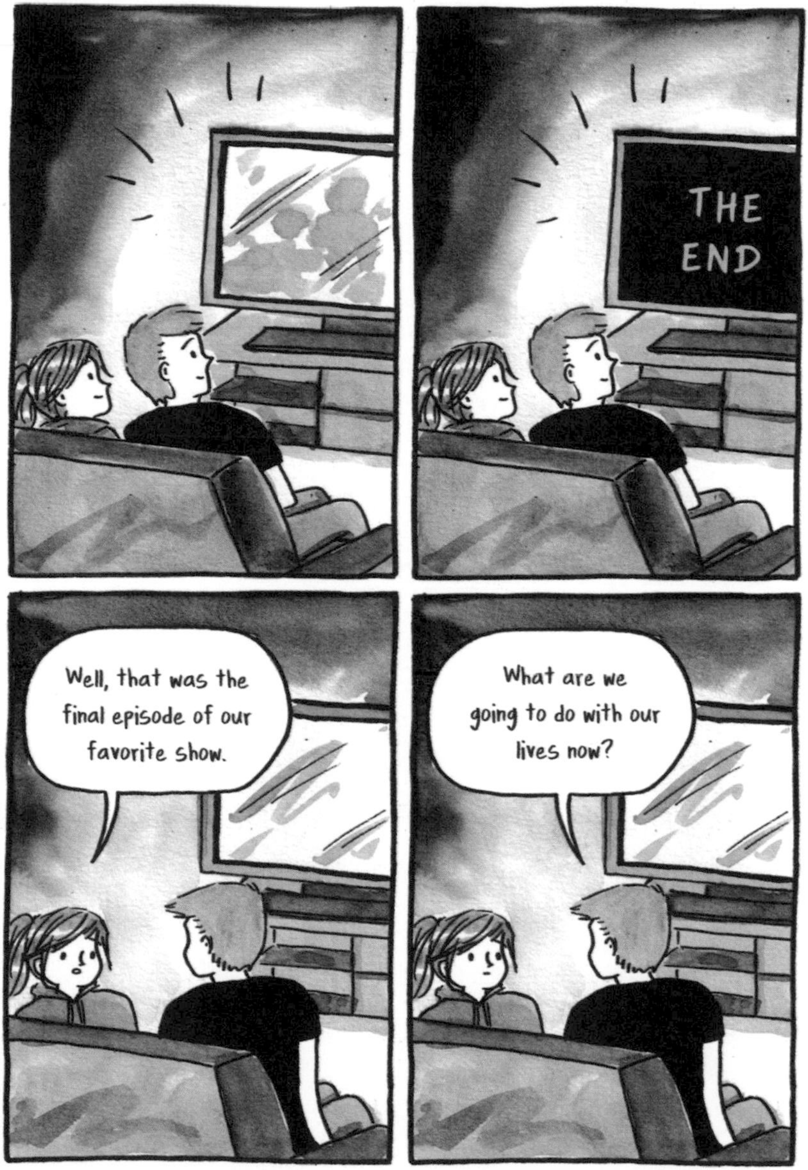
THE END
Well, that was the final episode of our favorite show.
What are we going to do with our lives now?

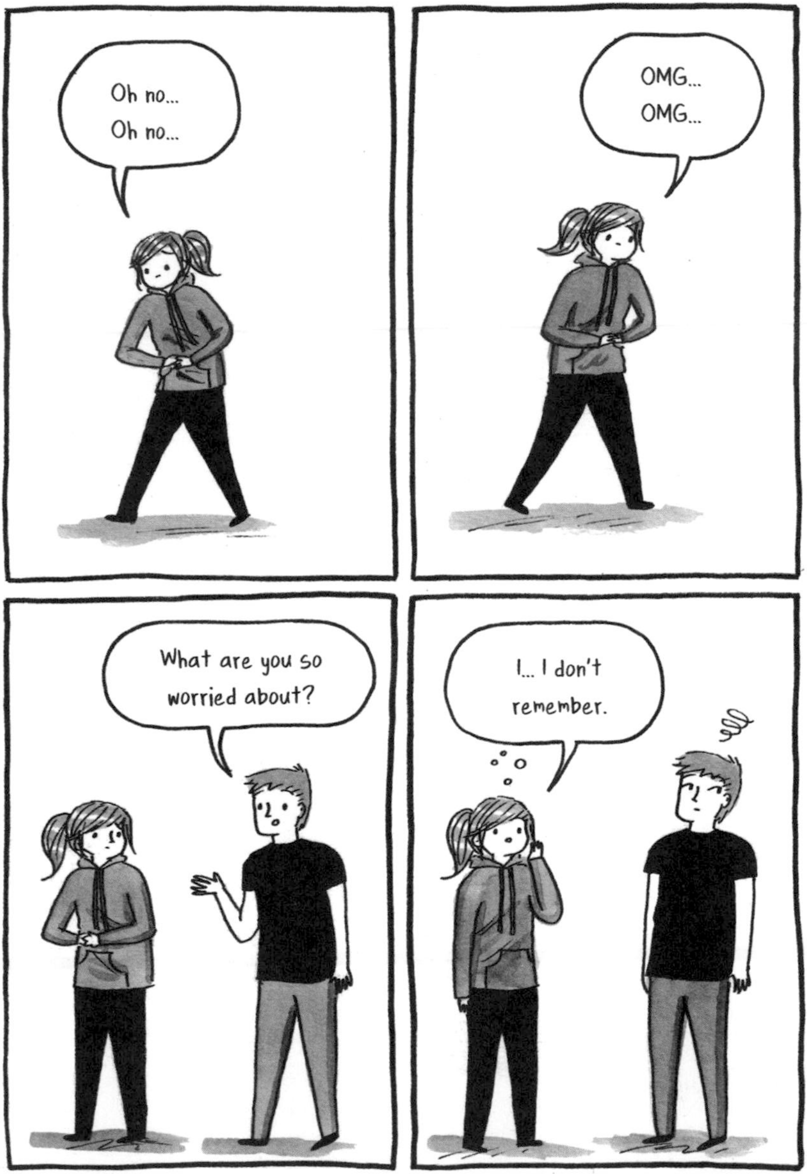
Oh no...
Oh no...
OMG...
OMG...
What are you so worried about?
I... I don't remember.

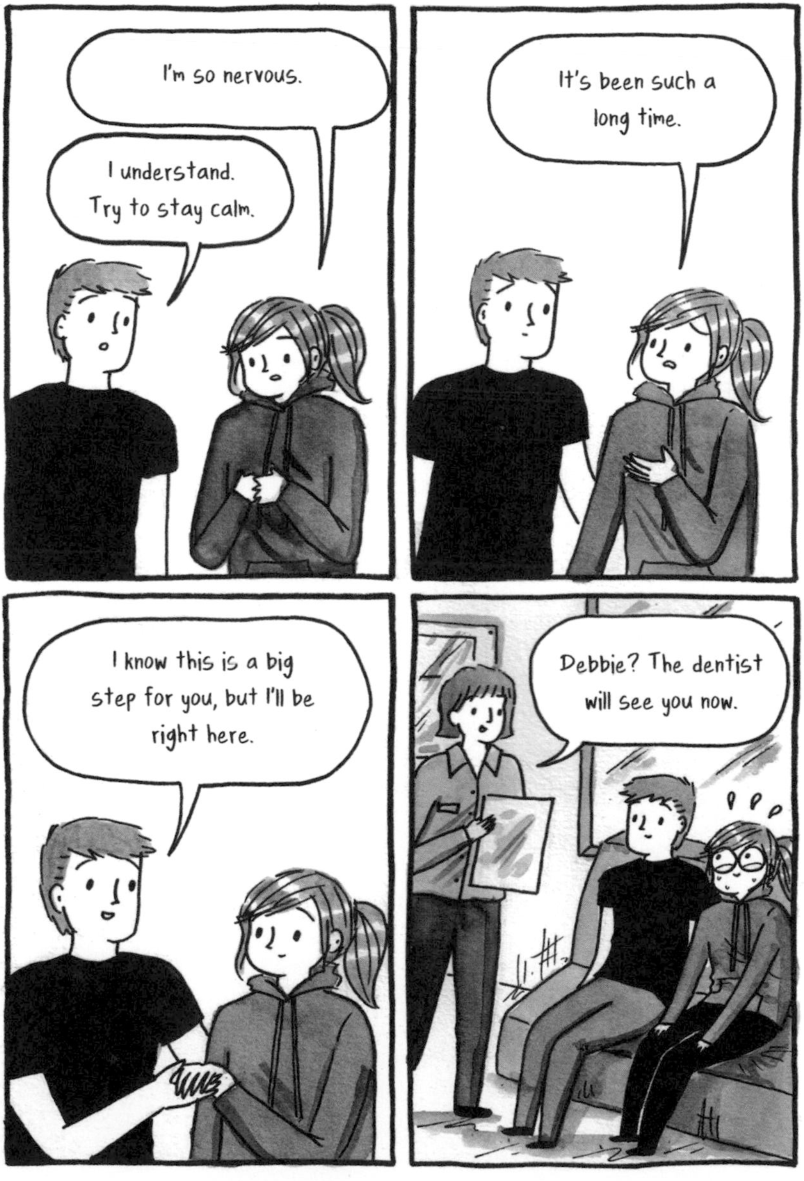
I'm so nervous.
I understand. Try to stay calm.
It's been such a long time.
I know this is a big step for you, but I'll be right here.
Debbie? The dentist will see you now.

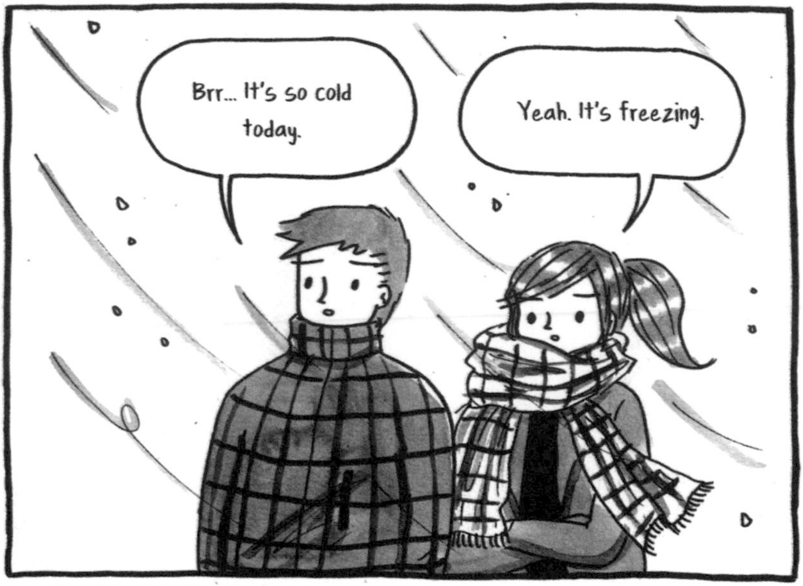
Brr... It's so cold today.
Yeah. It's freezing.

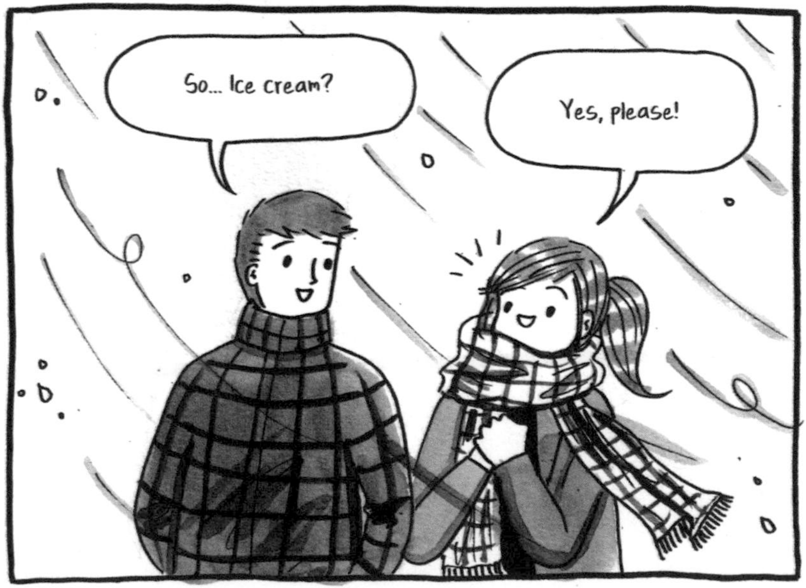
So... Ice cream?
Yes, please!

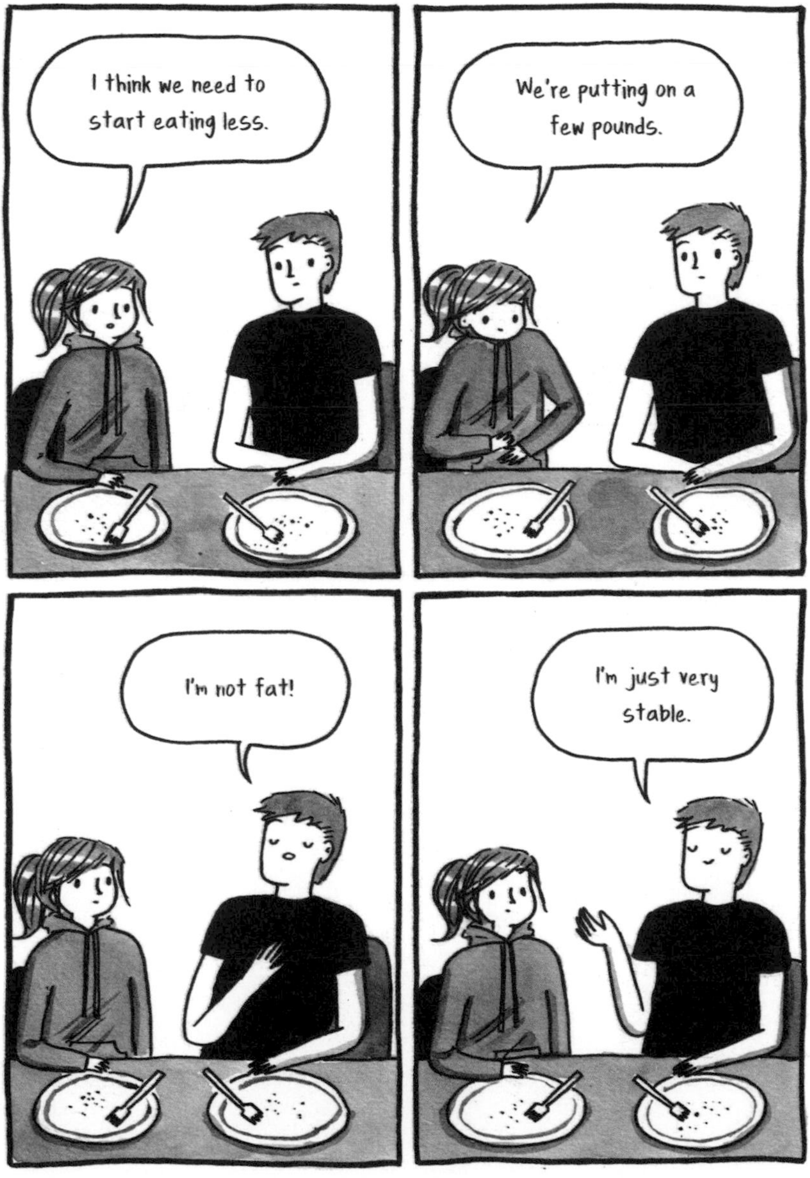
I think we need to start eating less.
We're putting on a few pounds.
I'm not fat!
I'm just very stable.

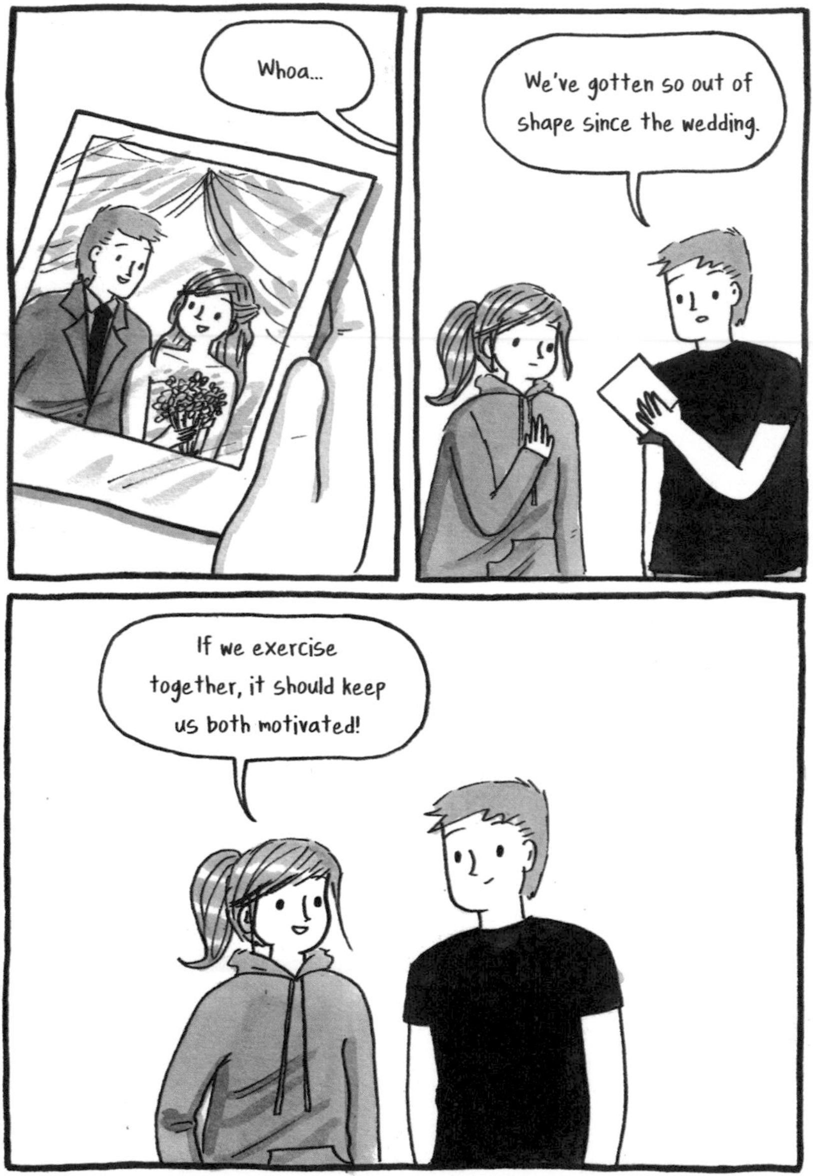
Whoa...
We've gotten so out of shape since the wedding.
If we exercise together, it should keep us both motivated!

Couples Workout

Expectation

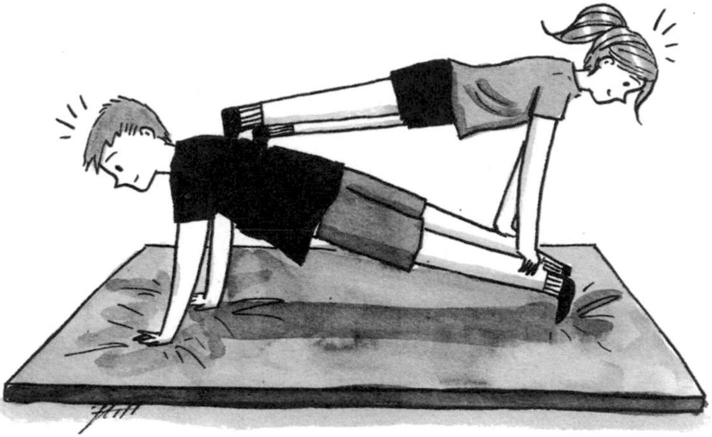

Reality

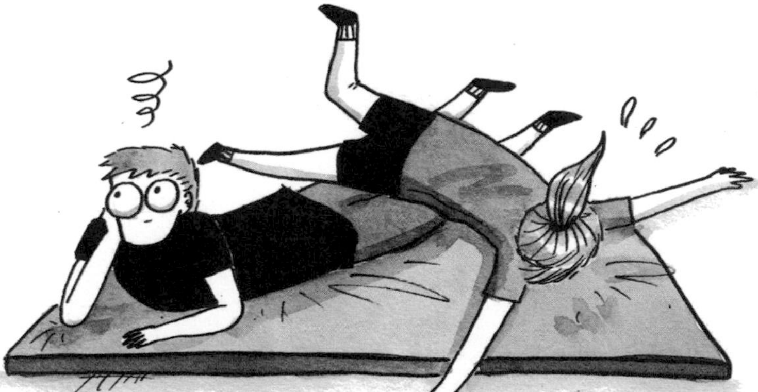

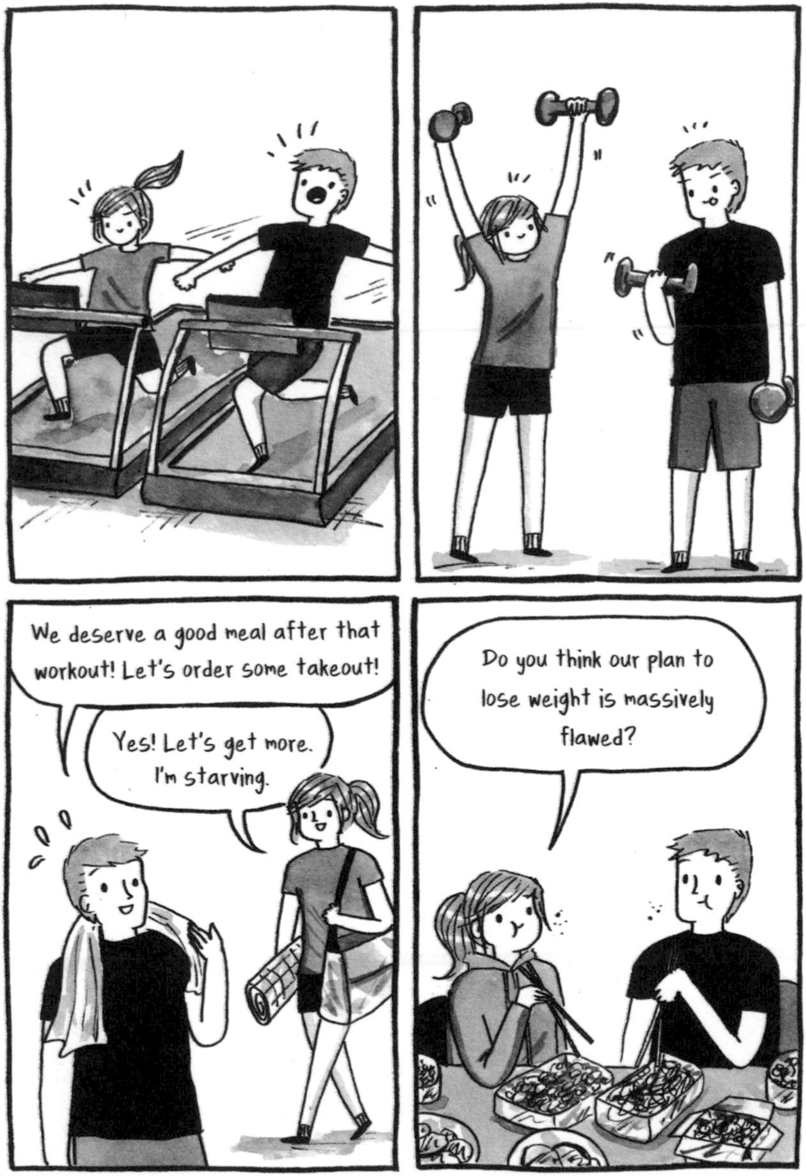
We deserve a good meal after that workout! Let's order some takeout!
Yes! Let's get more. I'm starving.
Do you think our plan to lose weight is massively flawed?

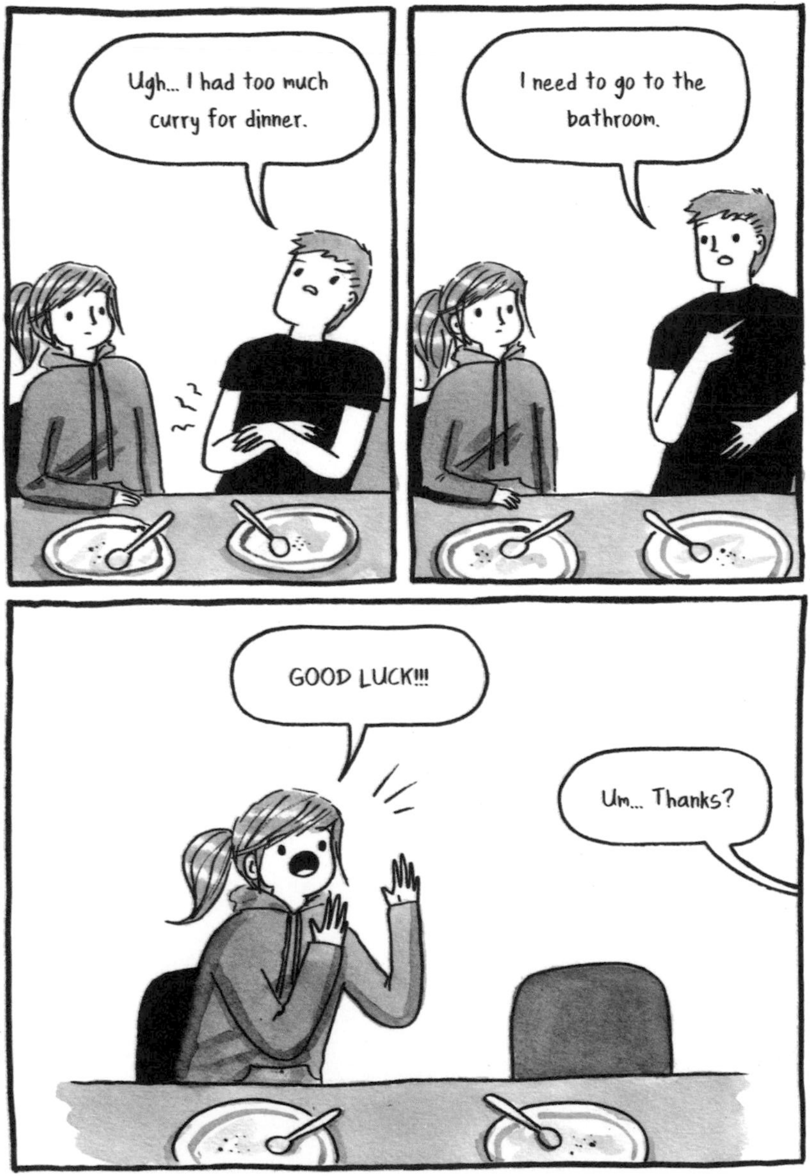
Ugh... I had too much curry for dinner.
I need to go to the bathroom.
GOOD LUCK!!!
Um... Thanks?

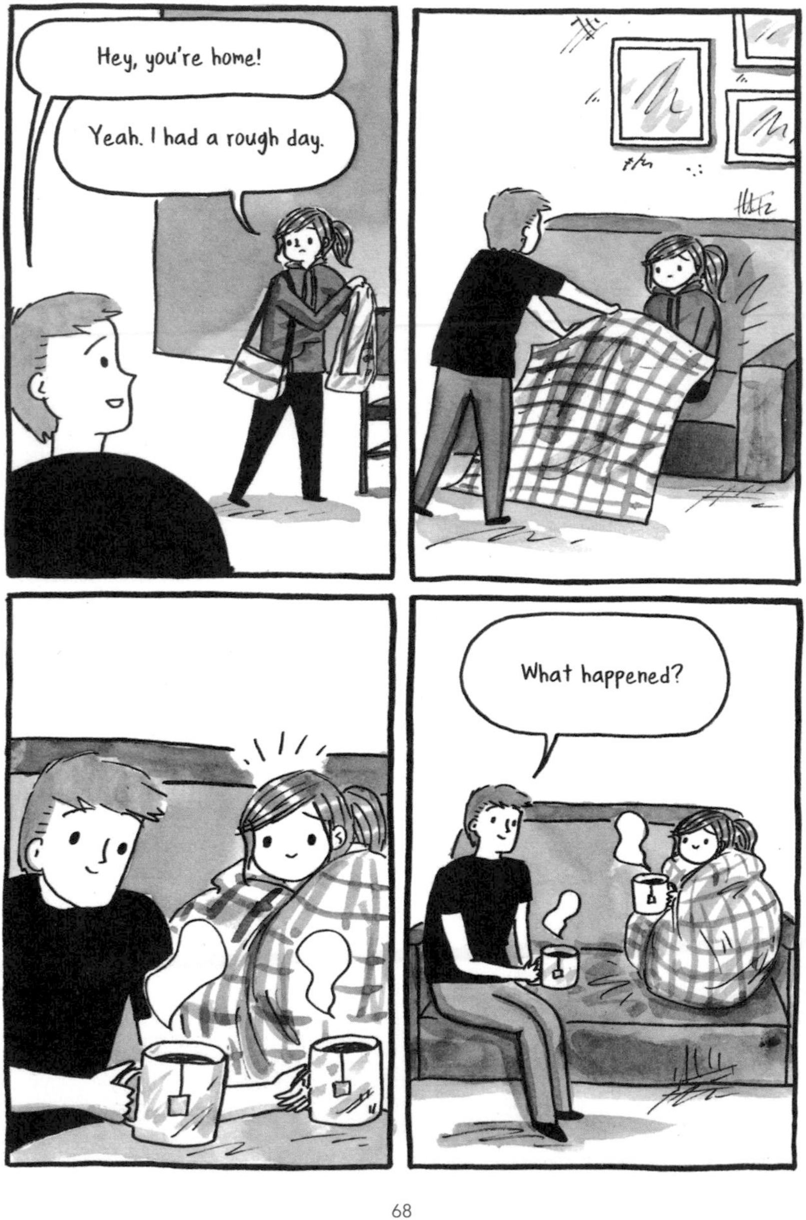
Hey, you're home!
Yeah. I had a rough day.
What happened?

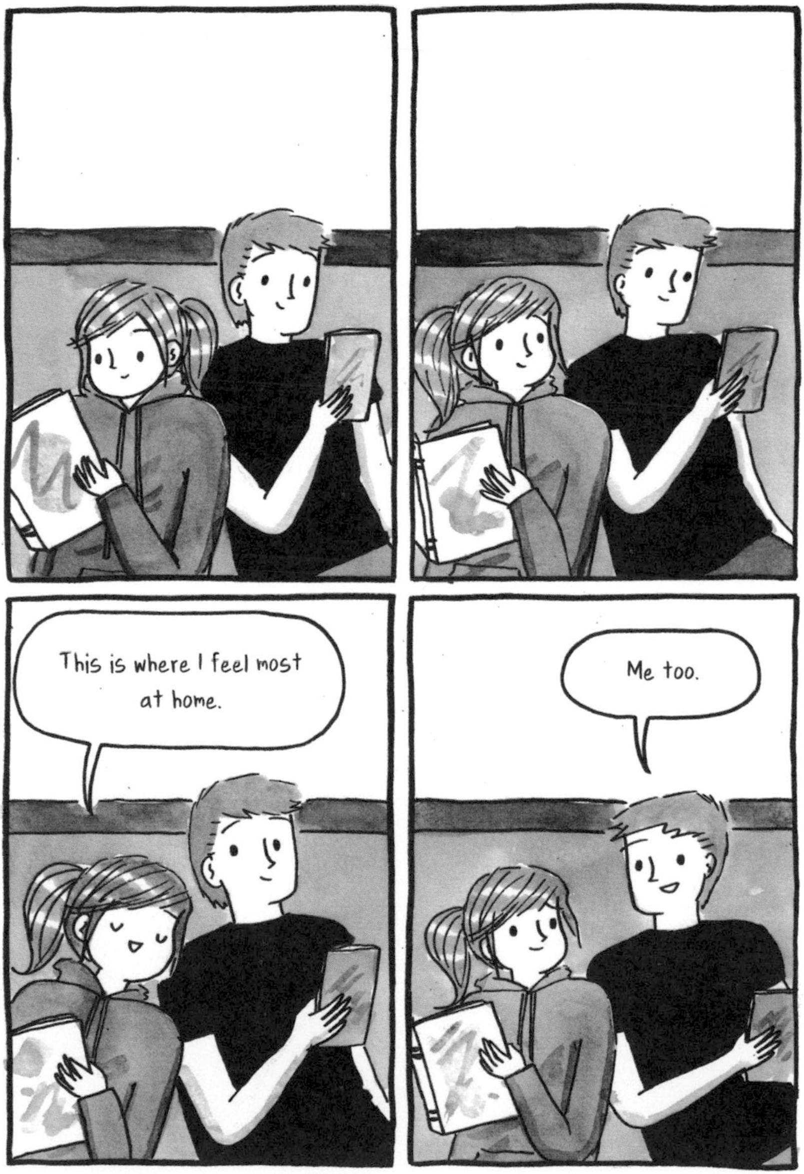
This is where I feel most at home.
Me too.

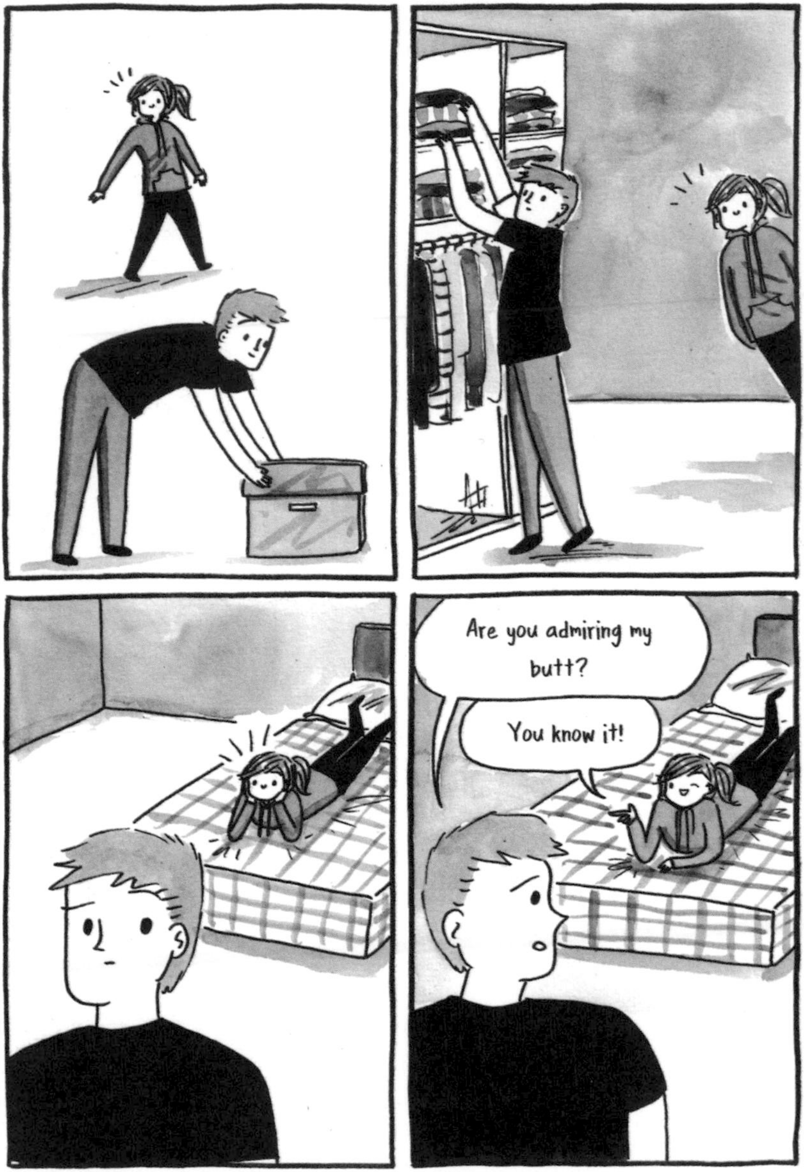
Are you admiring my butt?
You know it!

Romantic Massage

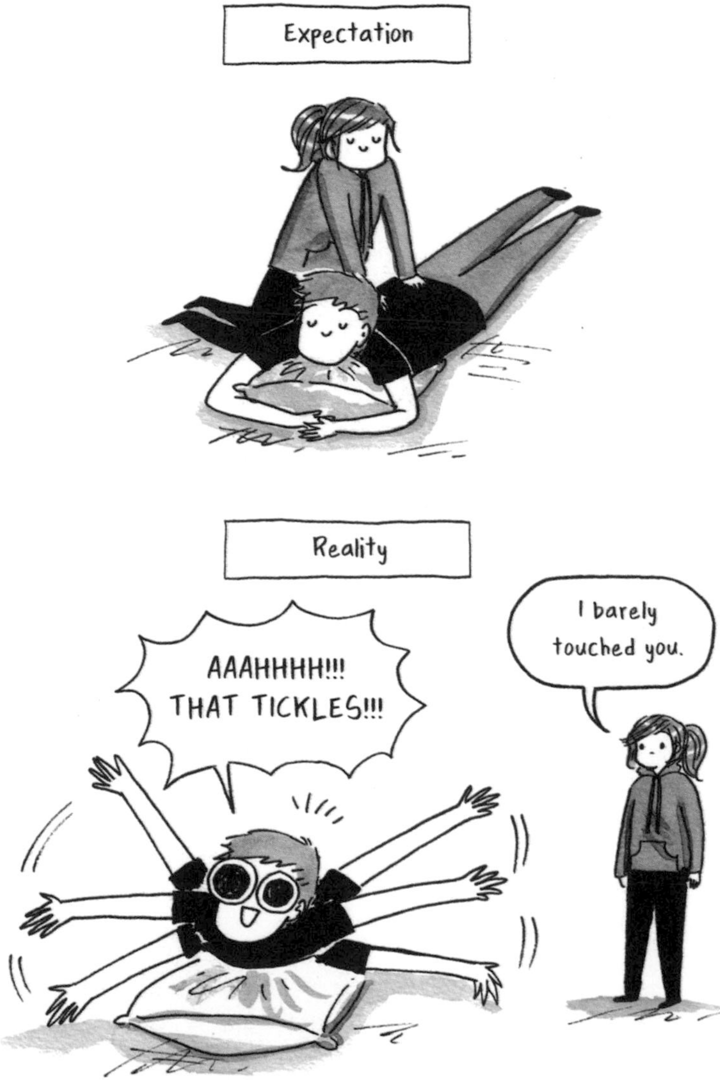
Expectation
Reality
AAAHHHH!!! THAT TICKLES!!!
I barely touched you.

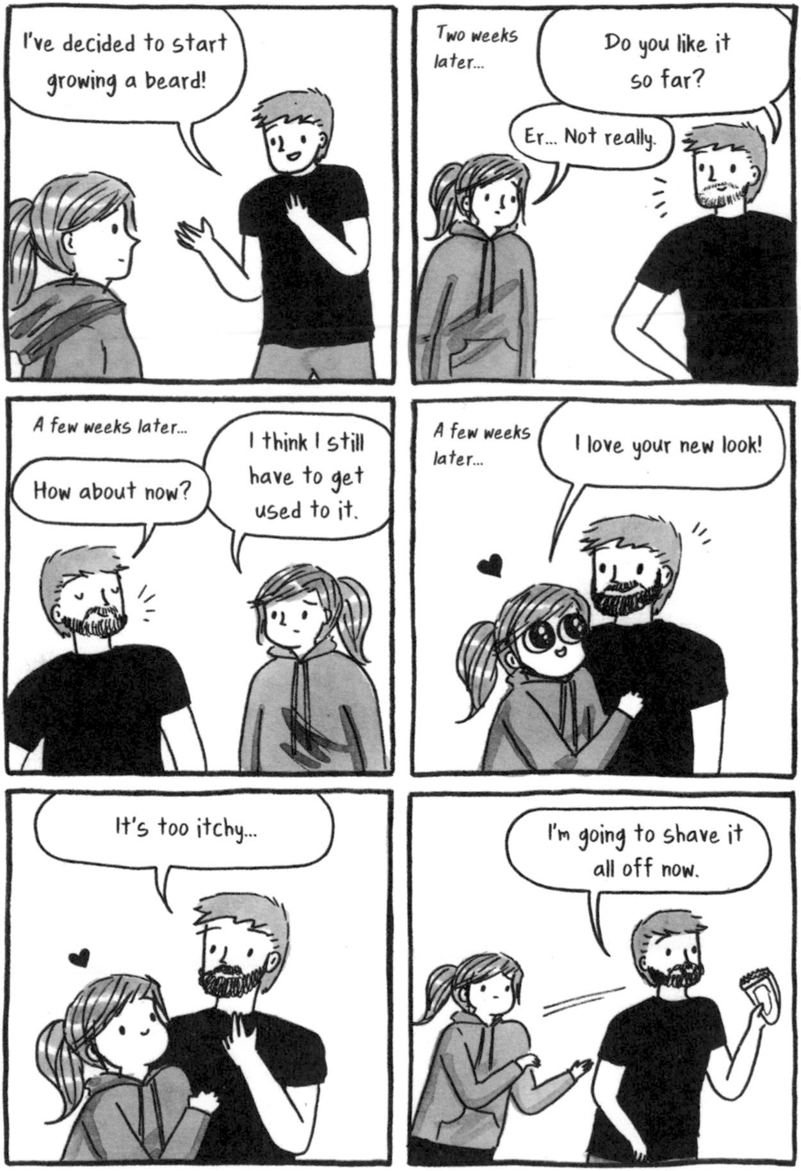
I've decided to start growing a beard!
Two weeks later...
Do you like it so far?
Er... Not really.
A few weeks later...
How about now?
I think I still have to get used to it.
A few weeks later...
I love your new look!
It's too itchy...
I'm going to shave it all off now.

Me

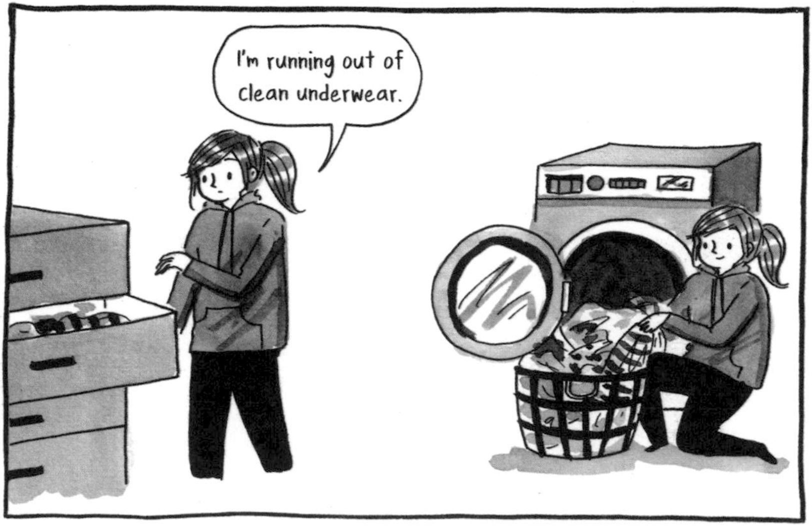
I'm running out of clean underwear.

Him

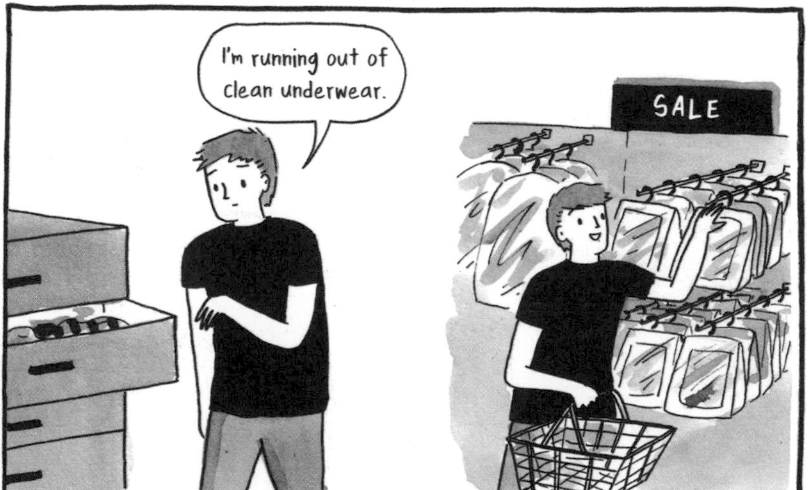
I'm running out of clean underwear.
SALE

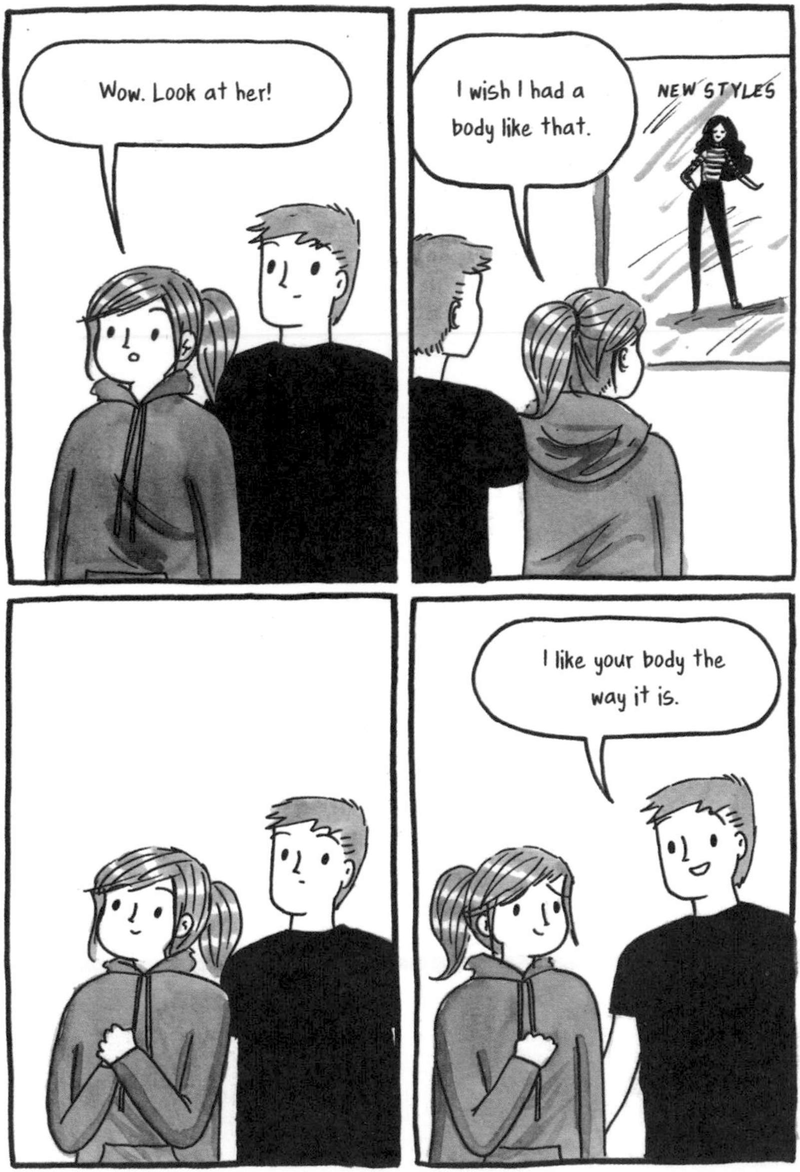
Wow. Look at her!
I wish I had a body like that.
NEW STYLES
I like your body the way it is.

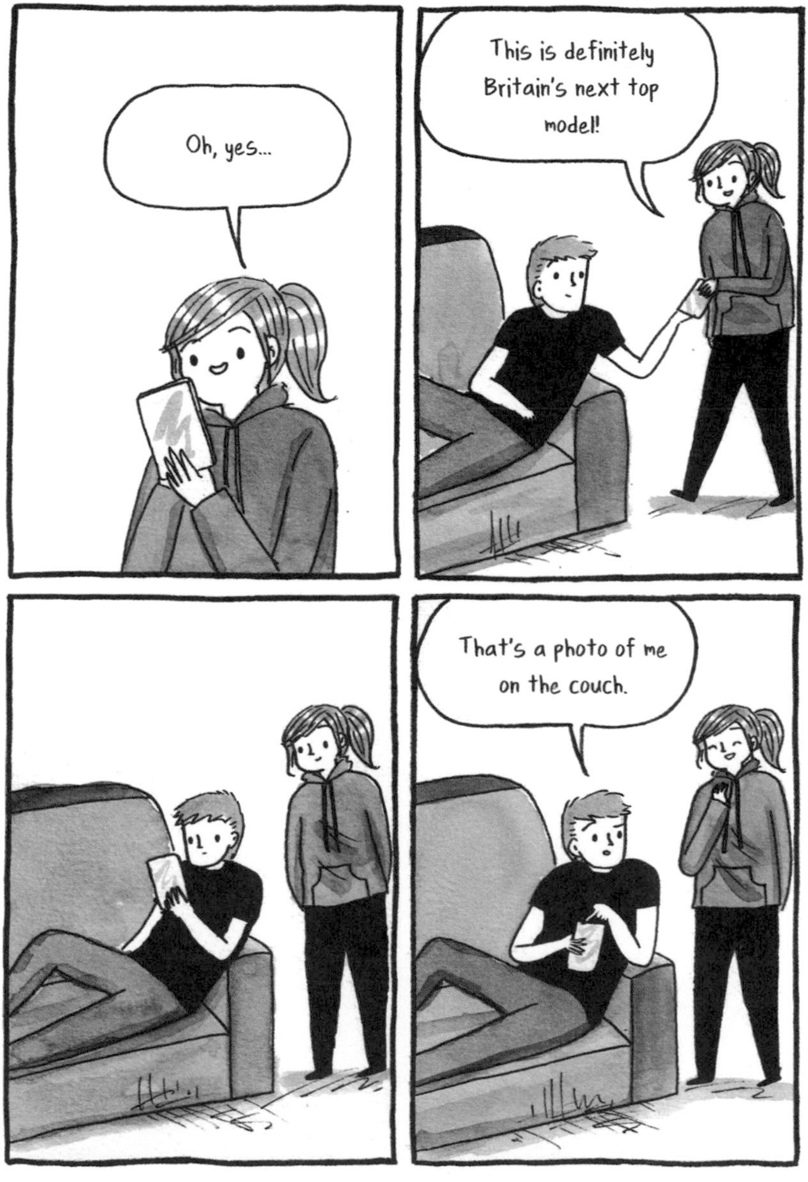
Oh, yes...
This is definitely Britain's next top model!
That's a photo of me on the couch.

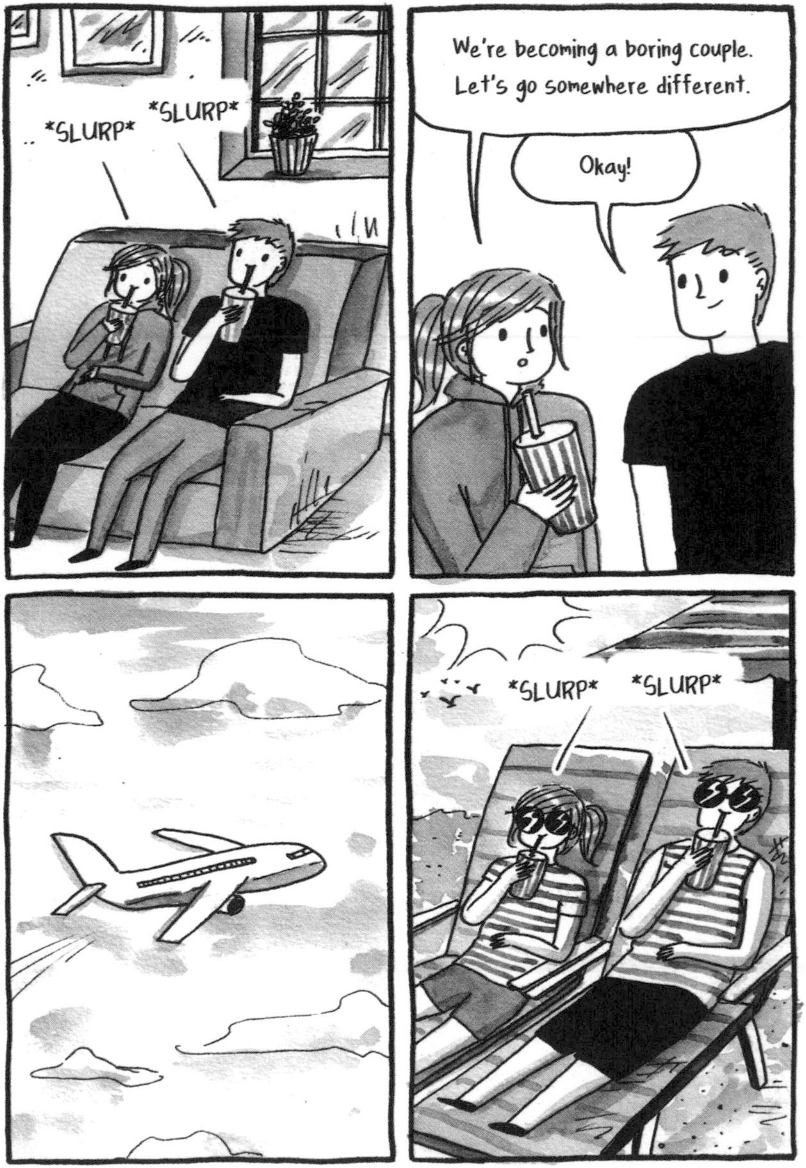
SLURP
SLURP
We're becoming a boring couple. Let's go somewhere different.
Okay!
SLURP
SLURP

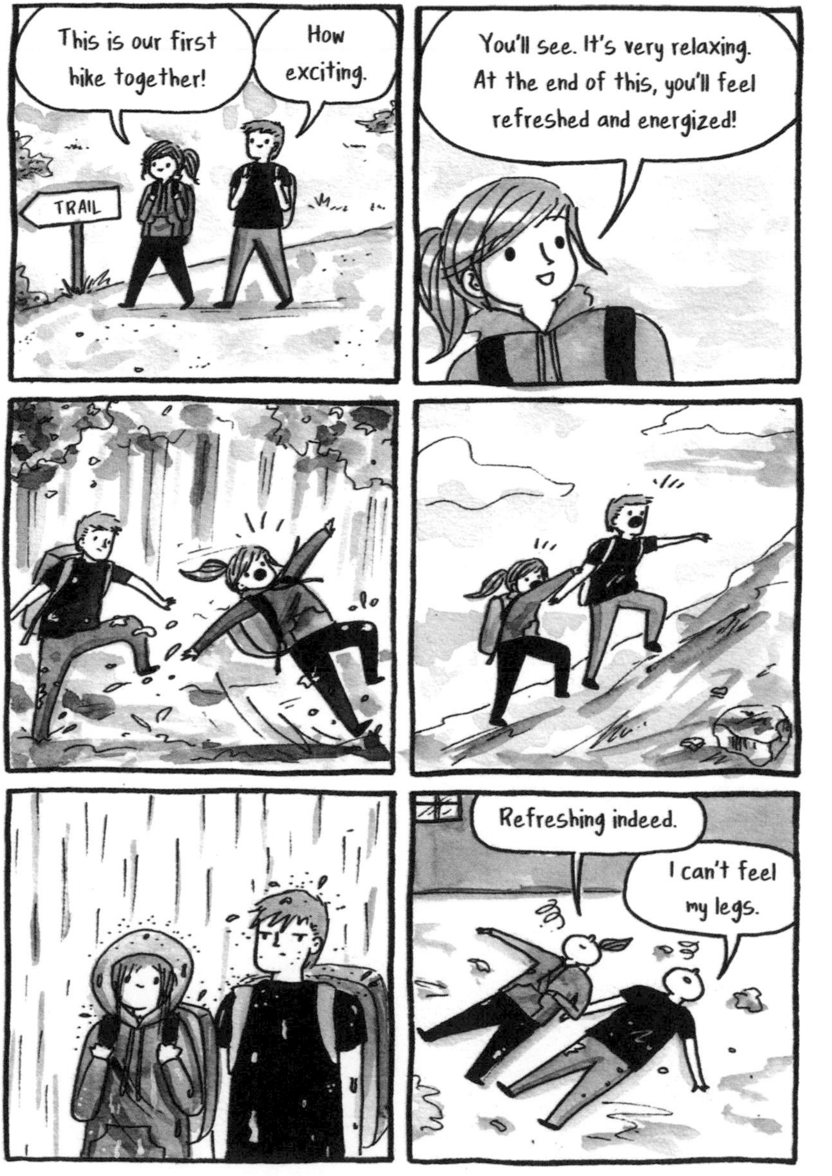
This is our first hike together!
How exciting.
TRAIL
You'll see. It's very relaxing. At the end of this, you'll feel refreshed and energized!
Refreshing indeed.
I can't feel my legs.

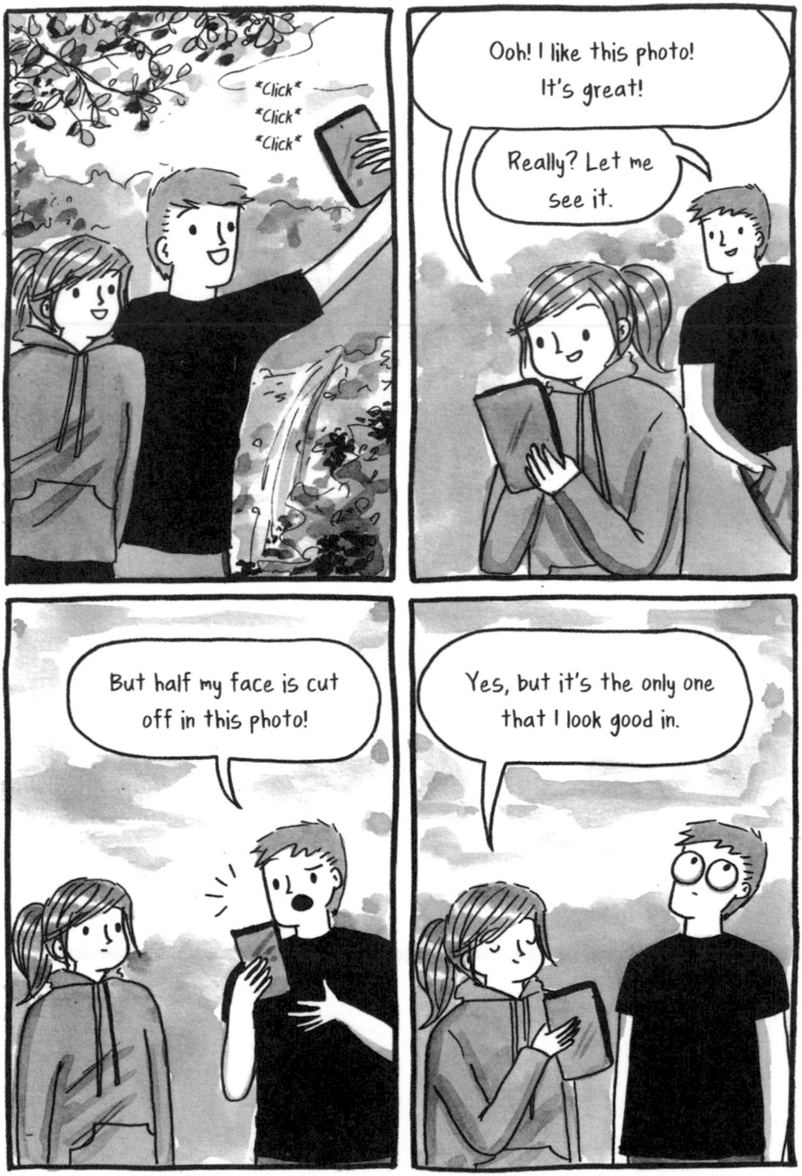
Click
Click
Click
Ooh! I like this photo! It's great!
Really? Let me see it.
But half my face is cut off in this photo!
Yes, but it's the only one that I look good in.

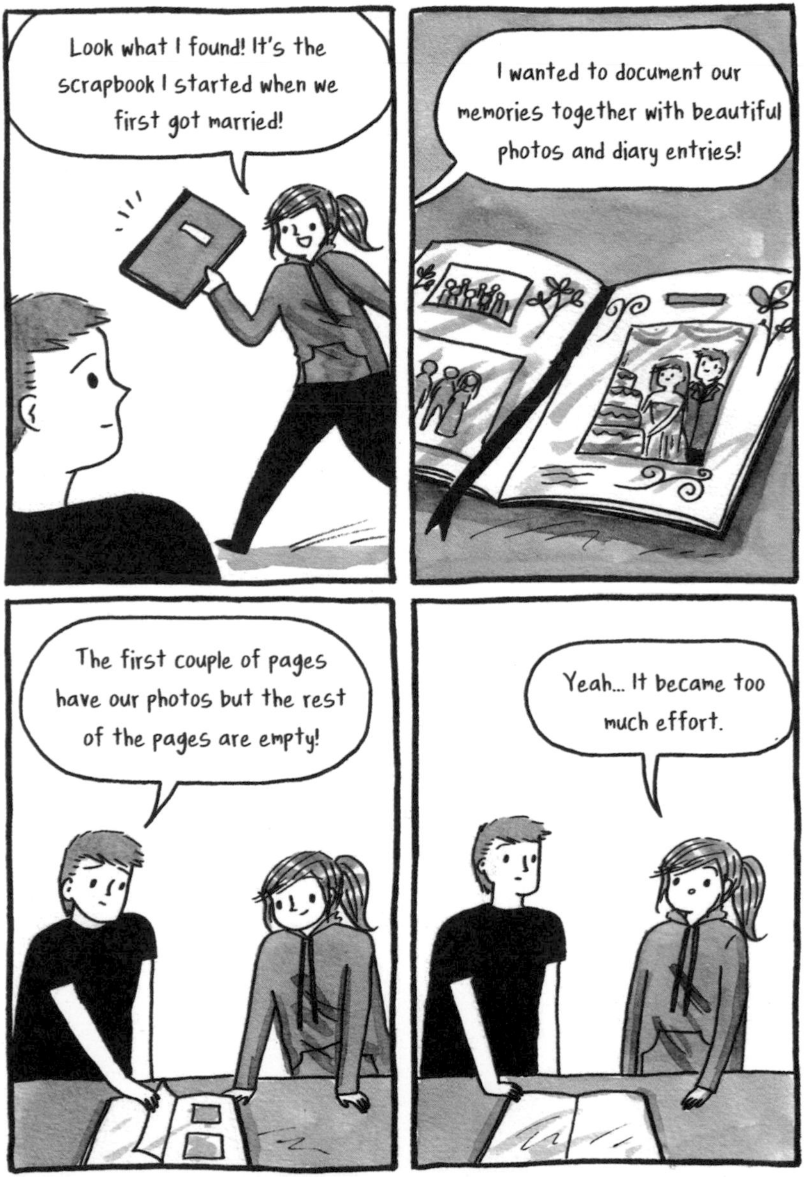
Look what I found! It's the scrapbook I started when we first got married!
I wanted to document our memories together with beautiful photos and diary entries!
The first couple of pages have our photos but the rest of the pages are empty!
Yeah... It became too much effort.

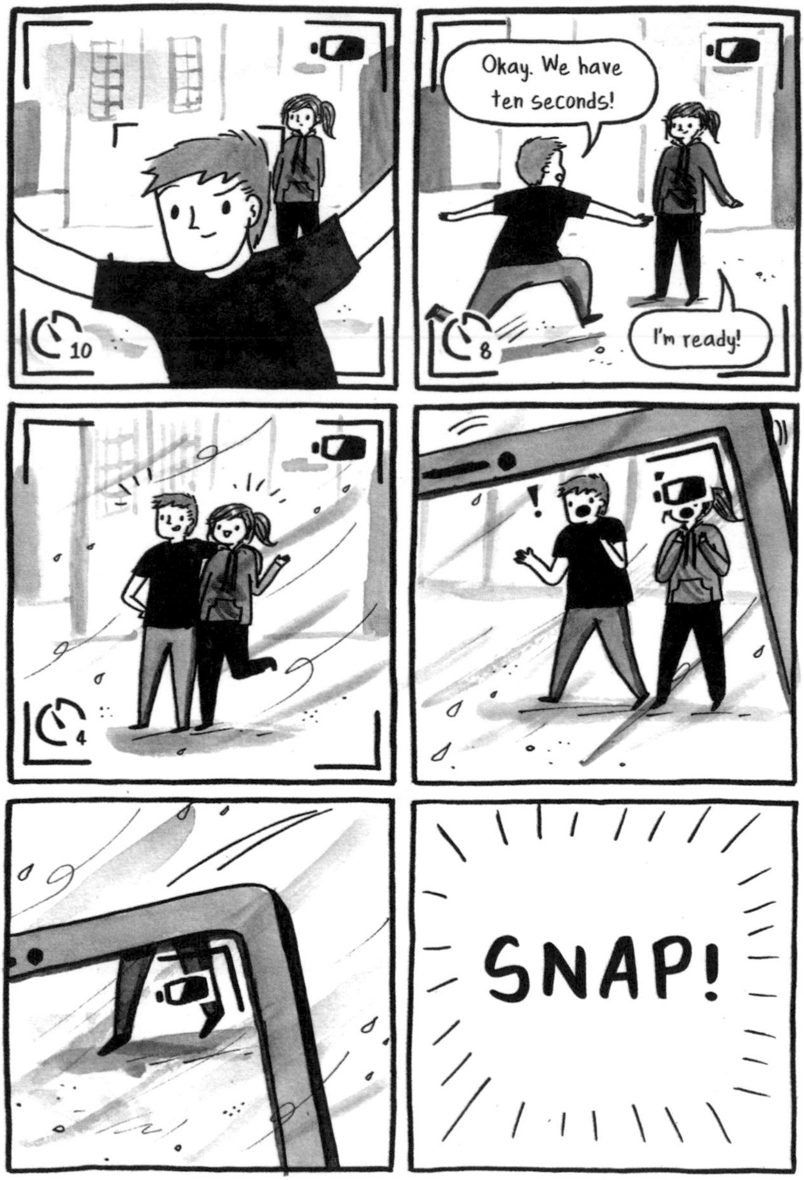
10
Okay. We have ten seconds!
8
I'm ready!
4
!
SNAP!

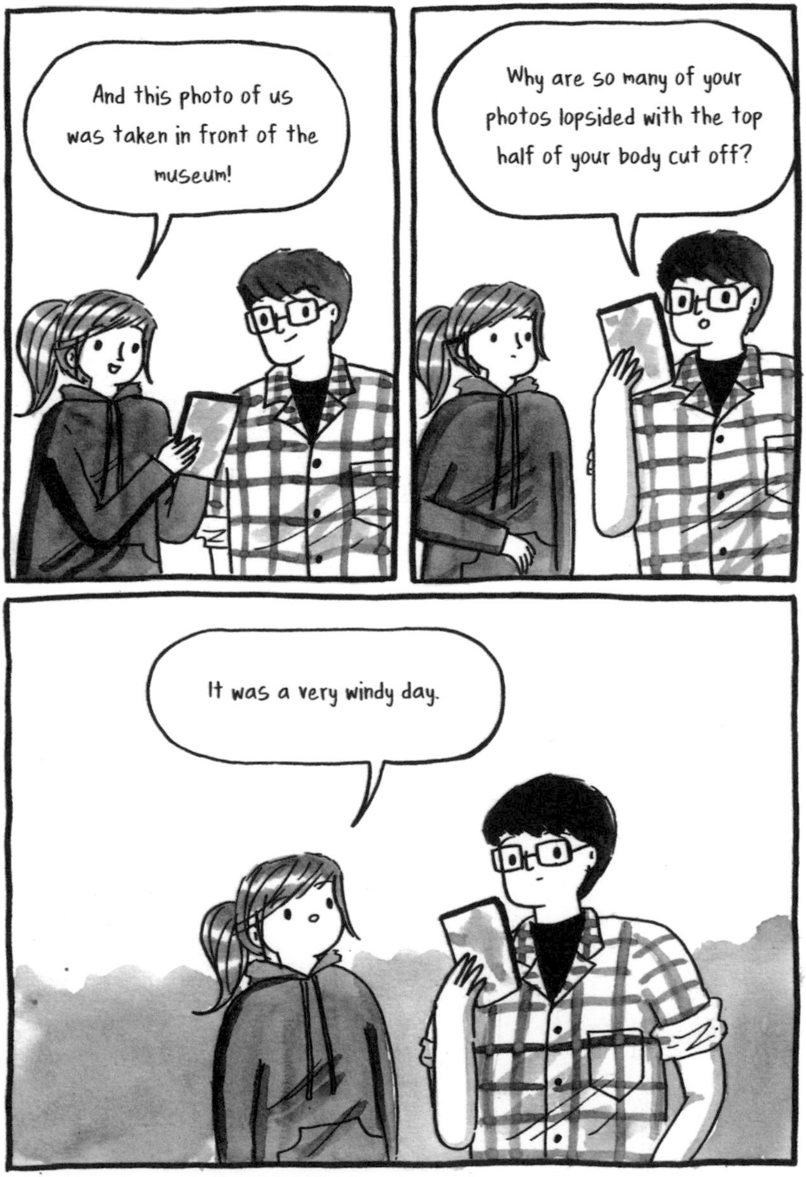
And this photo of us was taken in front of the museum!
Why are so many of your photos lopsided with the top half of your body cut off?
It was a very windy day.

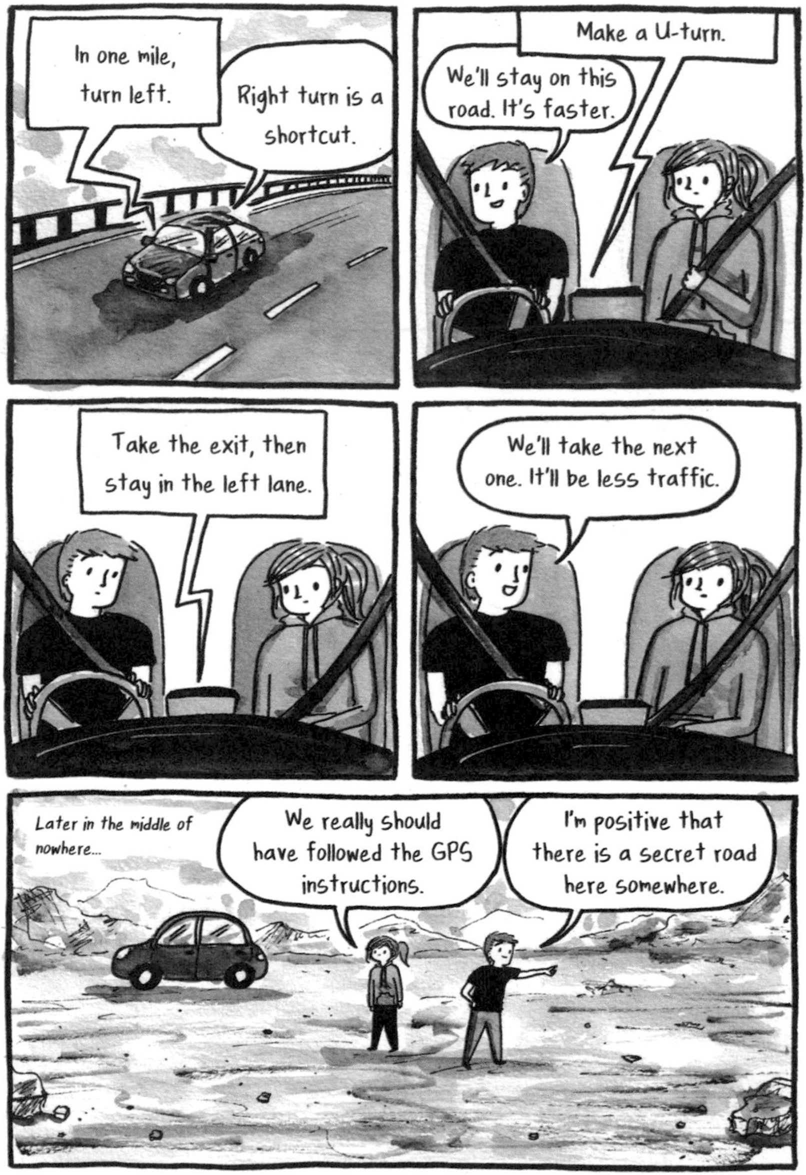

In one mile, turn left.
Right turn is a shortcut.
Make a U-turn.
We'll stay on this road. It's faster.
Take the exit, then stay in the left lane.
We'll take the next one. It'll be less traffic.
Later in the middle of nowhere...
We really should have followed the GPS instructions.
I'm positive that there is a secret road here somewhere.

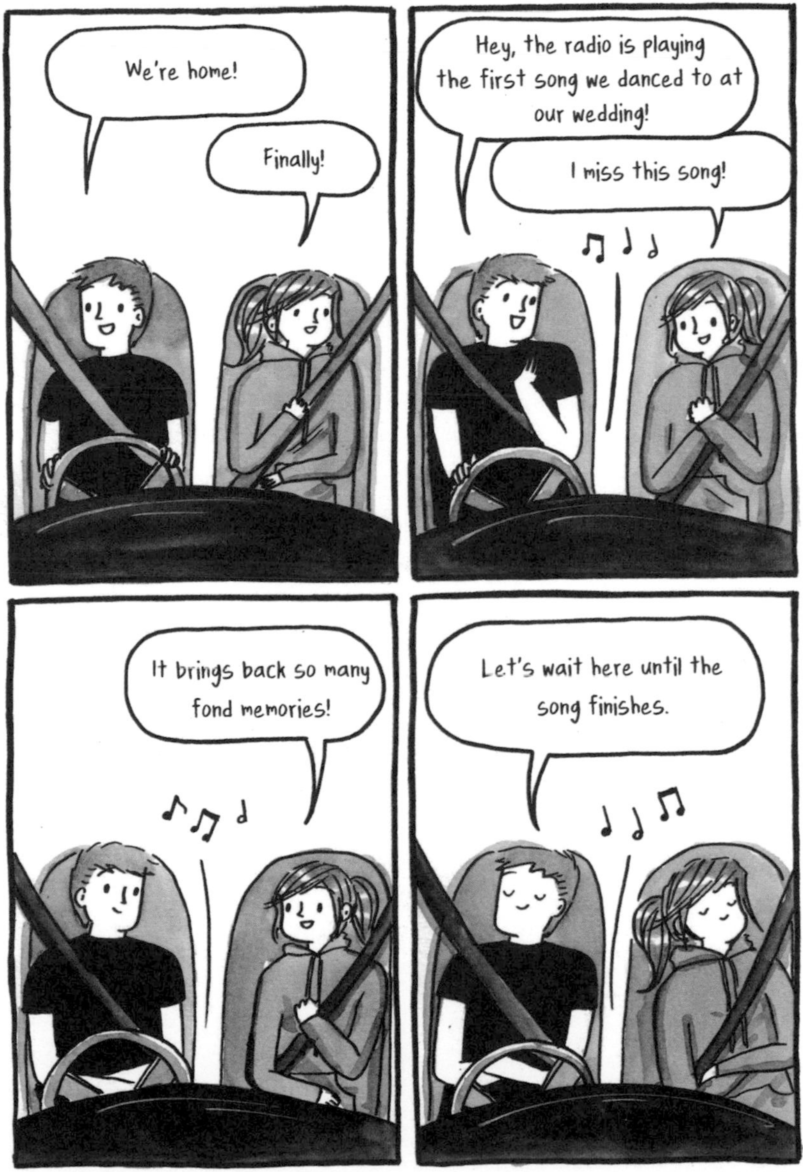

We're home!
Finally!
Hey, the radio is playing the first song we danced to at our wedding!
I miss this song!
It brings back so many fond memories!
Let's wait here until the song finishes.

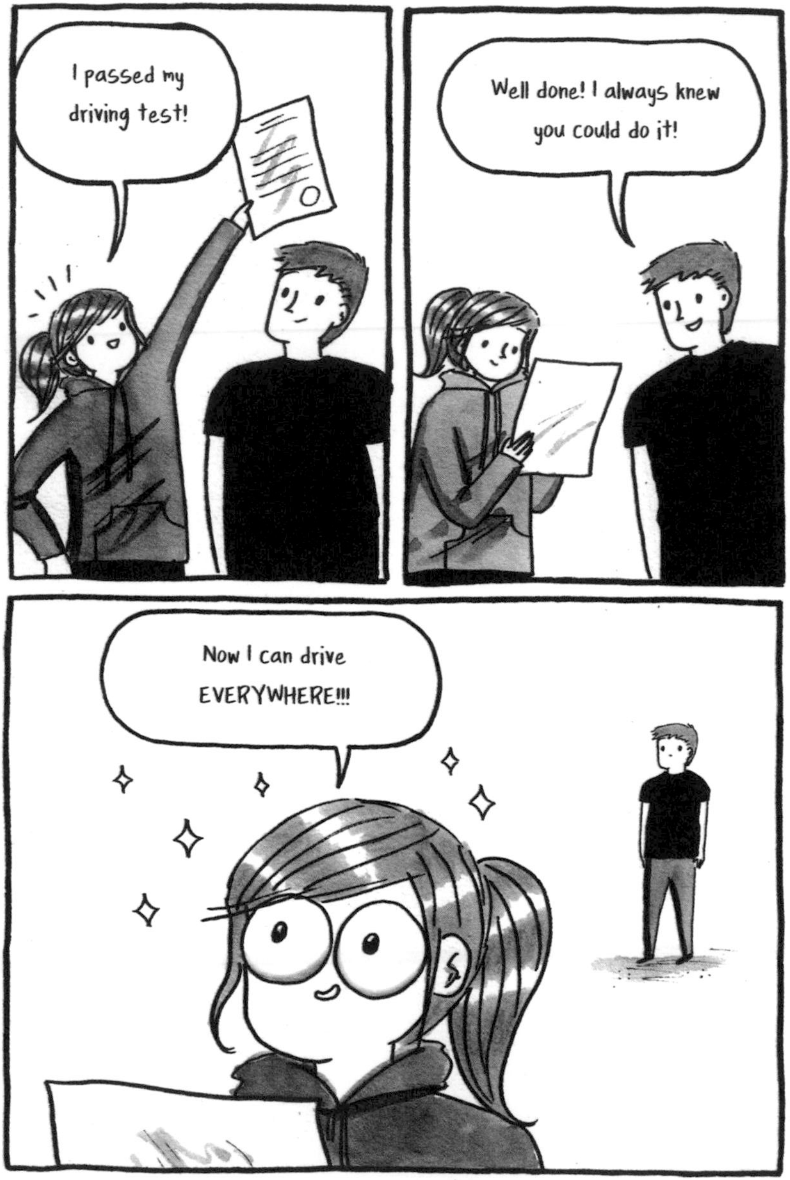
I passed my driving test!
Well done! I always knew you could do it!
Now I can drive EVERYWHERE!!!

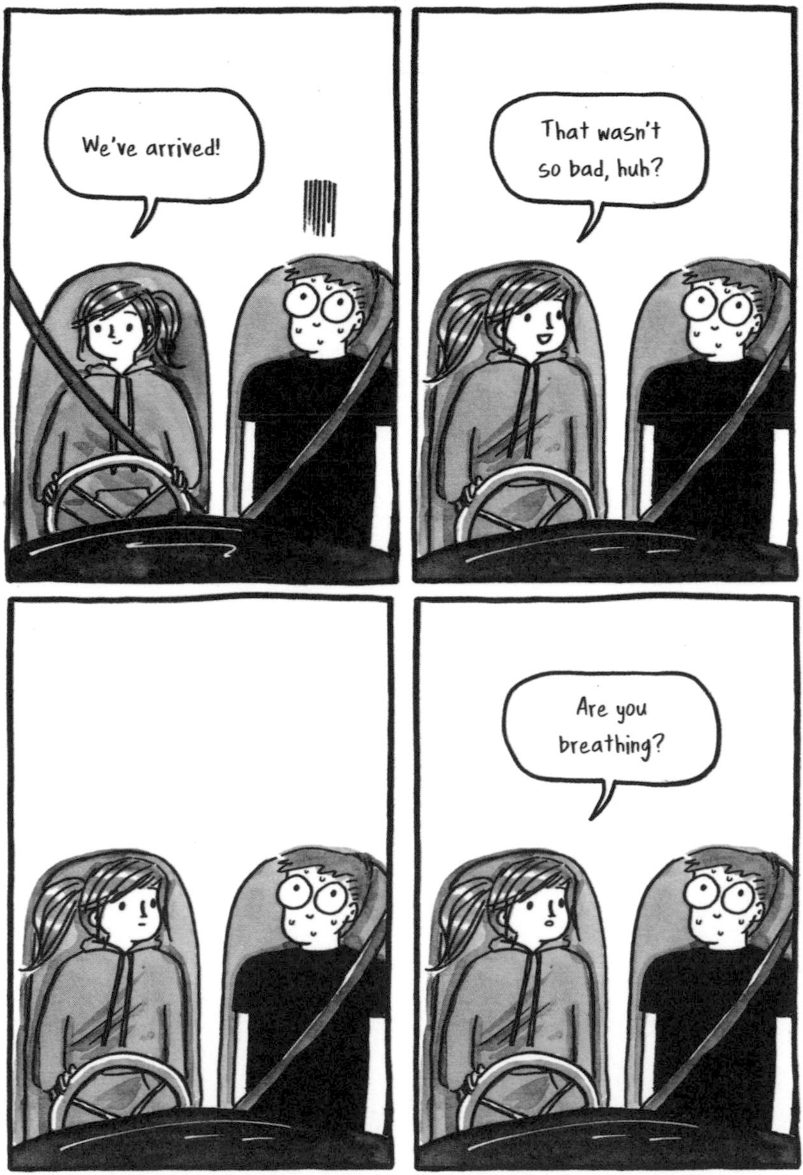
We've arrived!
That wasn't so bad, huh?
Are you breathing?

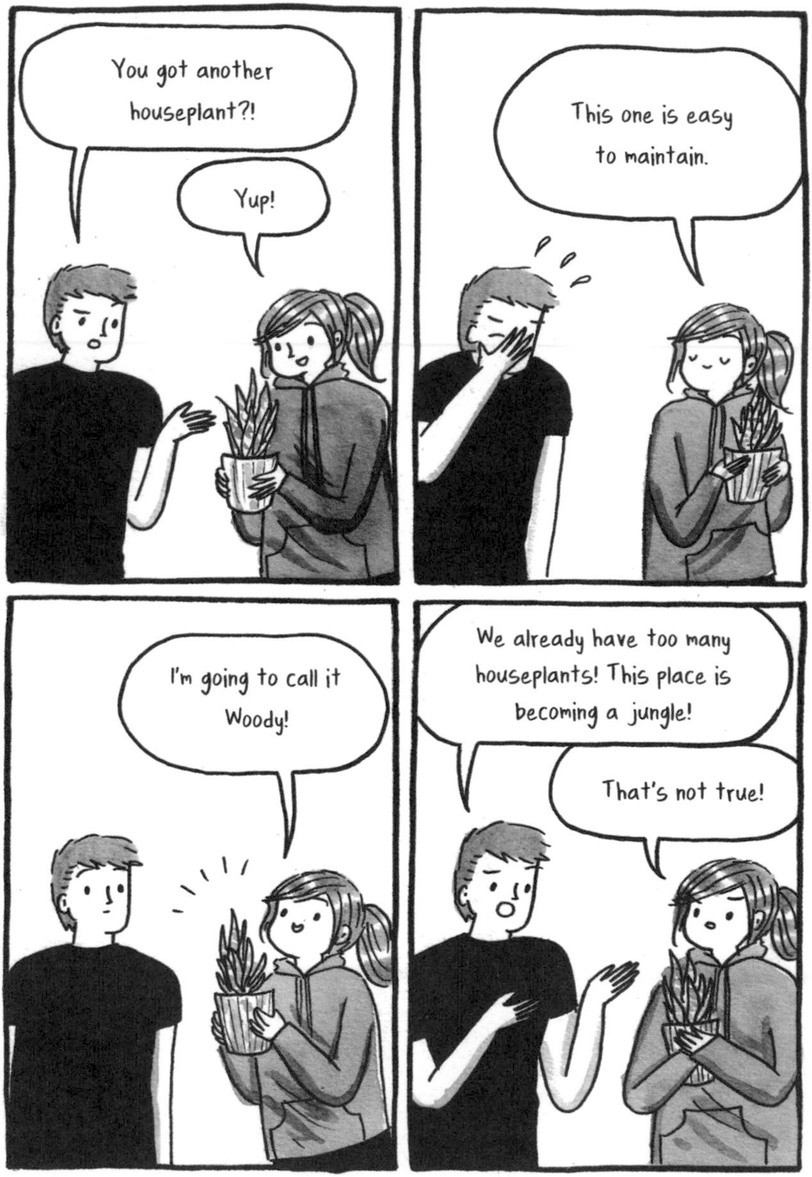
You got another houseplant?!
Yup!
This one is easy to maintain.
I'm going to call it Woody!
We already have too many houseplants! This place is becoming a jungle!
That's not true!

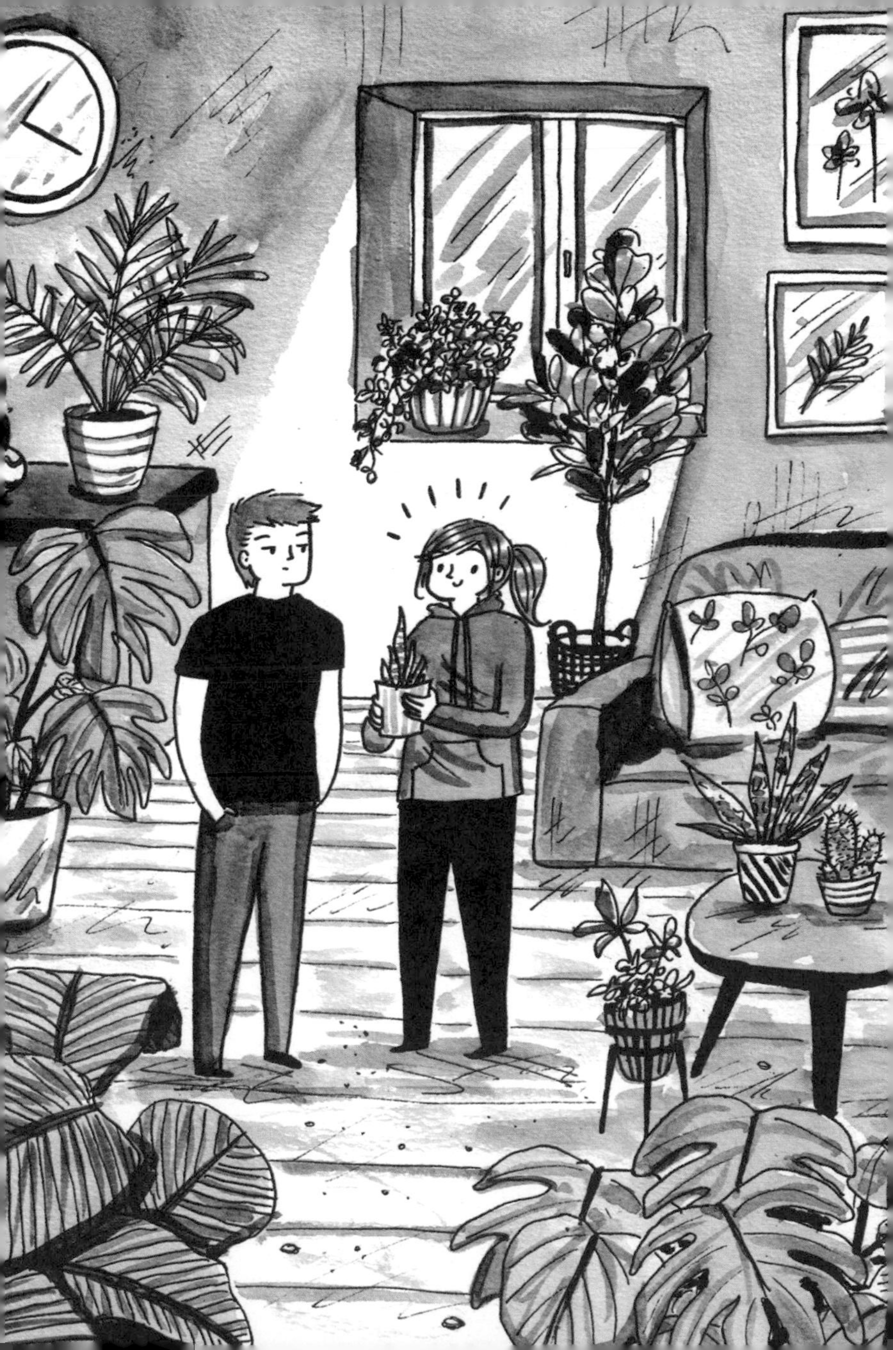

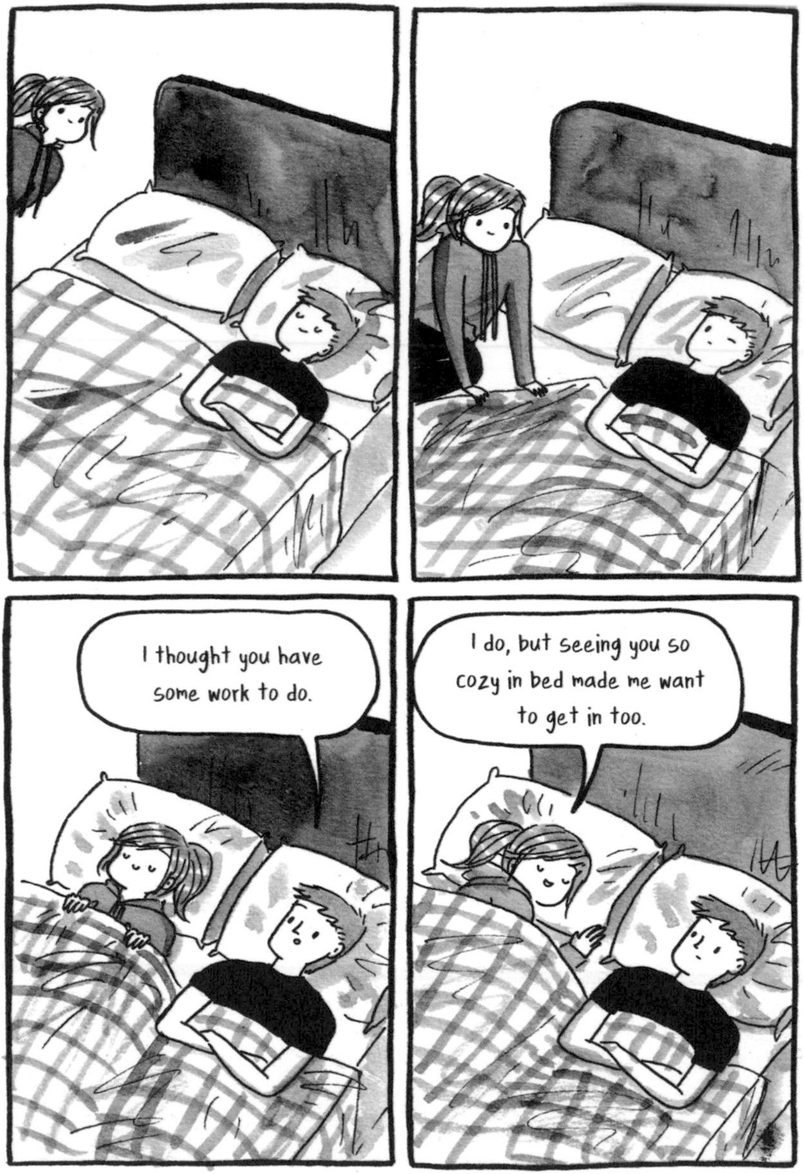
I thought you have some work to do.
I do, but seeing you so cozy in bed made me want to get in too.

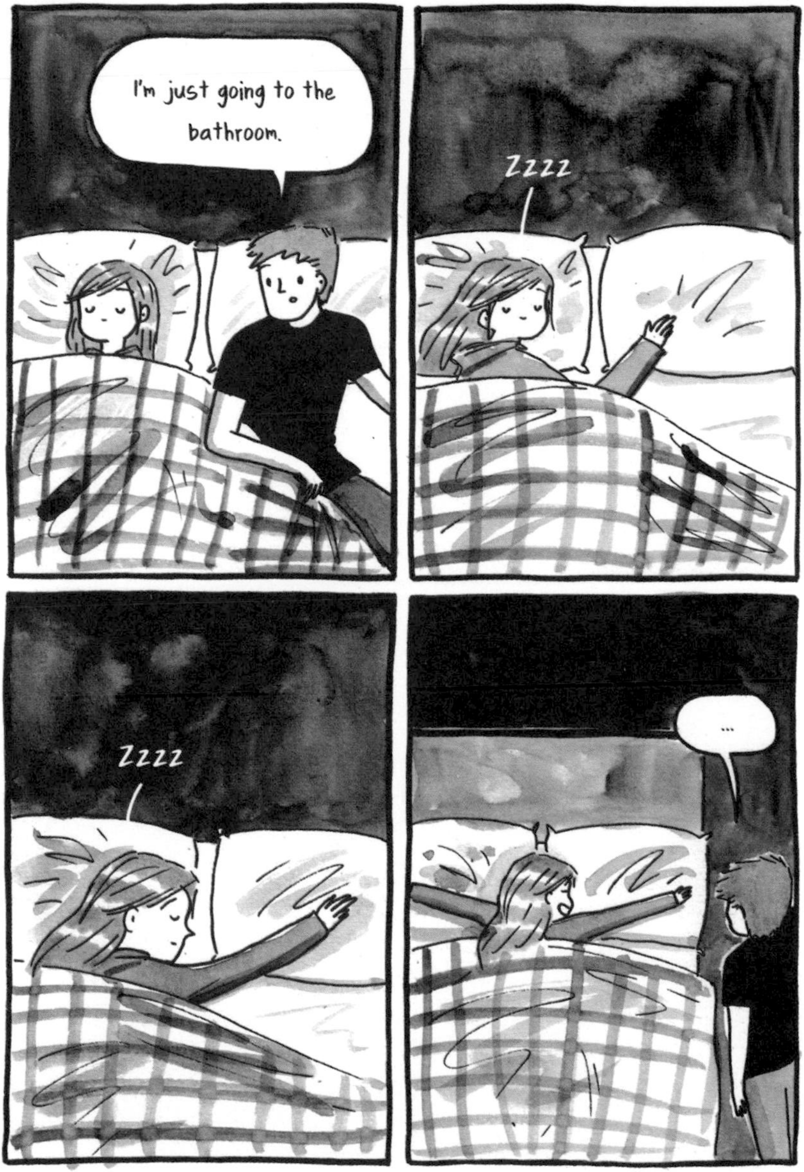
I'm just going to the bathroom.
Zzzz
Zzzz
...

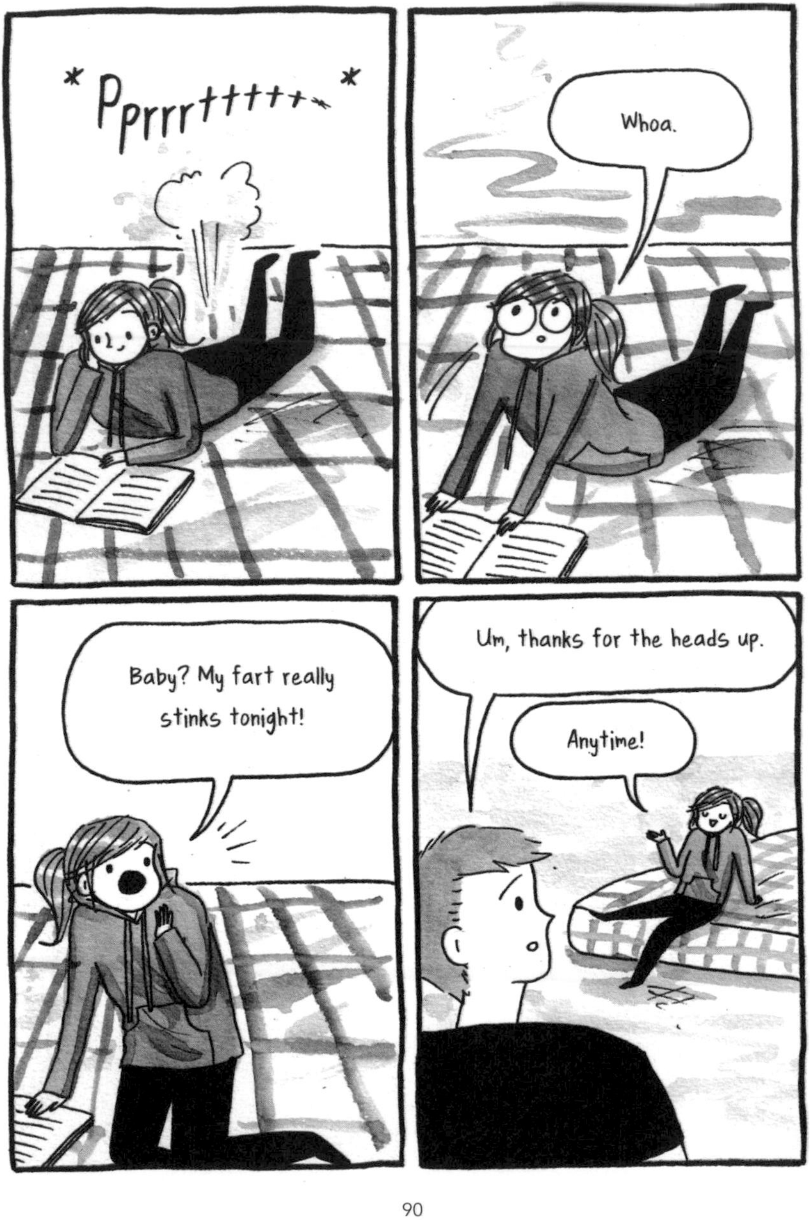
Pprrrttttt
Whoa.
Baby? My fart really stinks tonight!
Um, thanks for the heads up.
Anytime!

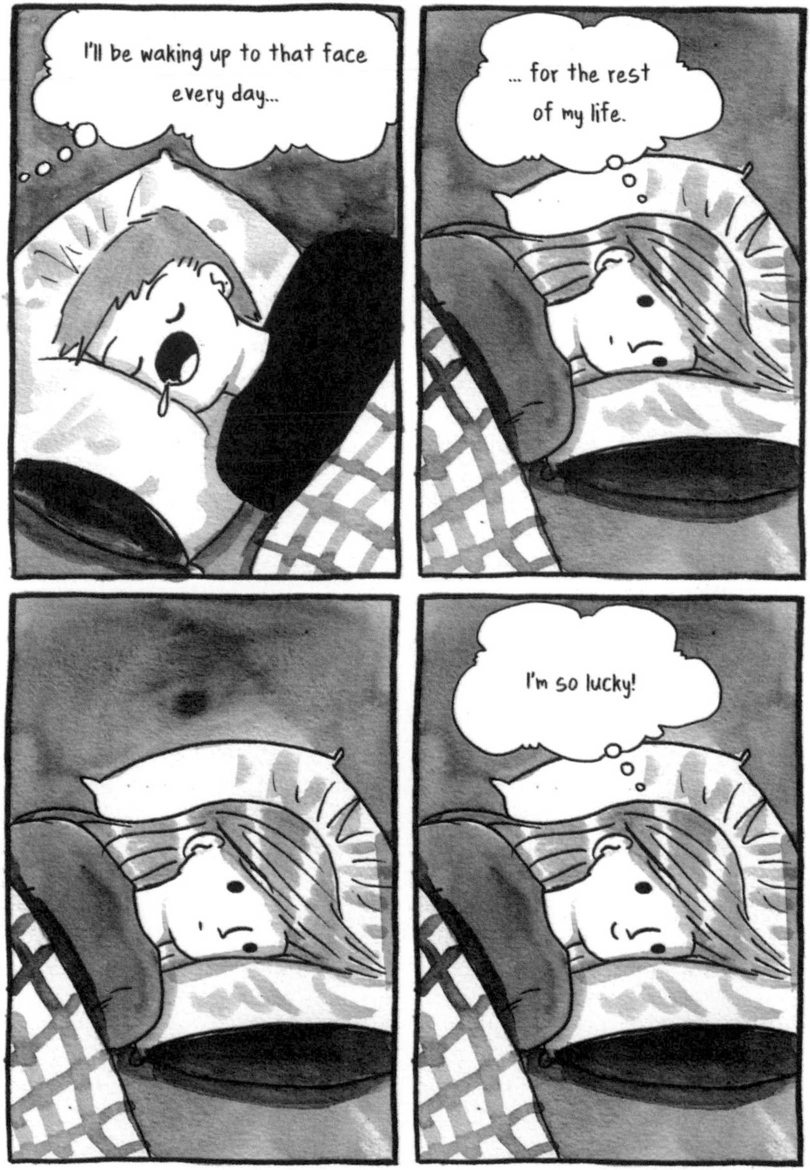
I'll be waking up to that face every day...
... for the rest of my life.
I'm so lucky!

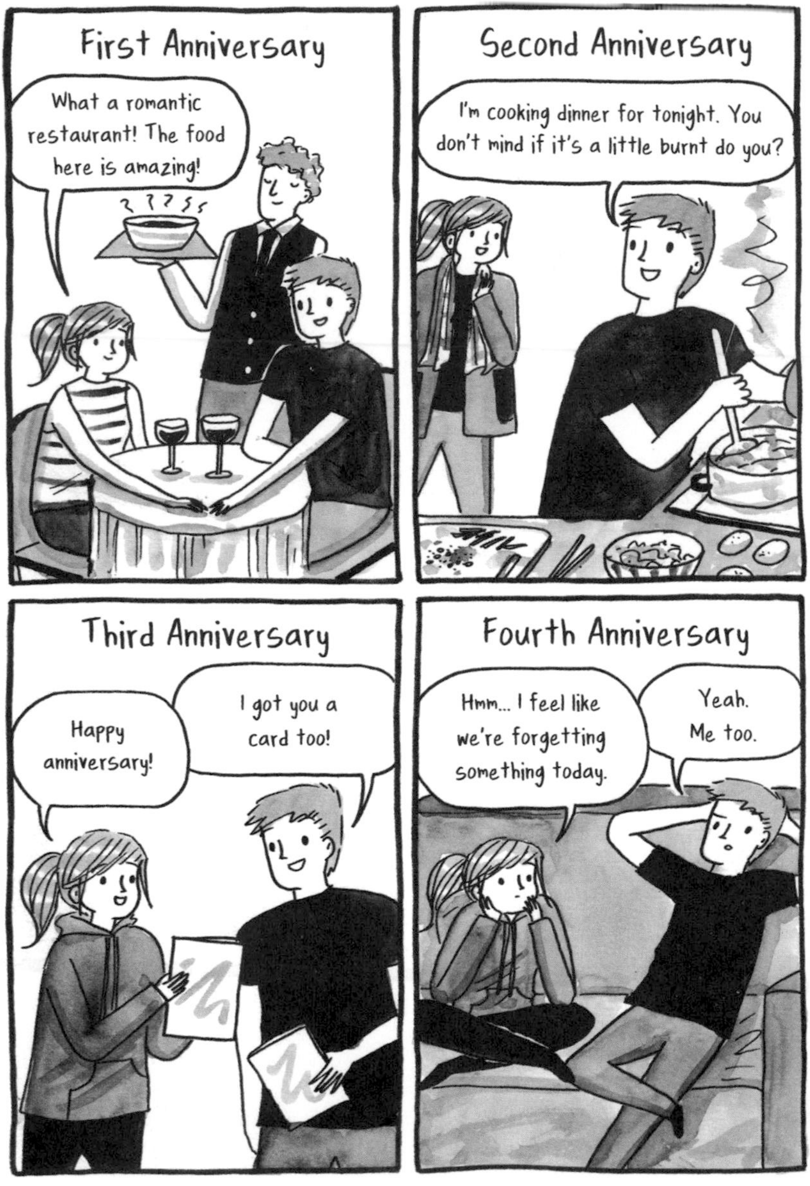

First Anniversary
What a romantic restaurant! The food here is amazing!
Second Anniversary
I'm cooking dinner for tonight. You don't mind if it's a little burnt do you?
Third Anniversary
Happy anniversary!
I got you a card too!
Fourth Anniversary
Hmm... I feel like we're forgetting something today.
Yeah. Me too.

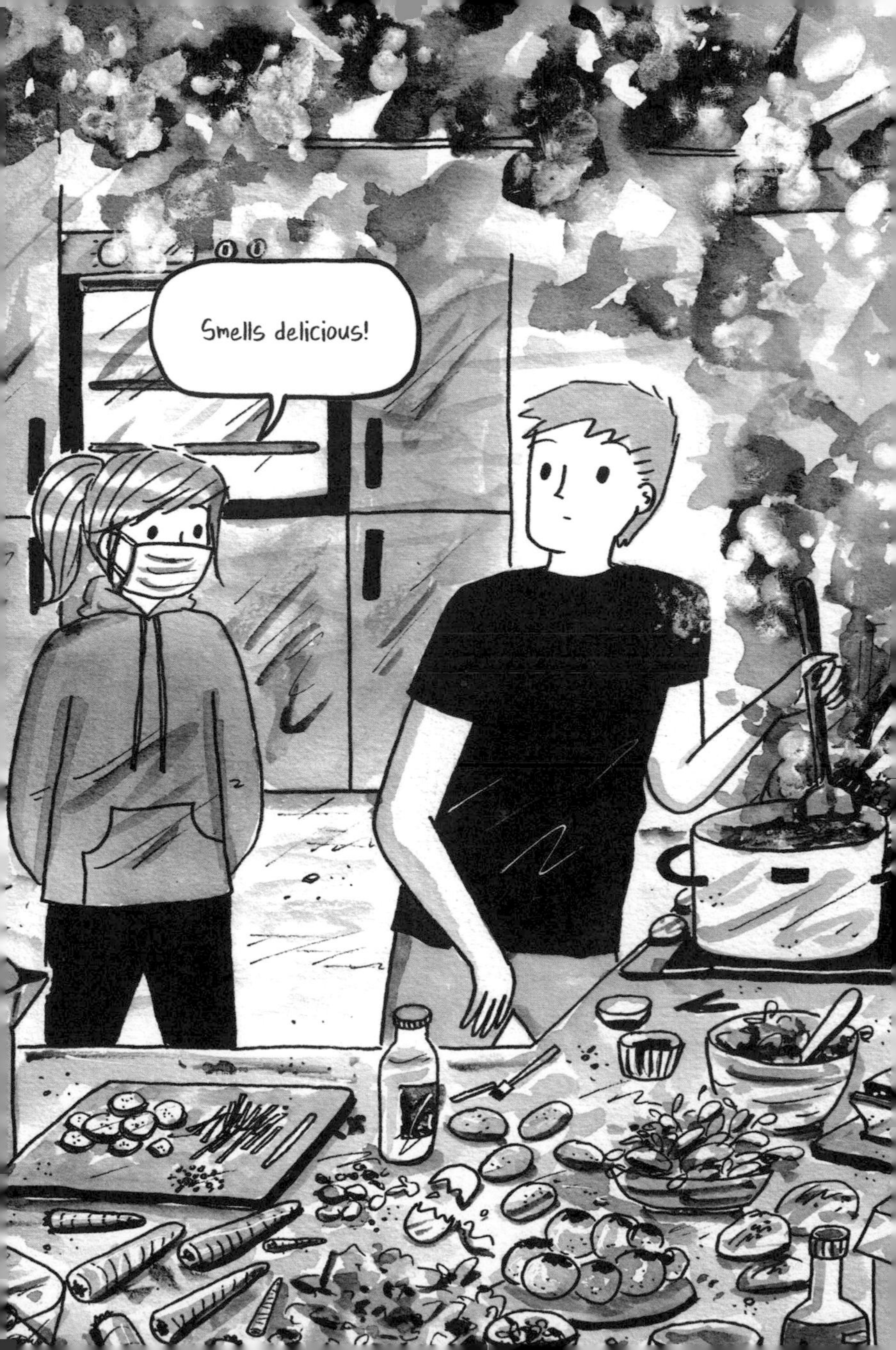
Smells delicious!

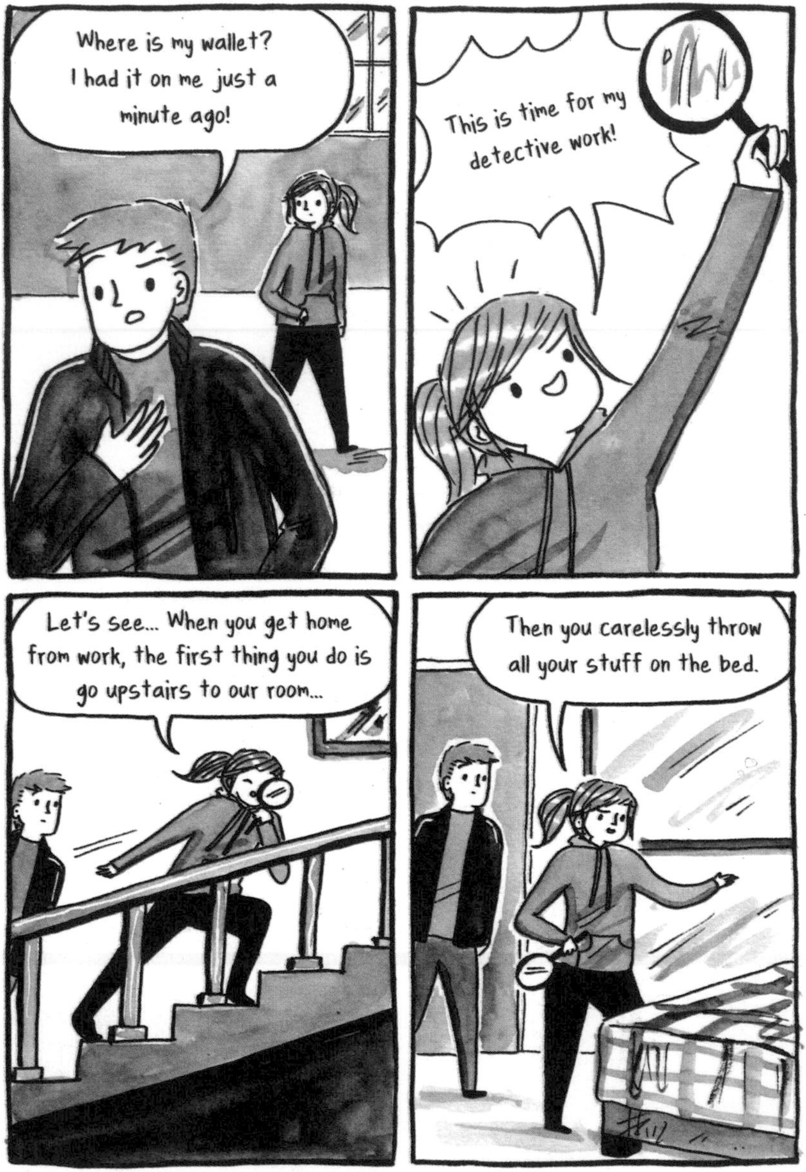
Where is my wallet? I had it on me just a minute ago!
This is time for my detective work!
Let's see... When you get home from work, the first thing you do is go upstairs to our room...
Then you carelessly throw all your stuff on the bed.

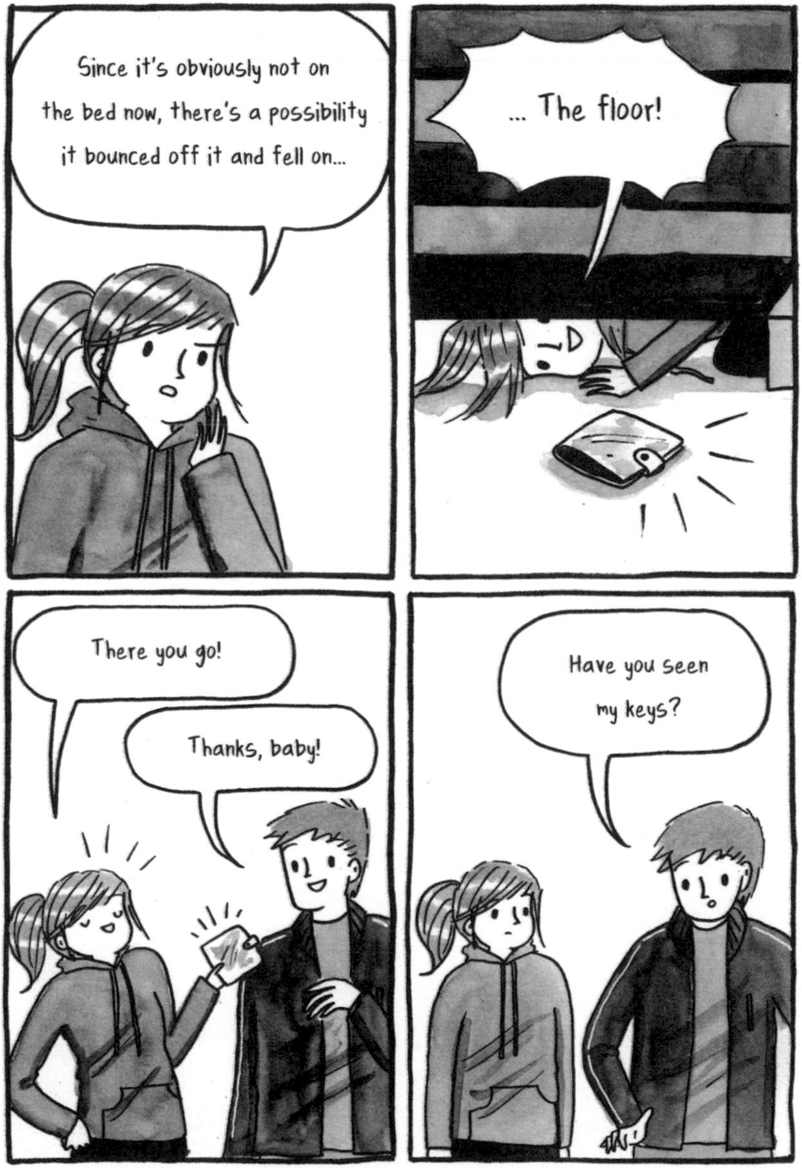
Since it's obviously not on the bed now, there's a possibility it bounced off it and fell on...
... The floor!
There you go!
Thanks, baby!
Have you seen my keys?

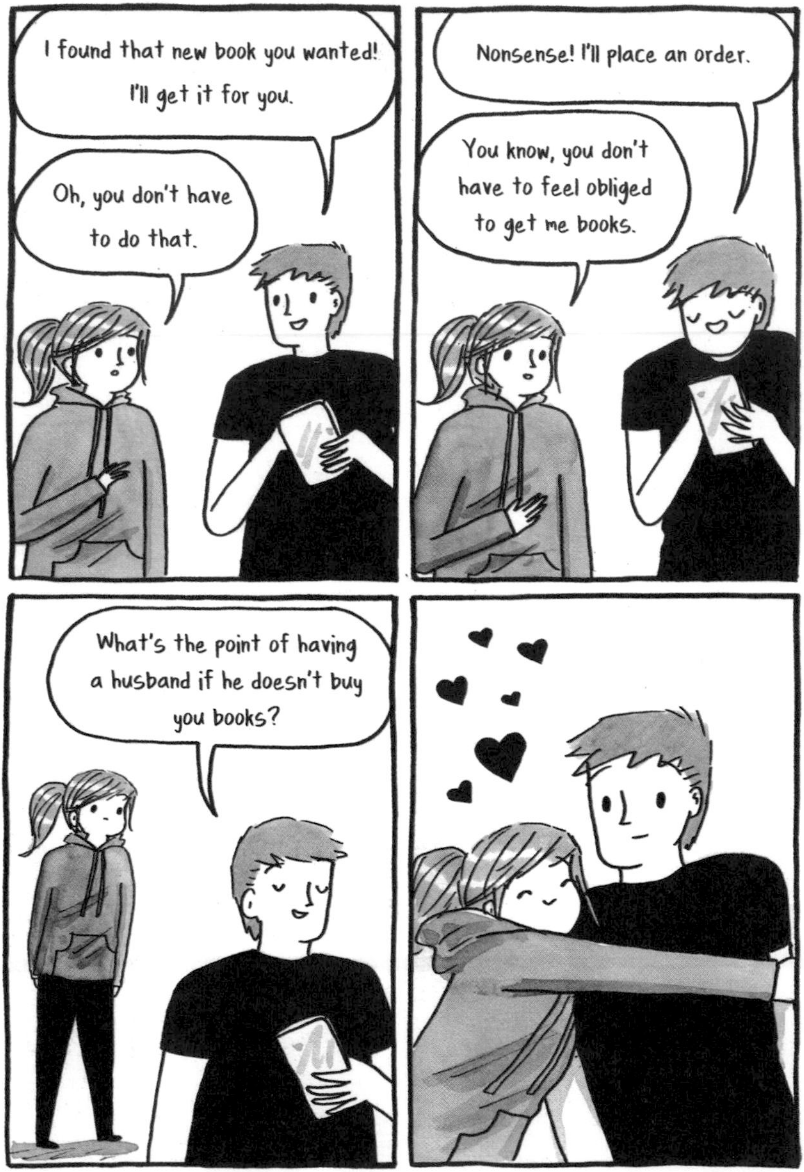
I found that new book you wanted! I'll get it for you.
Oh, you don't have to do that.
Nonsense! I'll place an order.
You know, you don't have to feel obliged to get me books.
What's the point of having a husband if he doesn't buy you books?

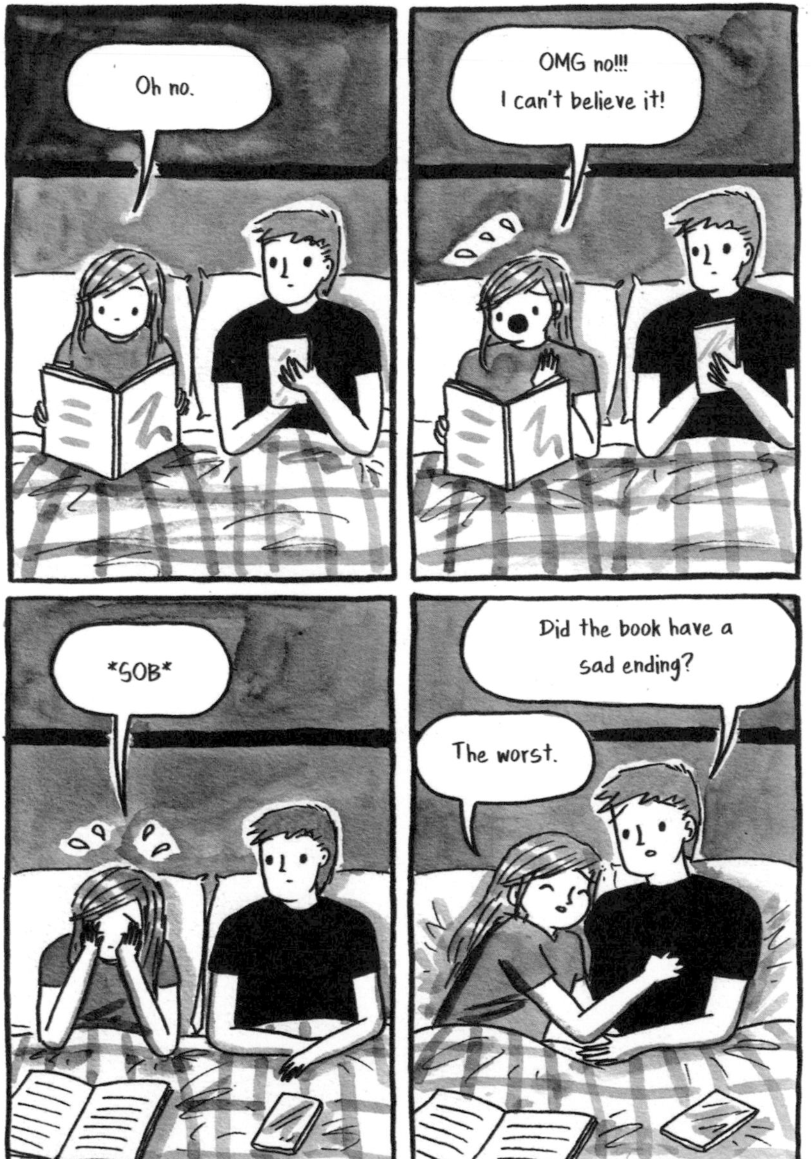
Oh no.
OMG no!!!
I can't believe it!
SOB
Did the book have a sad ending?
The worst.

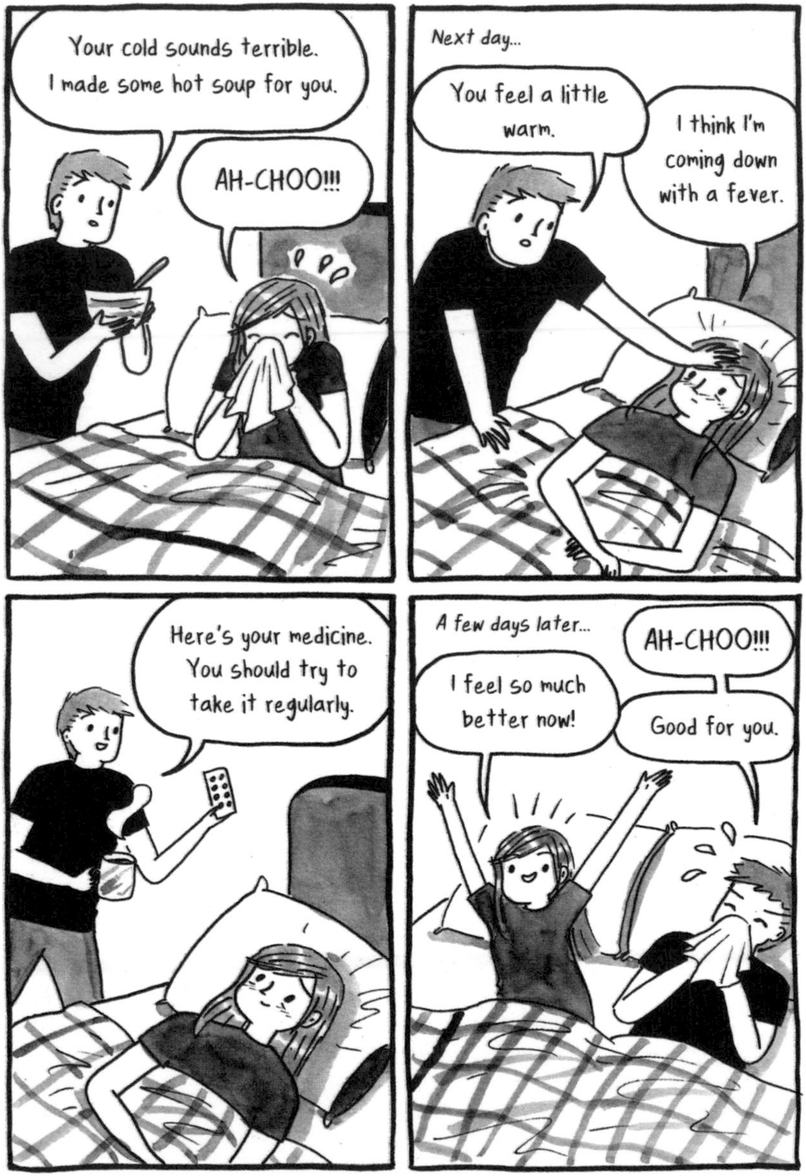
Your cold sounds terrible. I made some hot soup for you.
AH-CHOO!!!
Next day...
You feel a little warm.
I think I'm coming down with a fever.
Here's your medicine. You should try to take it regularly.
A few days later...
I feel so much better now!
AH-CHOO!!!
Good for you.

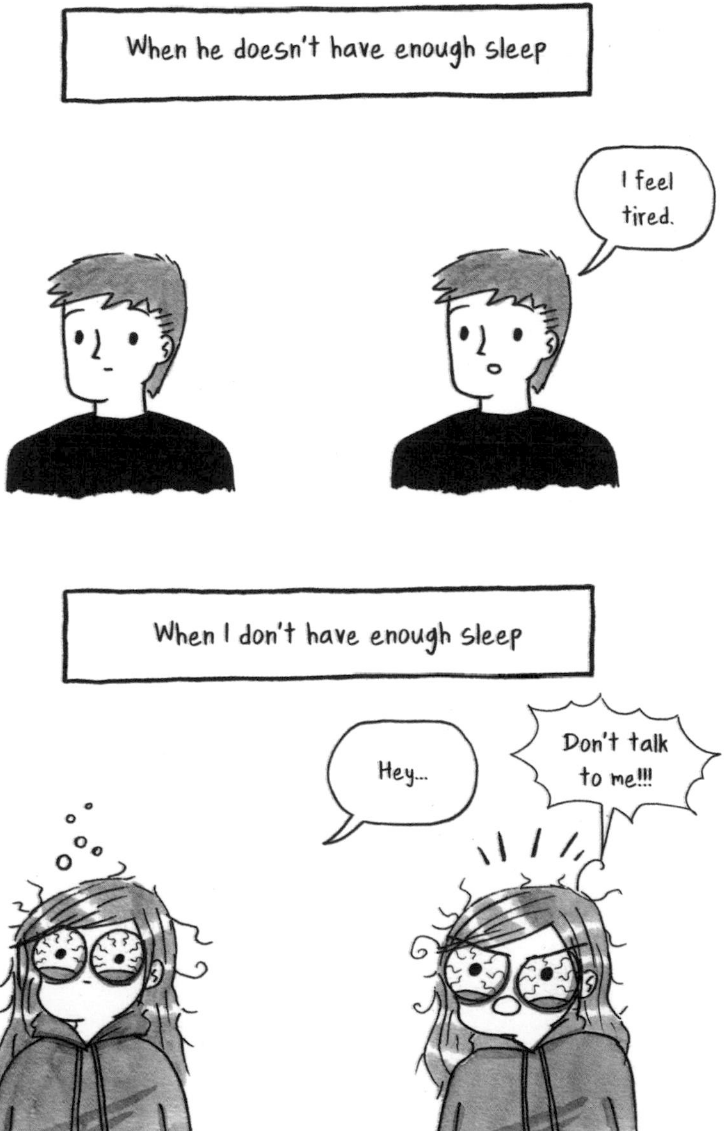
When he doesn't have enough sleep
I feel tired.
When I don't have enough sleep
Hey...
Don't talk to me!!!

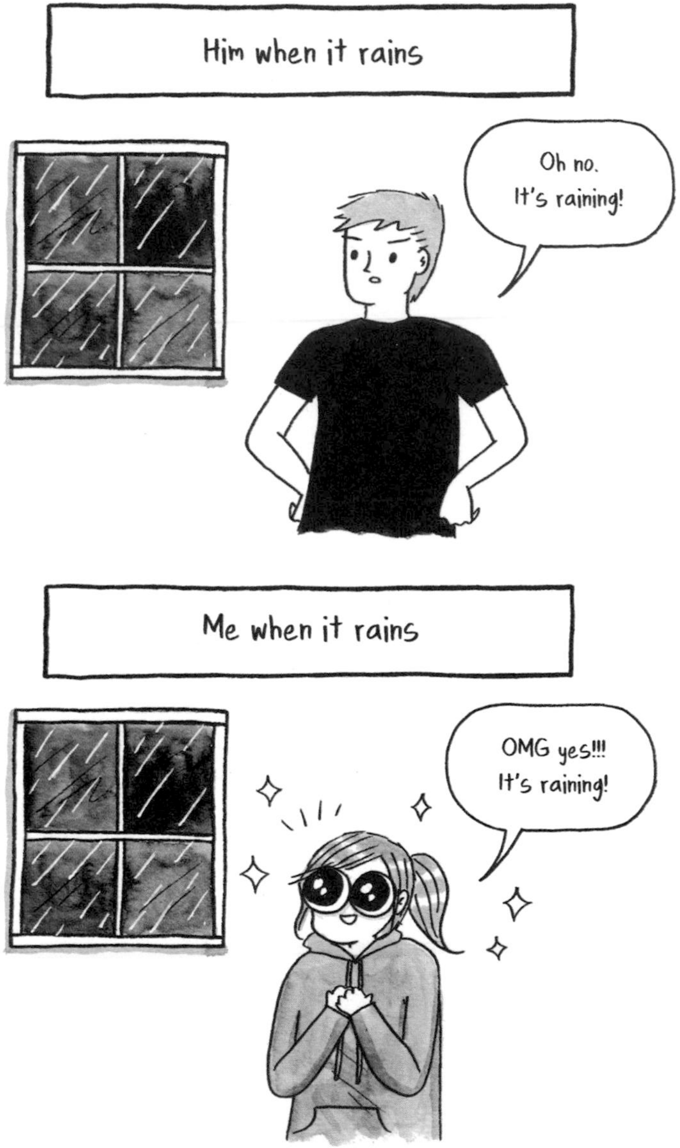
Him when it rains
Oh no. It's raining!
Me when it rains
OMG yes!!! It's raining!

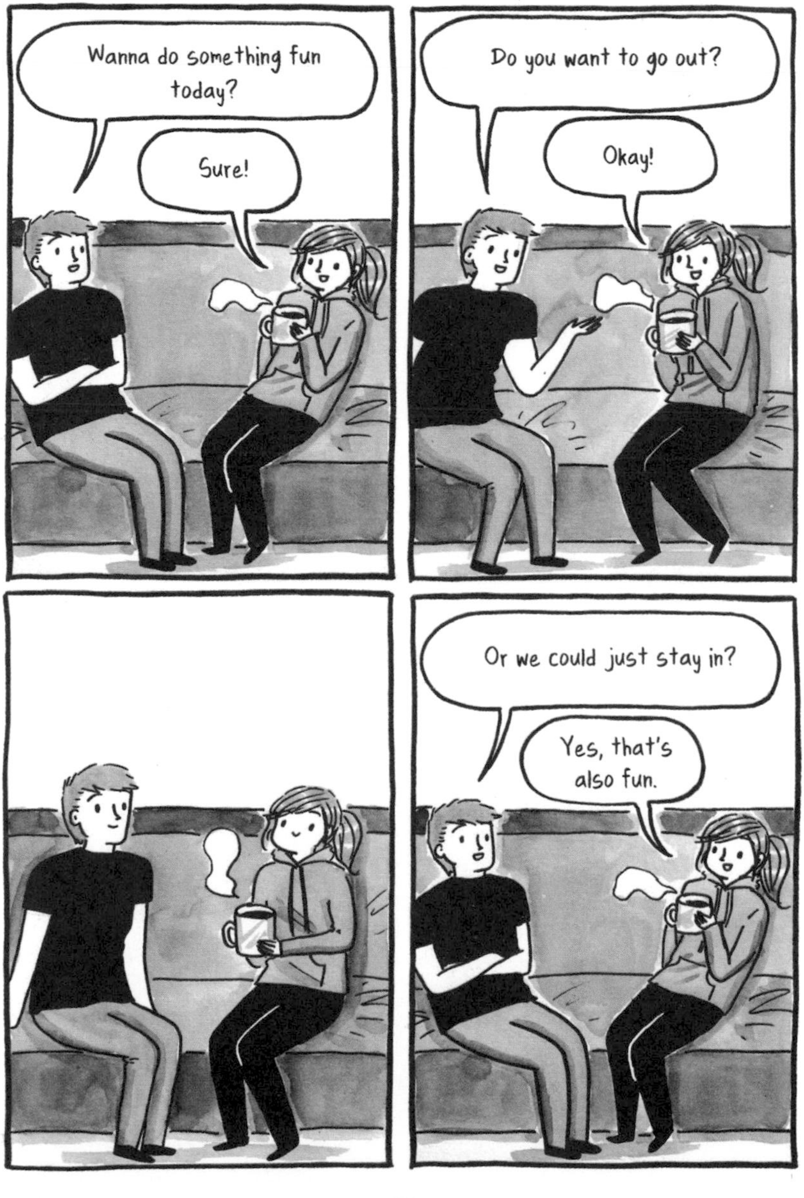
Wanna do something fun today?
Sure!
Do you want to go out?
Okay!
Or we could just stay in?
Yes, that's also fun.

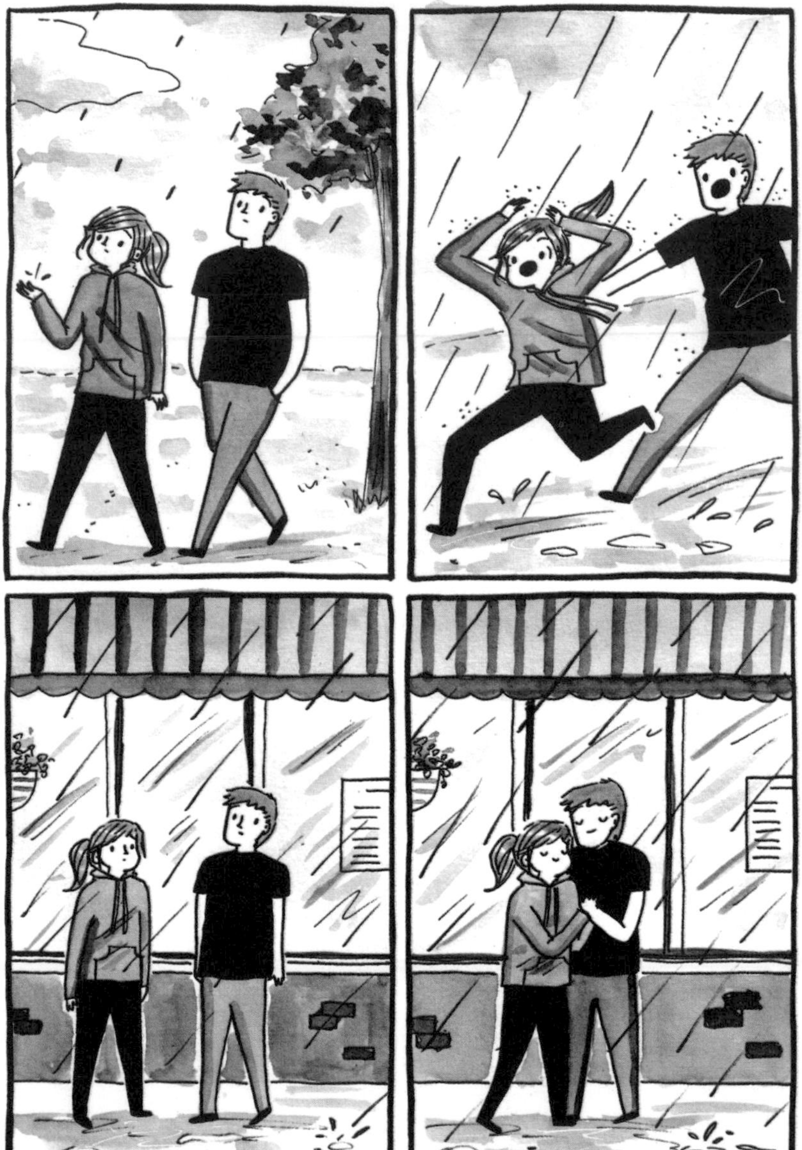

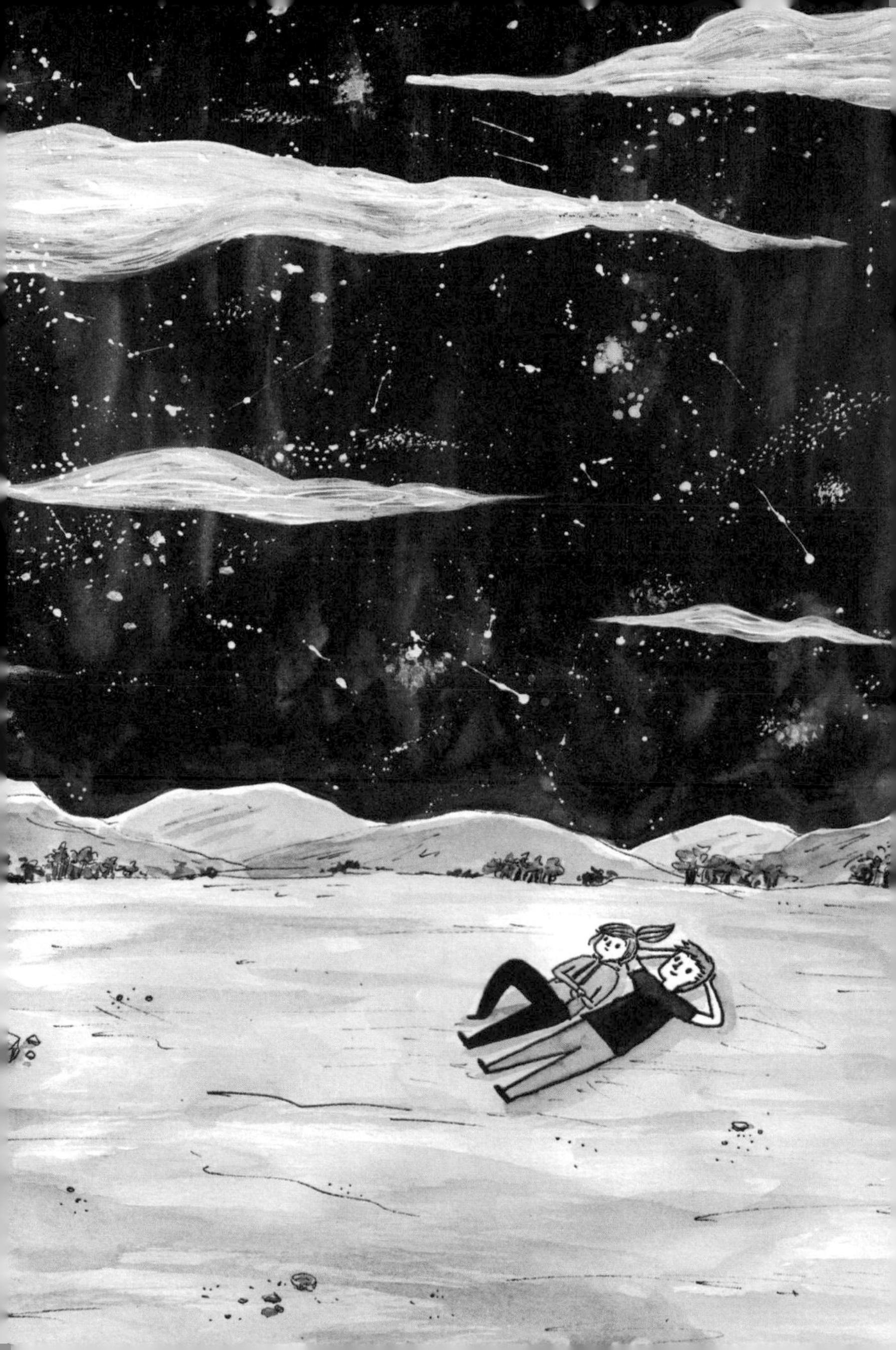

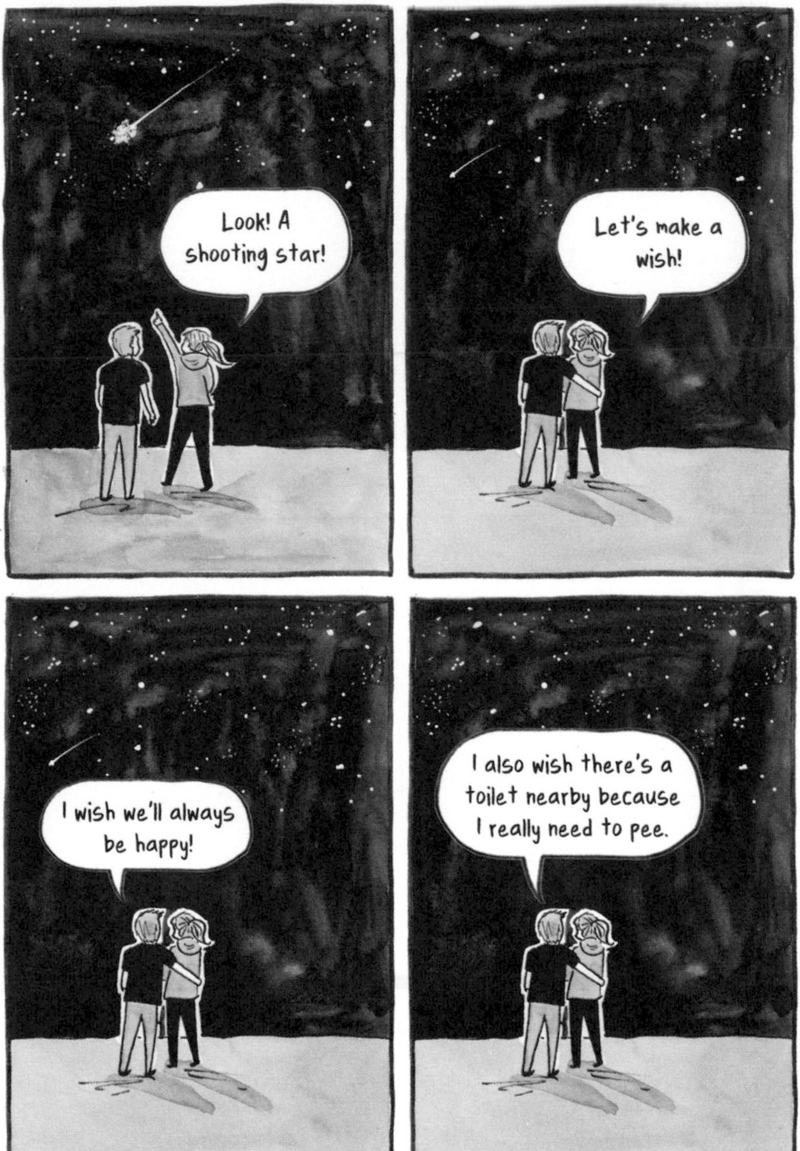
Look! A shooting star!
Let's make a wish!
I wish we'll always be happy!
I also wish there's a toilet nearby because I really need to pee.

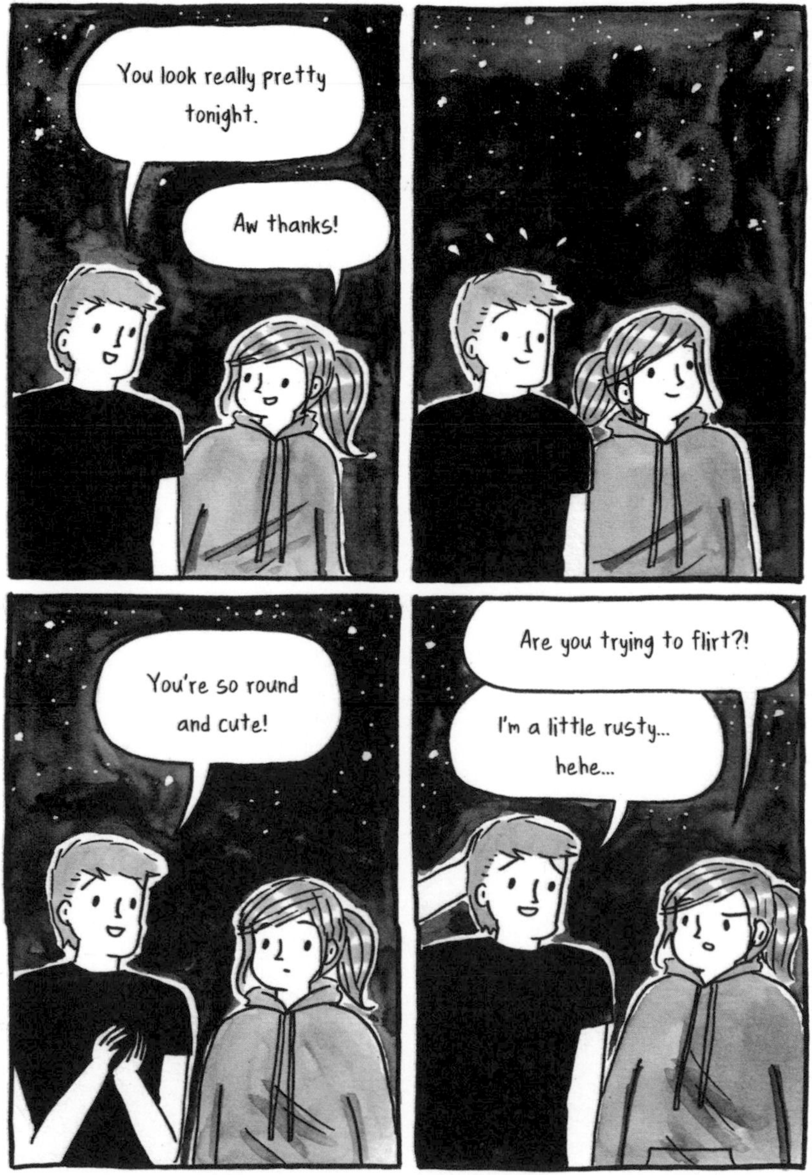

You look really pretty tonight.
Aw thanks!
You're so round and cute!
Are you trying to flirt?!
I'm a little rusty... hehe...

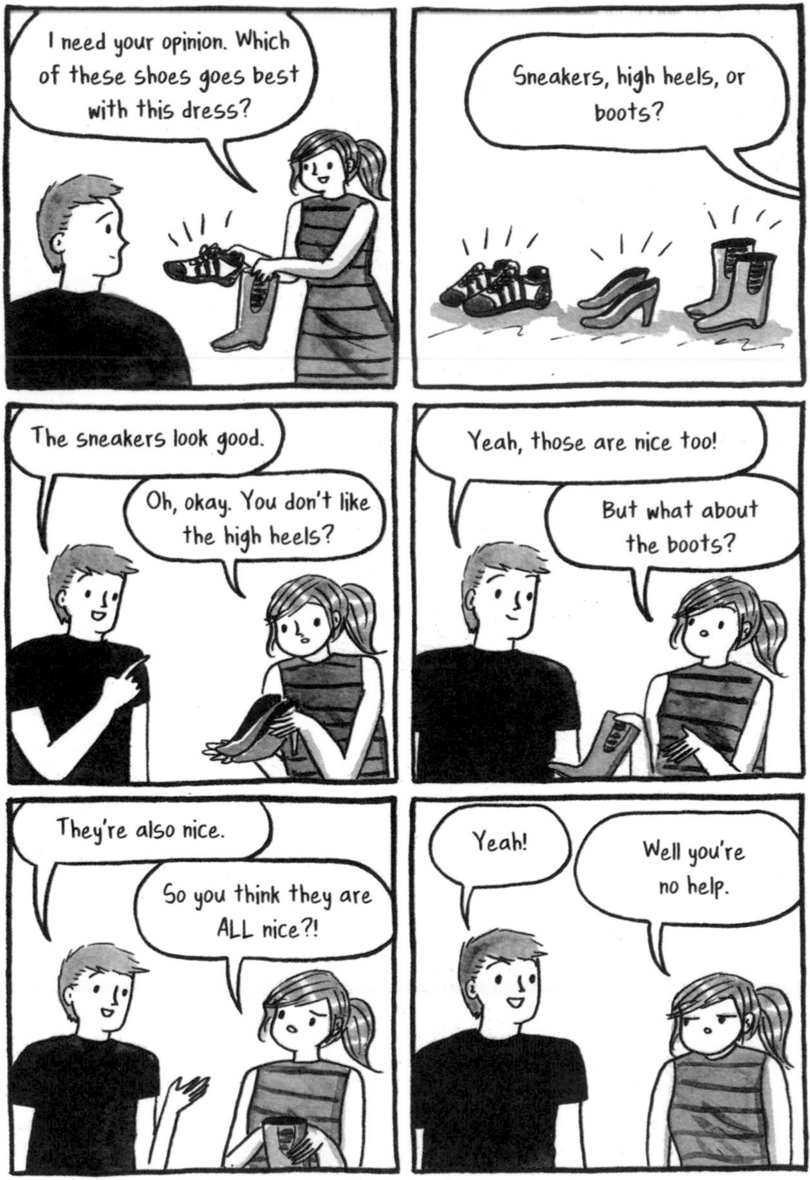
I need your opinion. Which of these shoes goes best with this dress?
Sneakers, high heels, or boots?
The sneakers look good.
Oh, okay. You don't like the high heels?
Yeah, those are nice too!
But what about the boots?
They're also nice.
So you think they are ALL nice?!
Yeah!
Well you're no help.

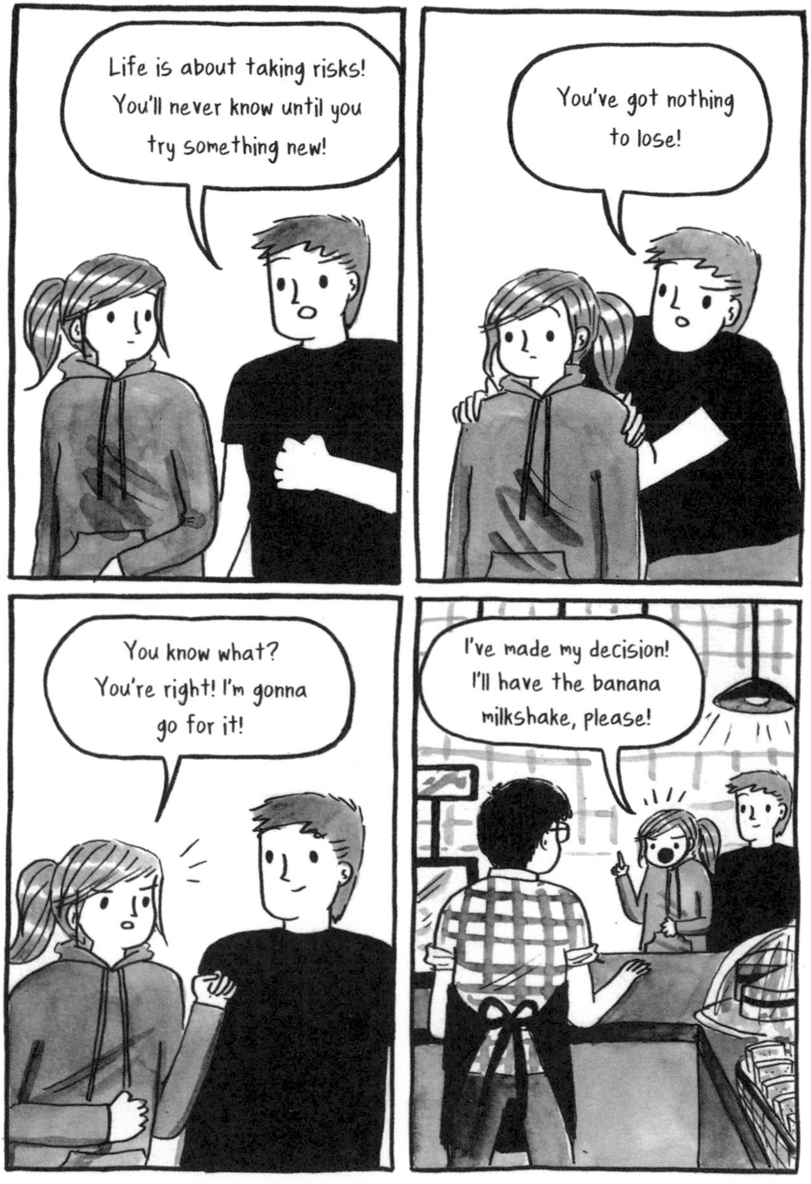
Life is about taking risks! You'll never know until you try something new!
You've got nothing to lose!
You know what? You're right! I'm gonna go for it!
I've made my decision! I'll have the banana milkshake, please!

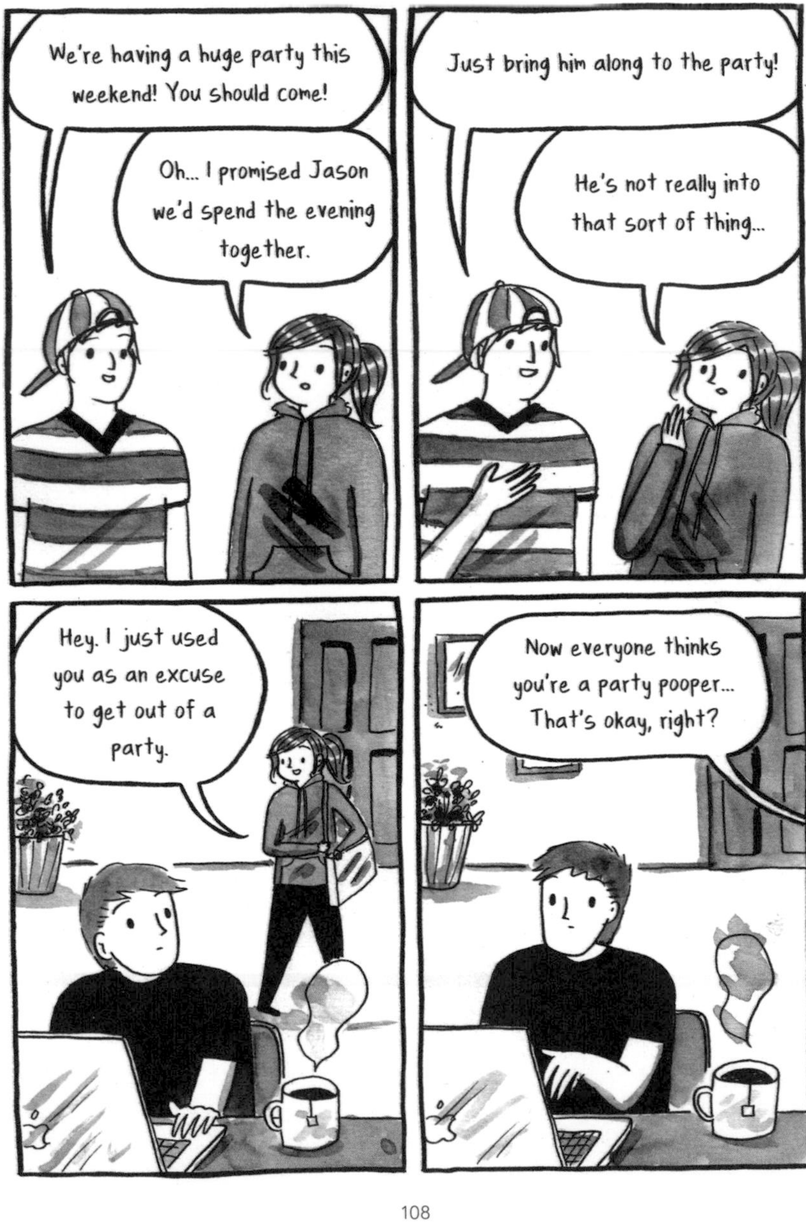
We're having a huge party this weekend! You should come!
Oh... I promised Jason we'd spend the evening together.
Just bring him along to the party!
He's not really into that sort of thing...
Hey. I just used you as an excuse to get out of a party.
Now everyone thinks you're a party pooper... That's okay, right?

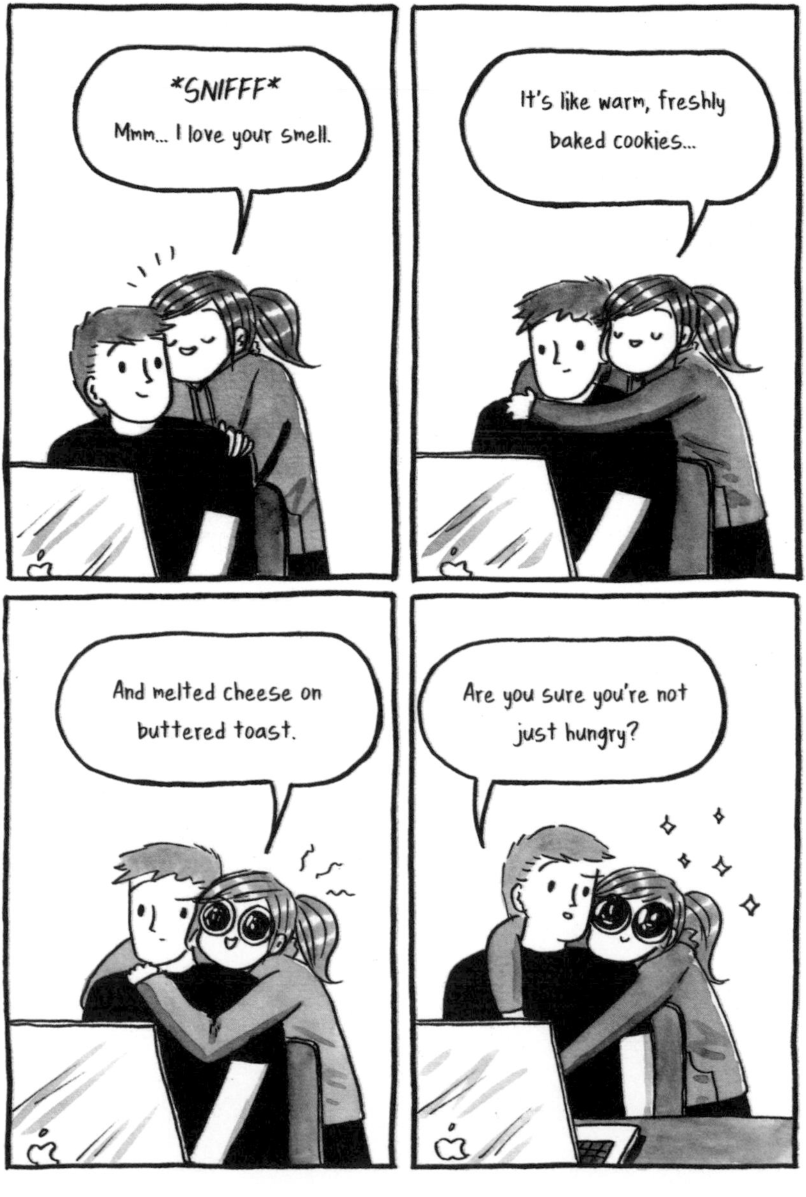
SNIFFF
Mmm... I love your smell.
It's like warm, freshly baked cookies...
And melted cheese on buttered toast.
Are you sure you're not just hungry?

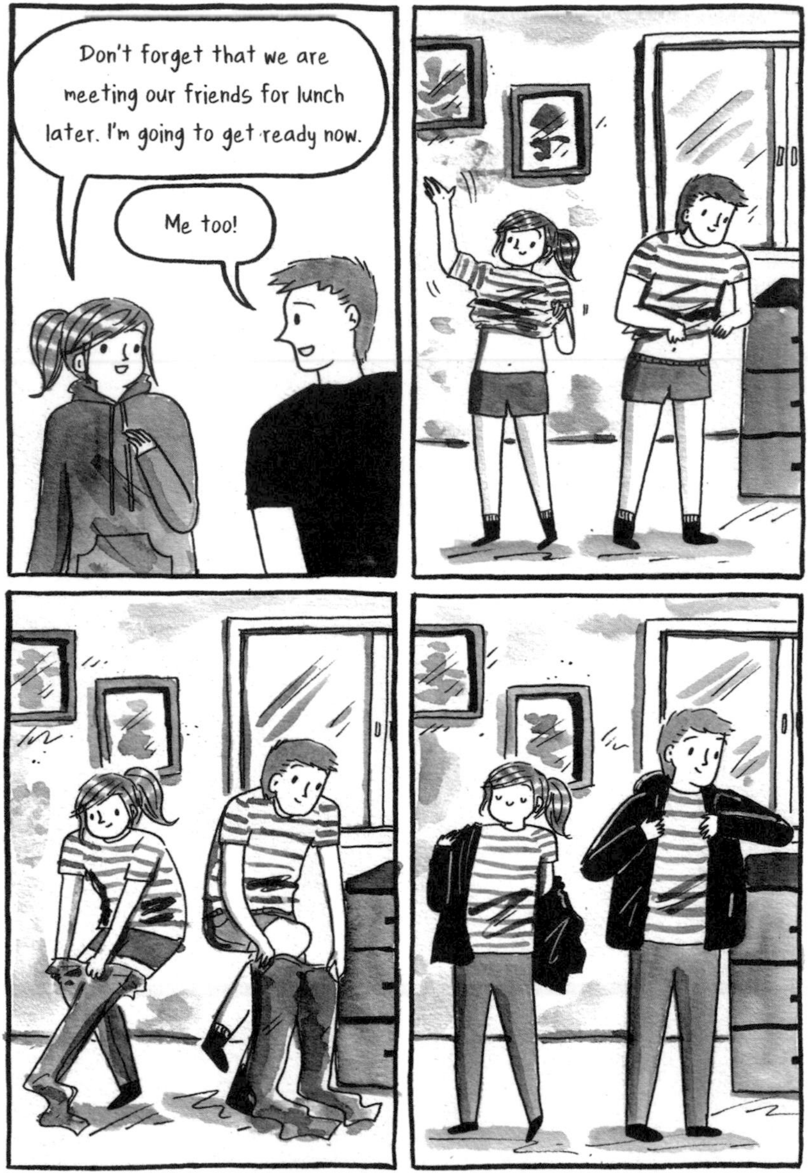
Don't forget that we are meeting our friends for lunch later. I'm going to get ready now.
Me too!

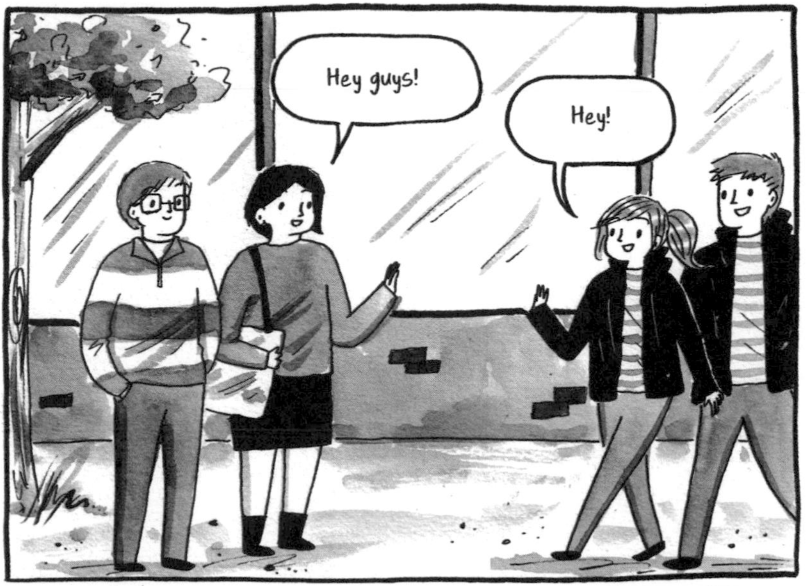
Hey guys!
Hey!

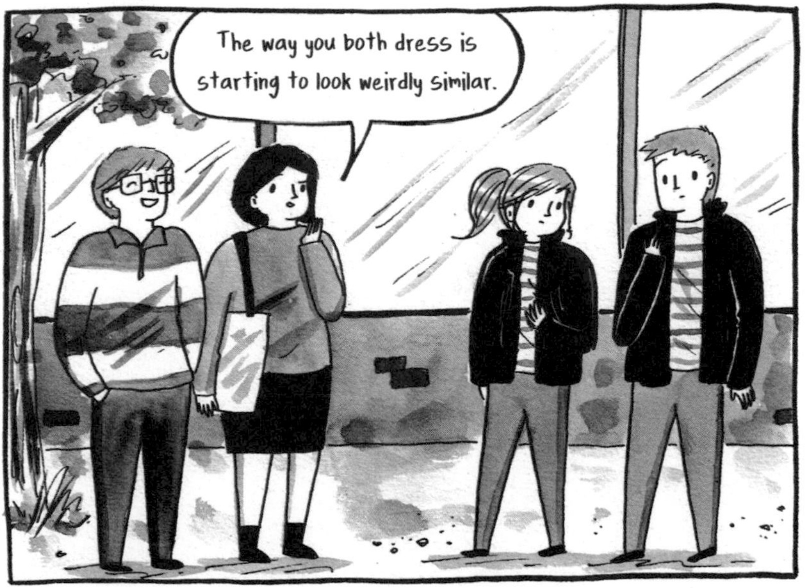
The way you both dress is starting to look weirdly similar.

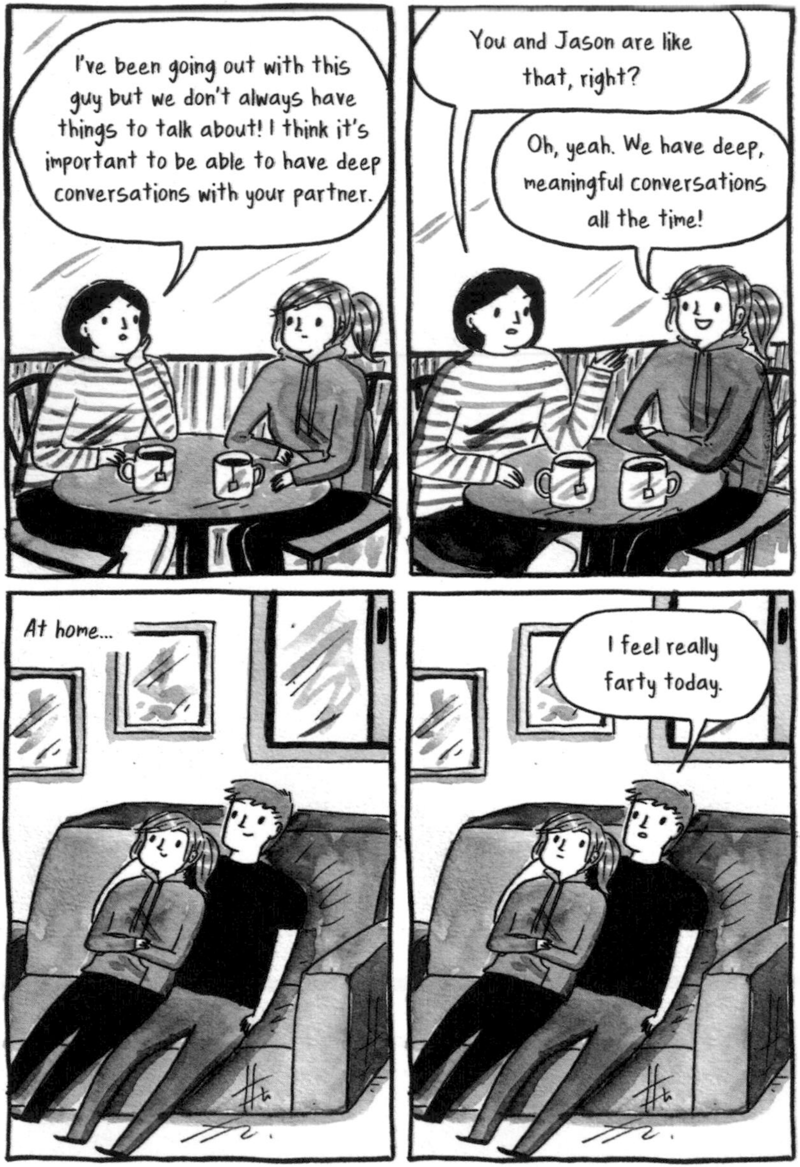

I've been going out with this guy but we don't always have things to talk about! I think it's important to be able to have deep conversations with your partner.
You and Jason are like that, right?
Oh, yeah. We have deep, meaningful conversations all the time!
At home...
I feel really farty today.

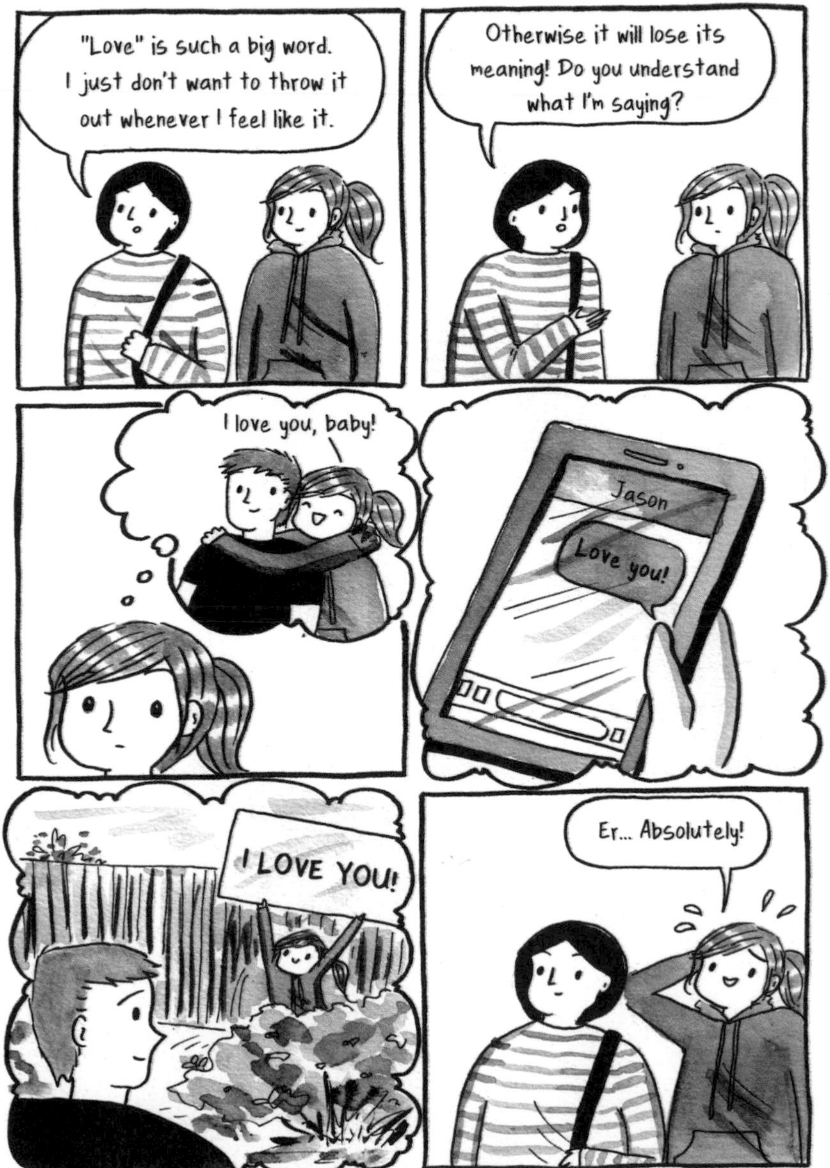
"Love" is such a big word. I just don't want to throw it out whenever I feel like it.
Otherwise it will lose its meaning! Do you understand what I'm saying?
I love you, baby!
Jason
Love you!
I LOVE YOU!
Er... Absolutely!

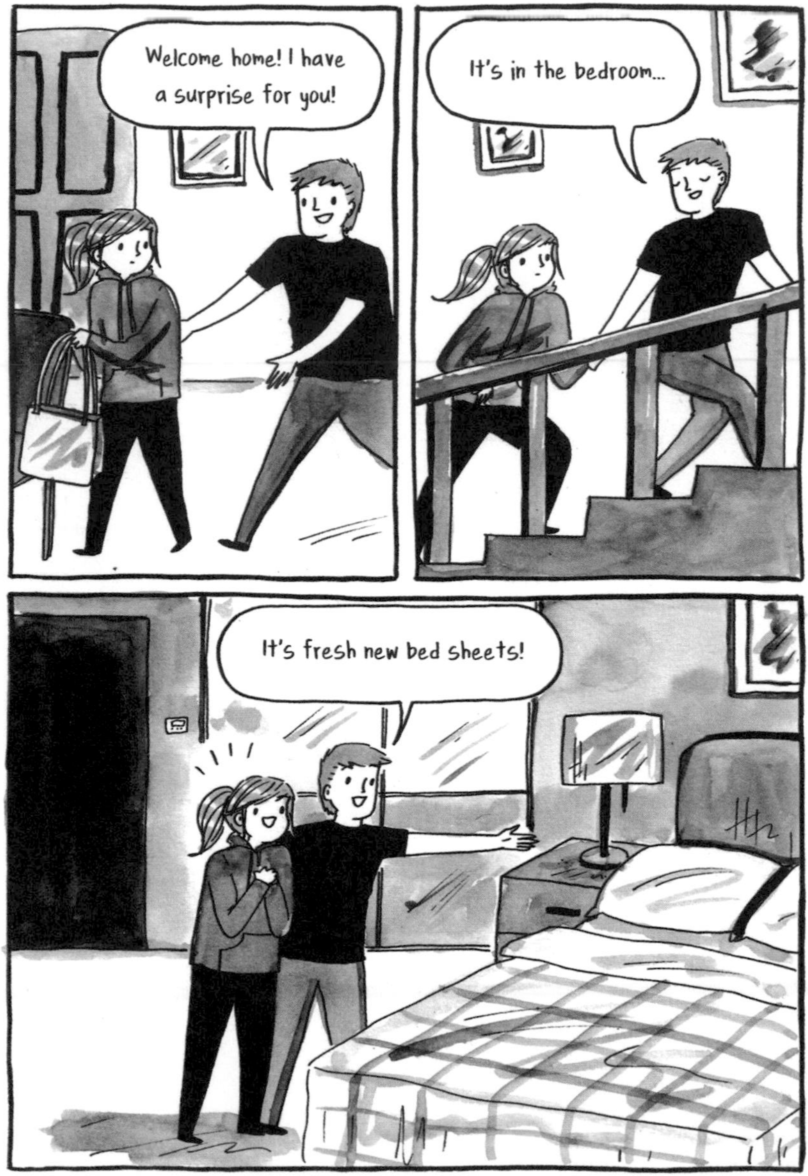
Welcome home! I have a surprise for you!
It's in the bedroom...
It's fresh new bed sheets!

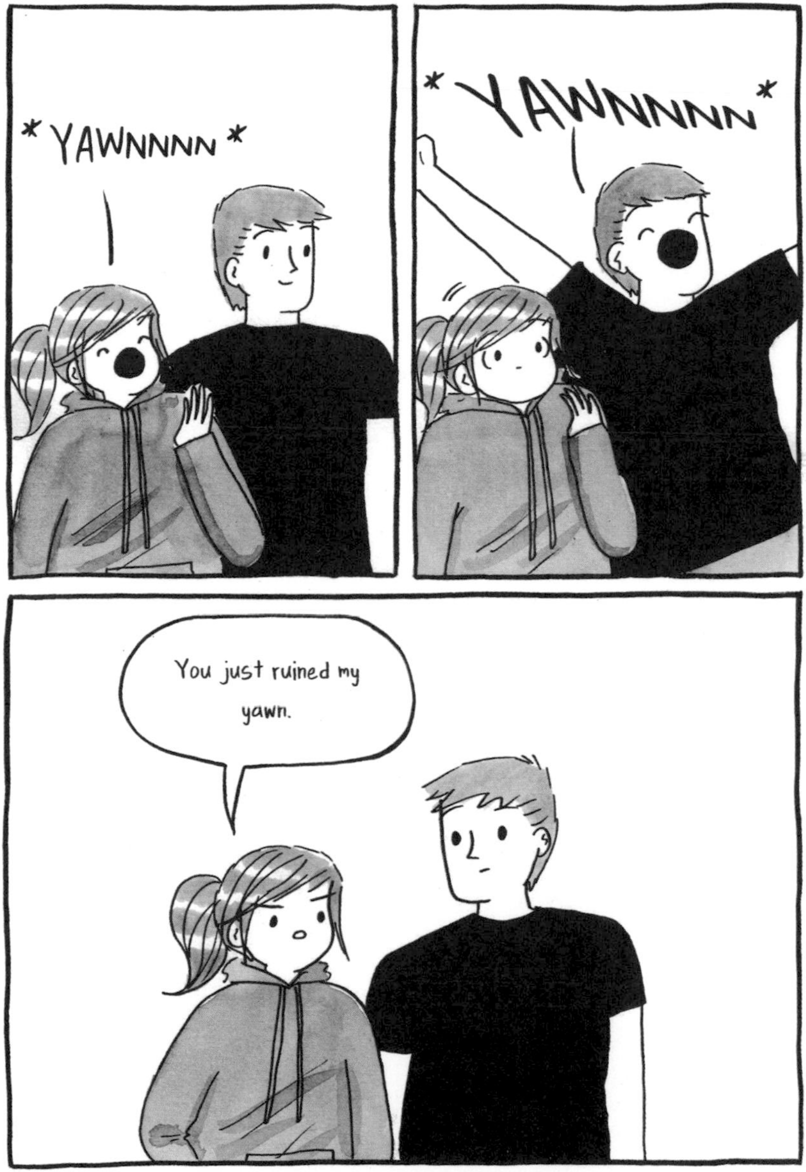
YAWNNNN
YAWNNNNN
You just ruined my yawn.

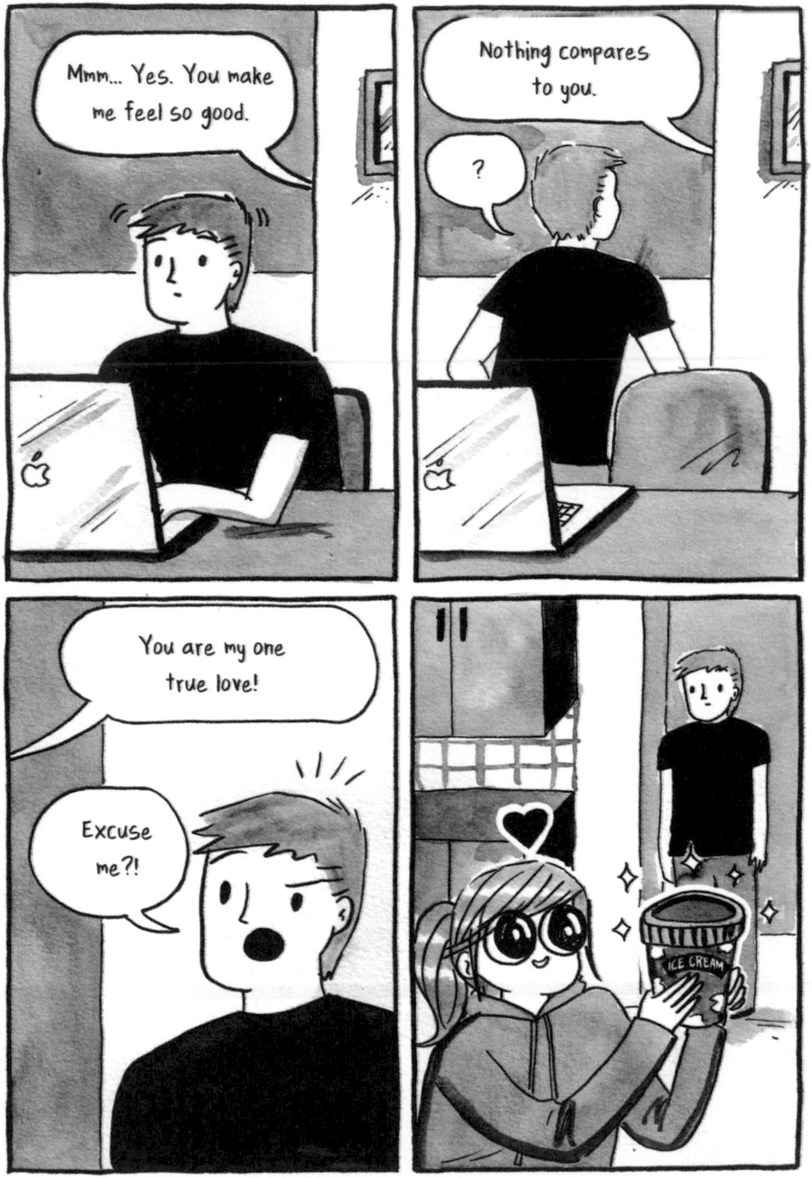
Mmm... Yes. You make me feel so good.
Nothing compares to you.
?
You are my one true love!
Excuse me?!
ICE CREAM

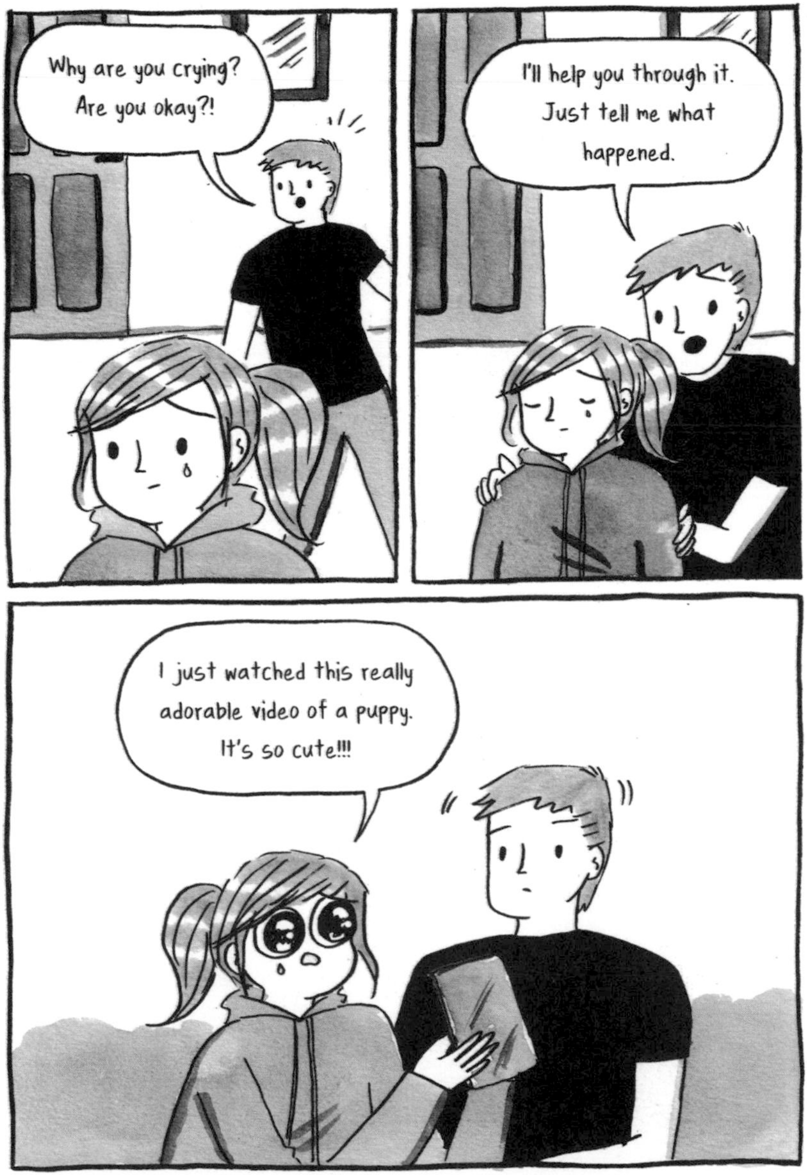
Why are you crying? Are you okay?!
I'll help you through it. Just tell me what happened.
I just watched this really adorable video of a puppy. It's so cute!!!

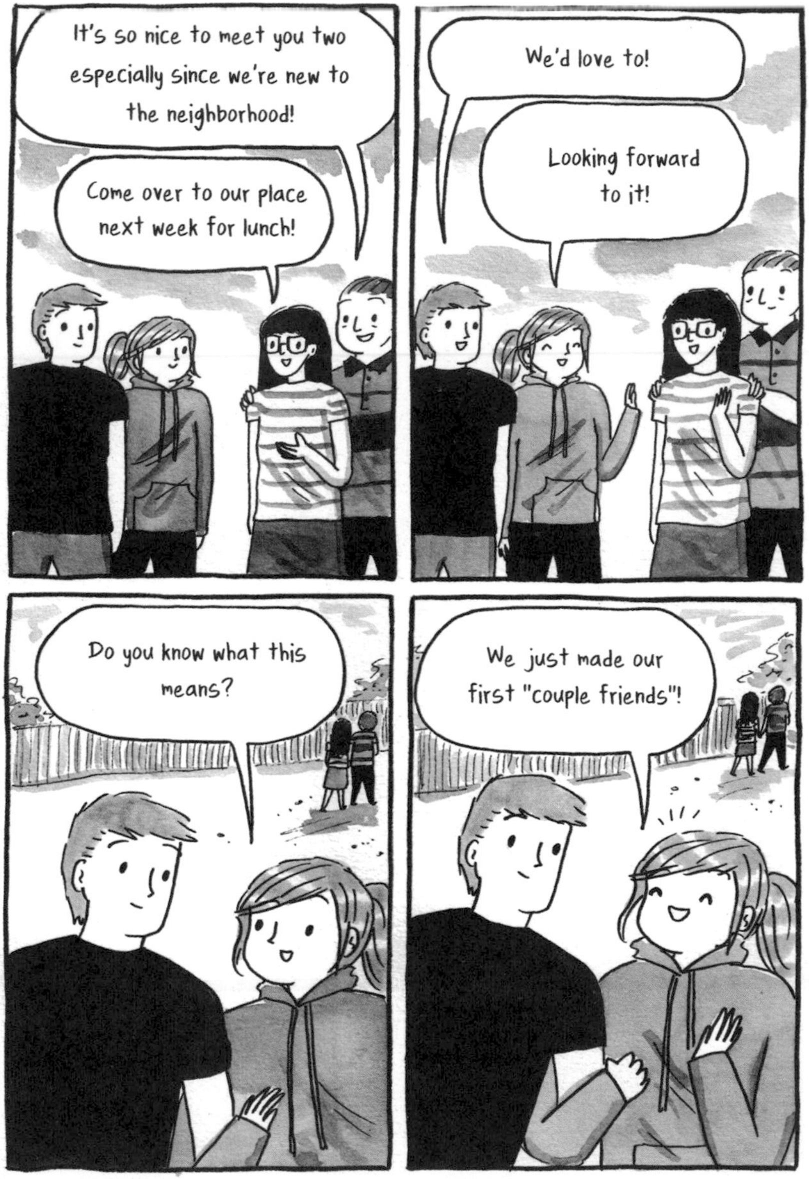
It's so nice to meet you two especially since we're new to the neighborhood!
Come over to our place next week for lunch!
We'd love to!
Looking forward to it!
Do you know what this means?
We just made our first "couple friends"!

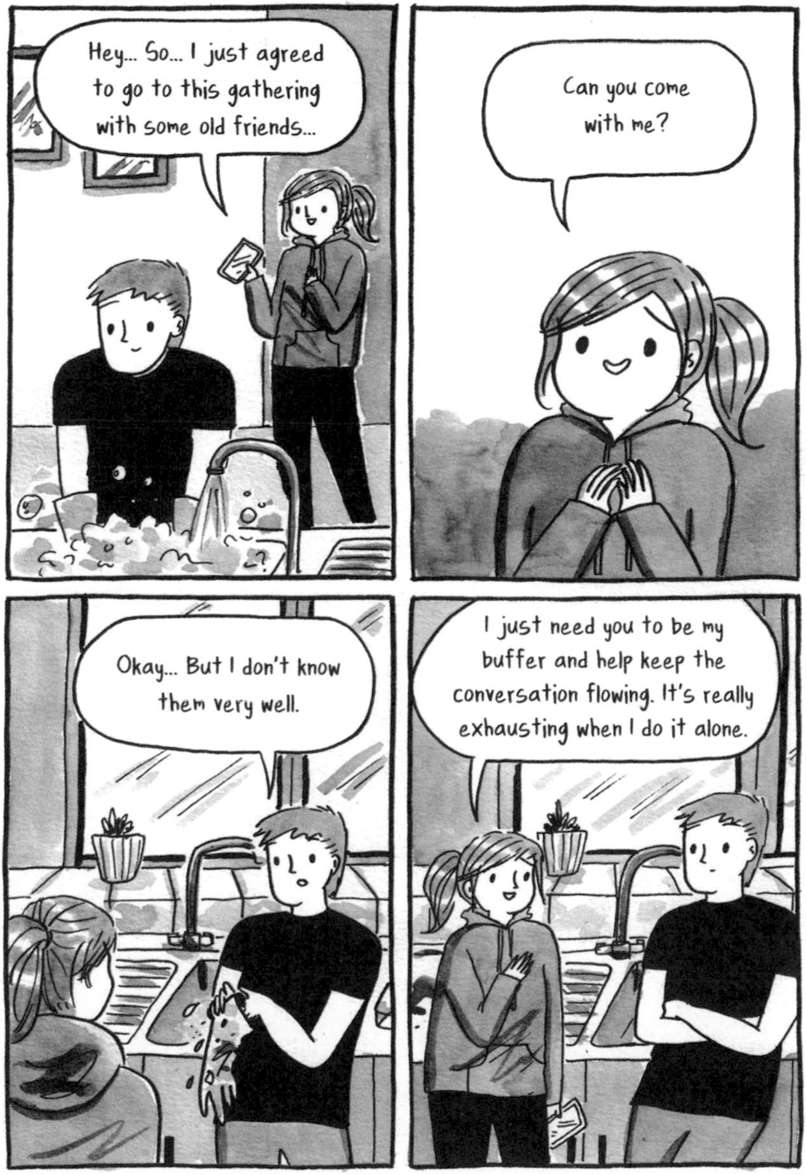
Hey... So... I just agreed to go to this gathering with some old friends...
Can you come with me?
Okay... But I don't know them very well.
I just need you to be my buffer and help keep the conversation flowing. It's really exhausting when I do it alone.

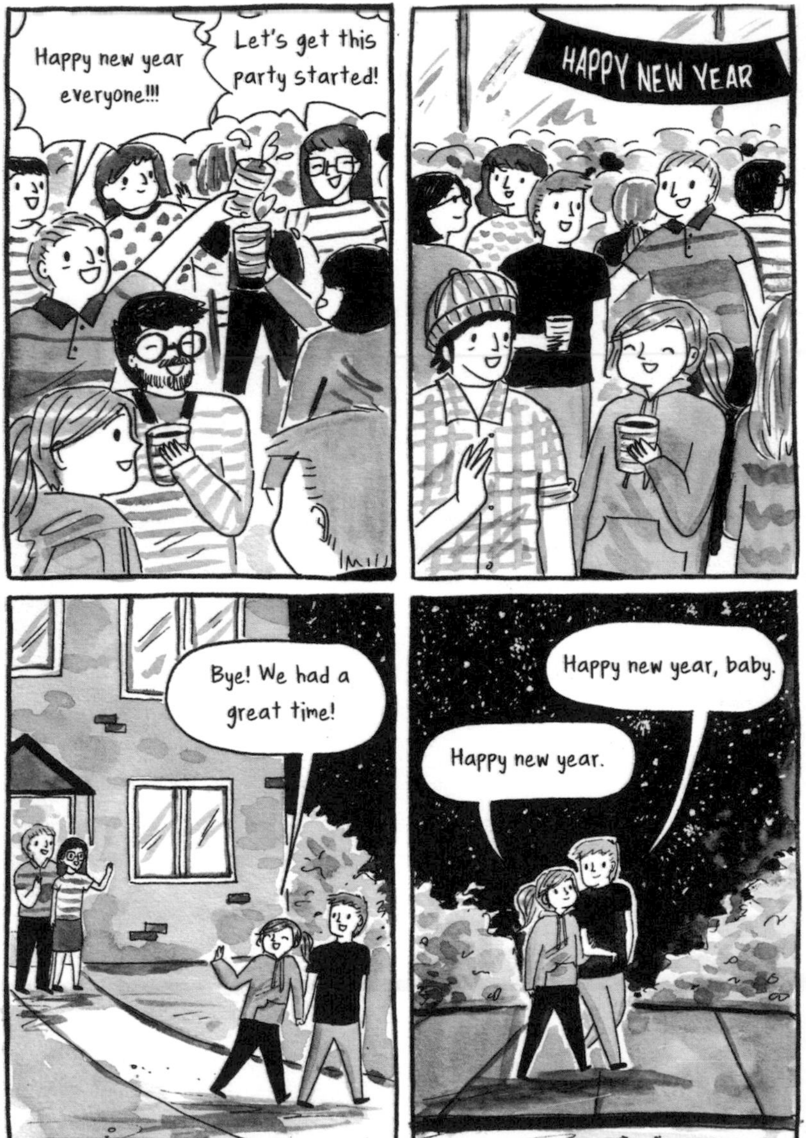
Happy new year everyone!!!
Let's get this party started!
HAPPY NEW YEAR
Bye! We had a great time!
Happy new year, baby.
Happy new year.

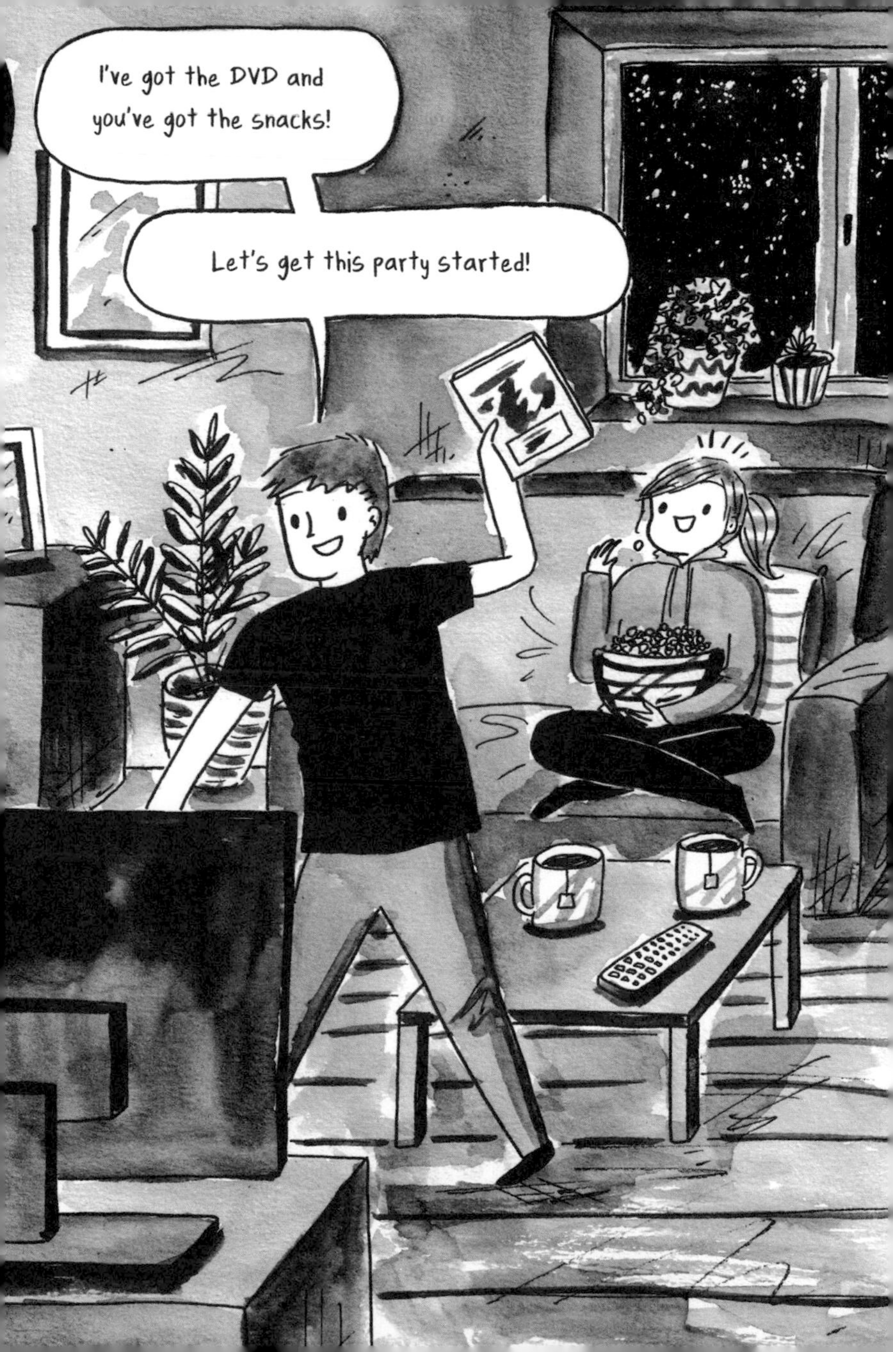
I've got the DVD and you've got the snacks!
Let's get this party started!

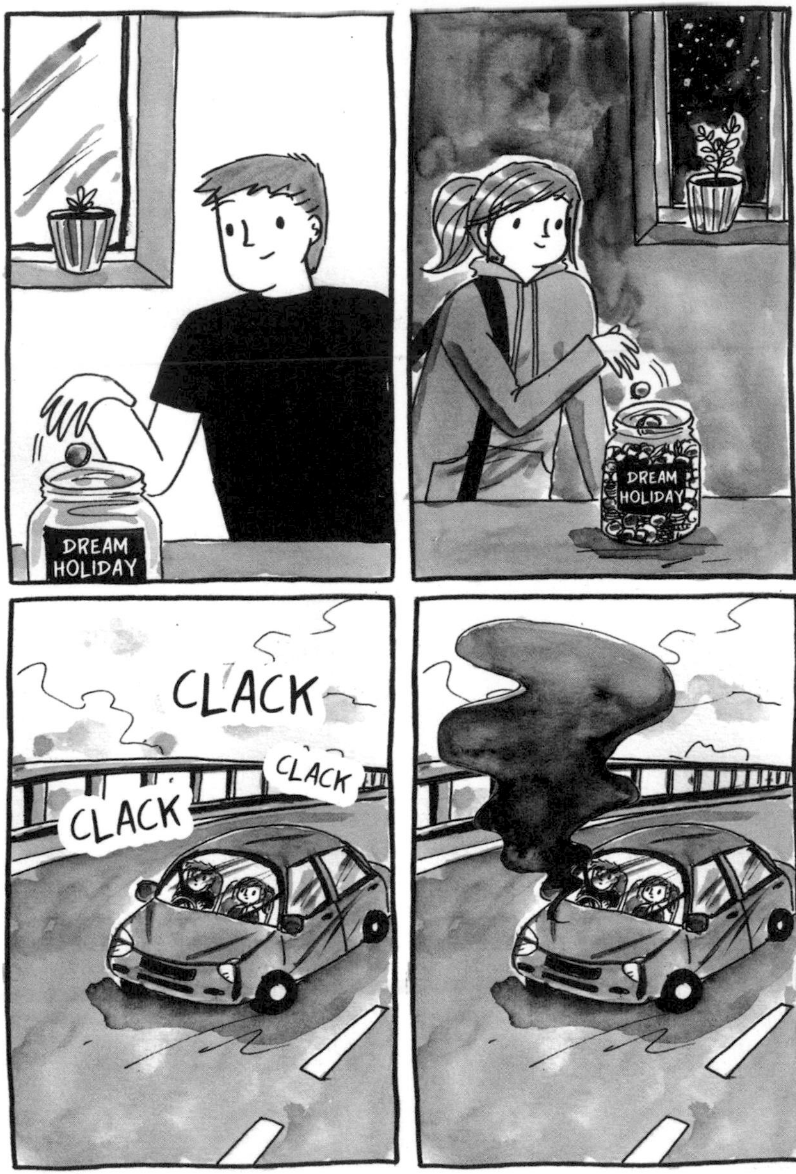
DREAM HOLIDAY
DREAM HOLIDAY
CLACK
CLACK
CLACK

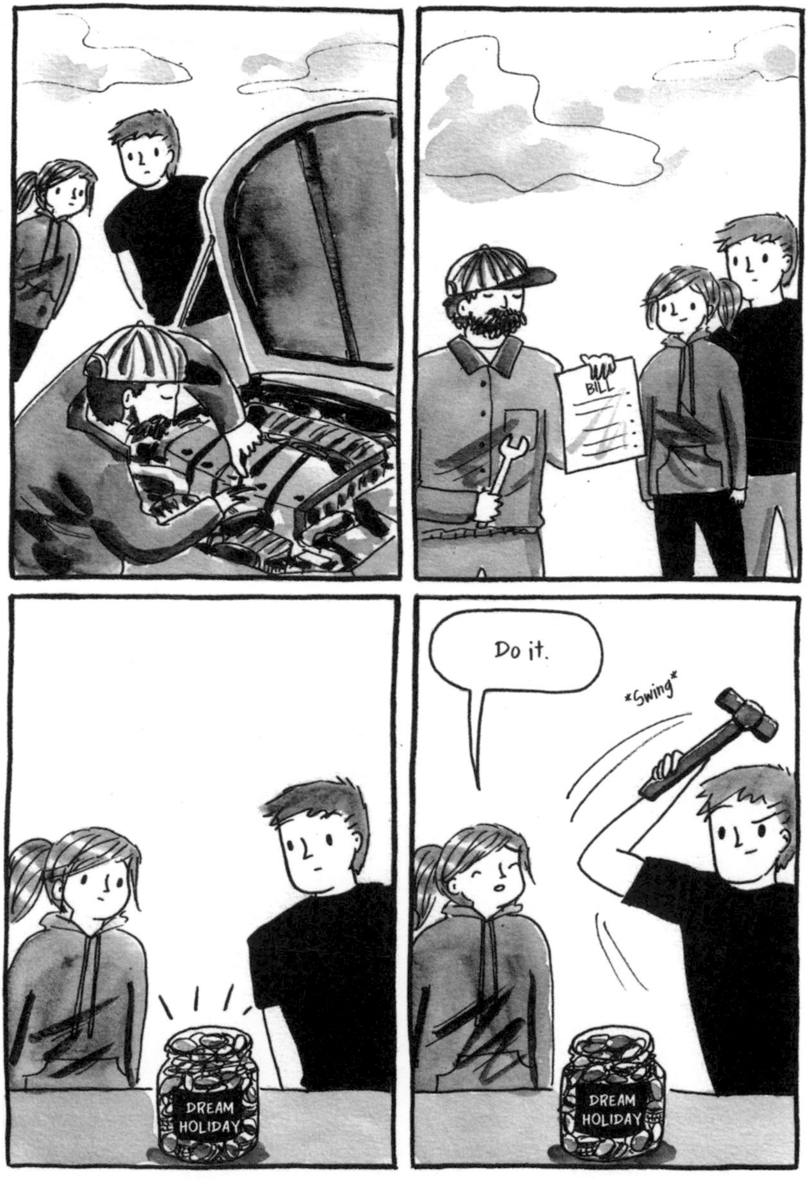
BILL
DREAM HOLIDAY
Do it.
Swing
DREAM HOLIDAY

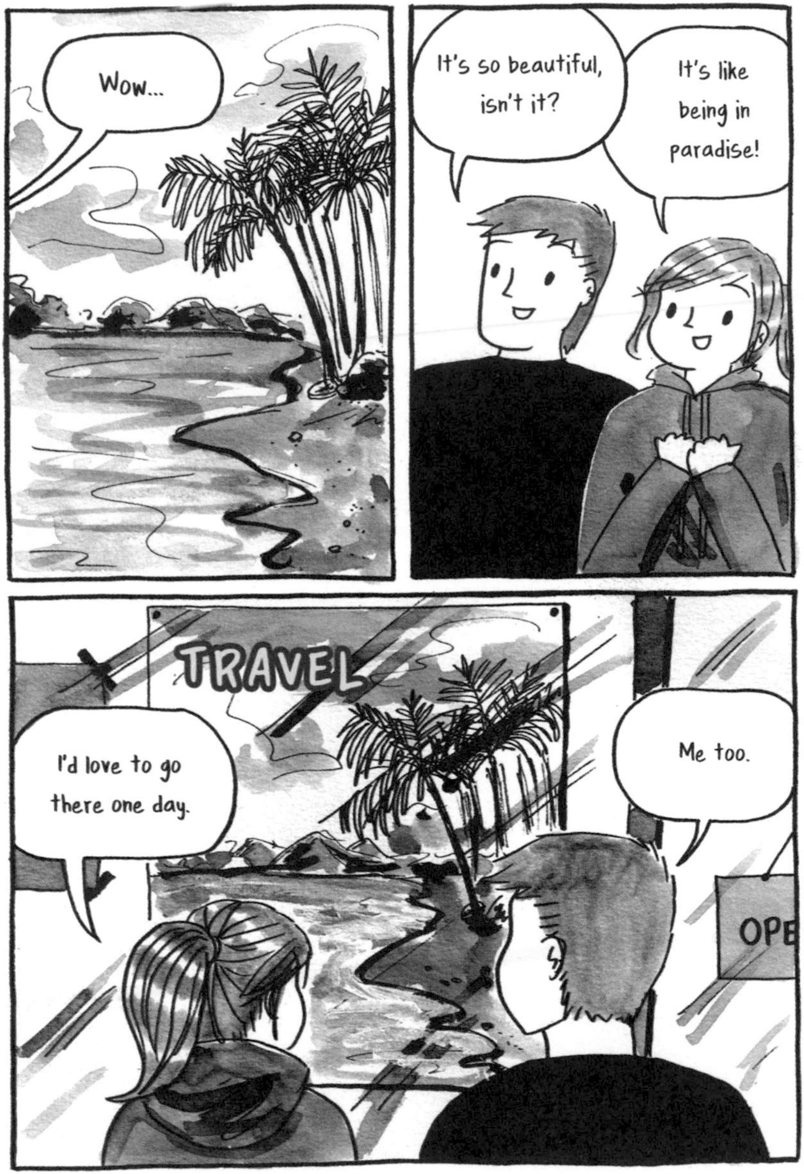
Wow...
It's so beautiful, isn't it?
It's like being in paradise!
TRAVEL
I'd love to go there one day.
Me too.
OPE

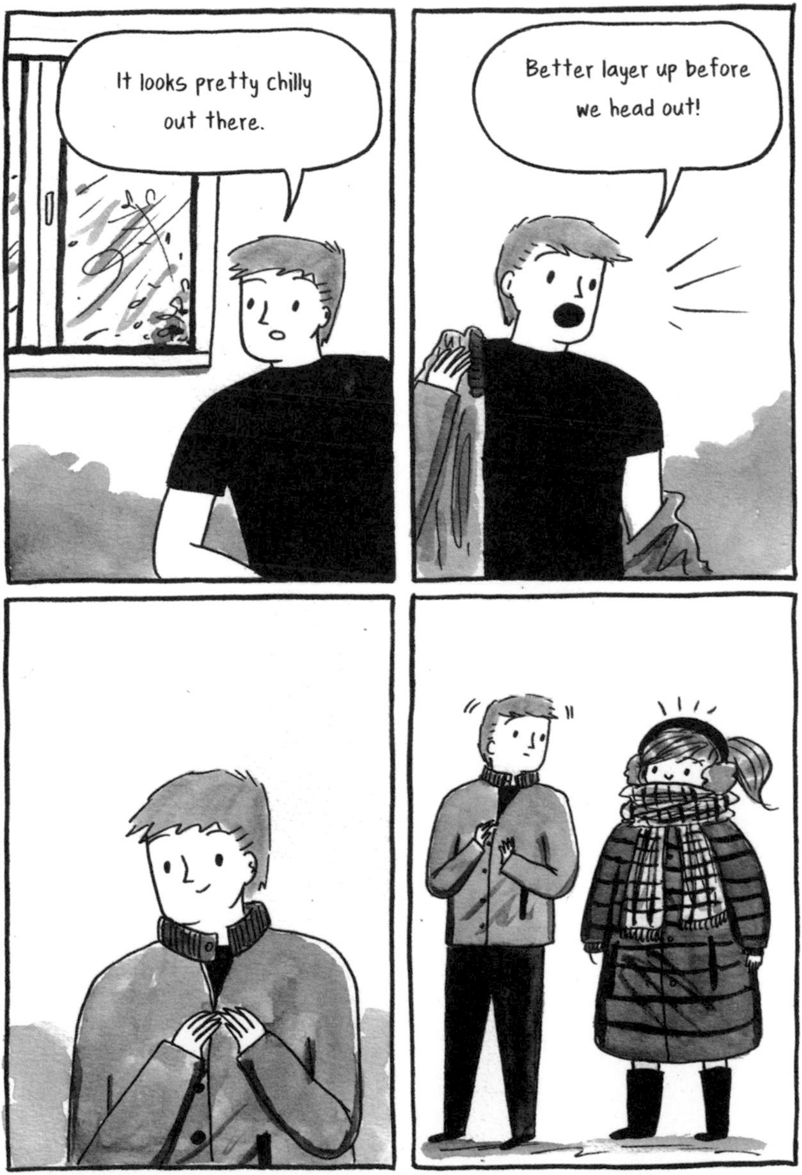
It looks pretty chilly out there.
Better layer up before we head out!

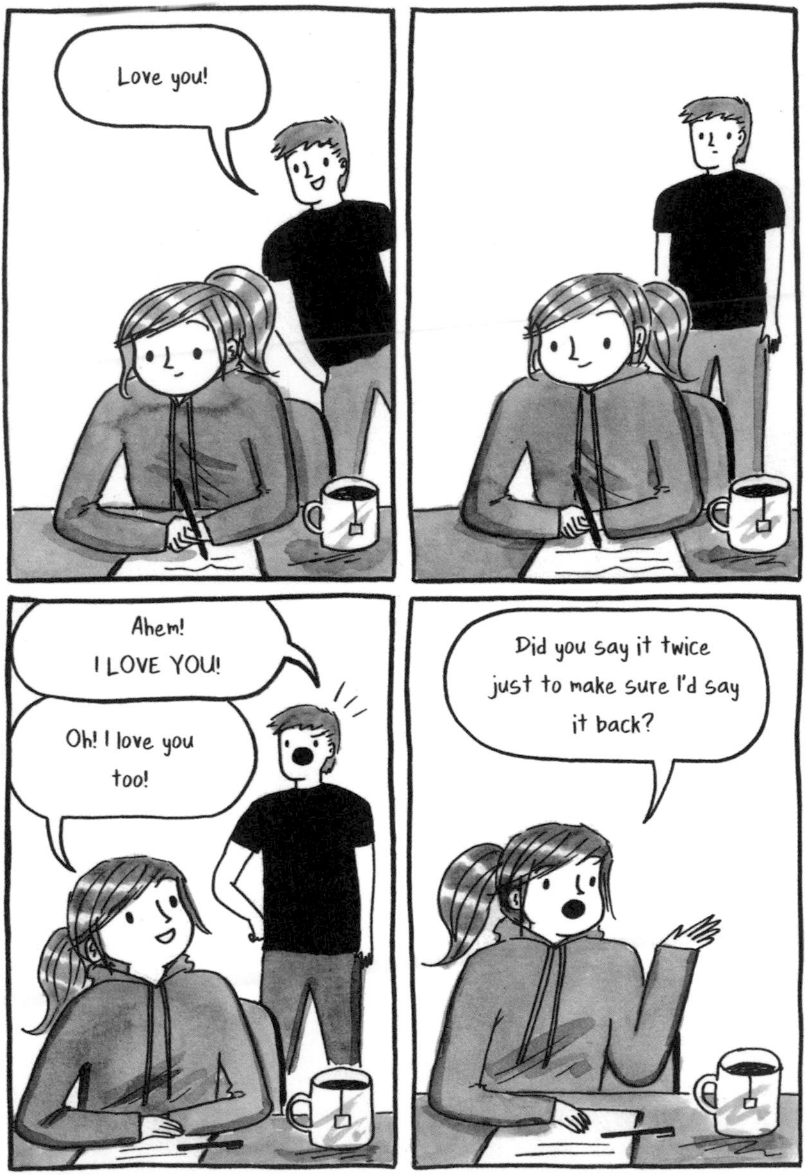
Love you!
Ahem! I LOVE YOU!
Oh! I love you too!
Did you say it twice just to make sure I'd say it back?

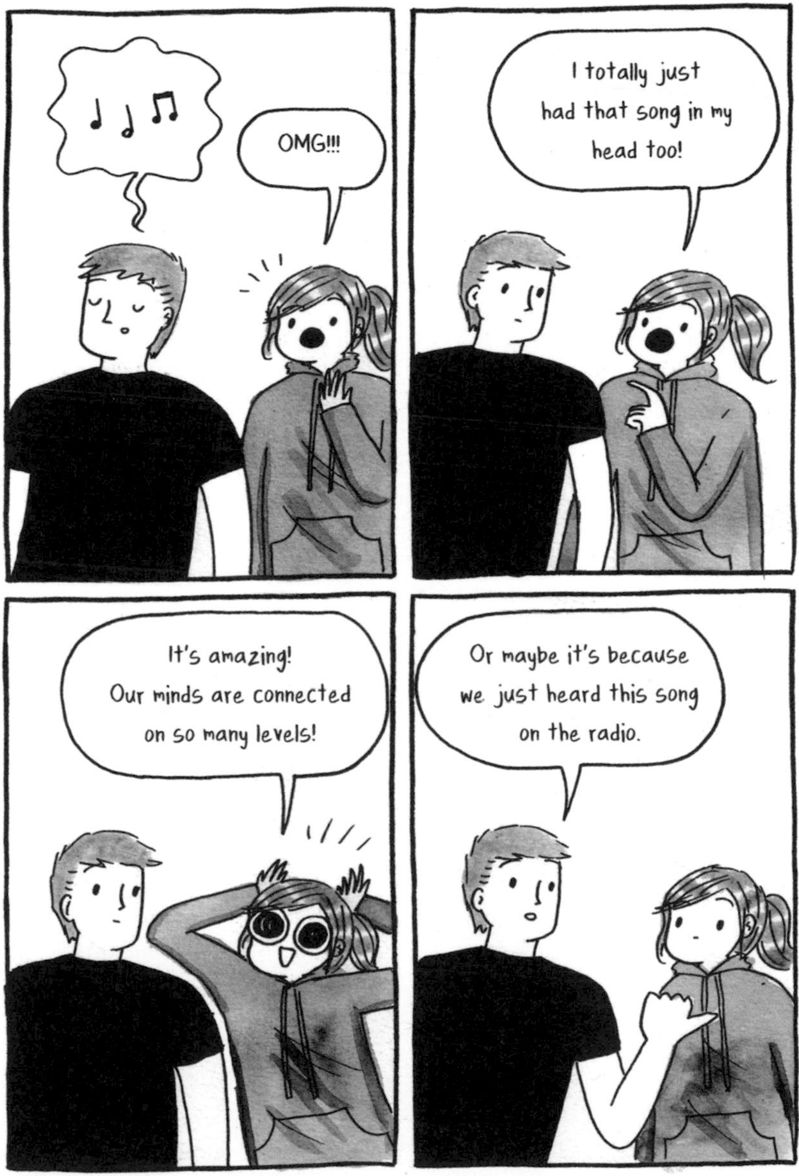
OMG!!!
I totally just had that song in my head too!
It's amazing! Our minds are connected on so many levels!
Or maybe it's because we just heard this song on the radio.

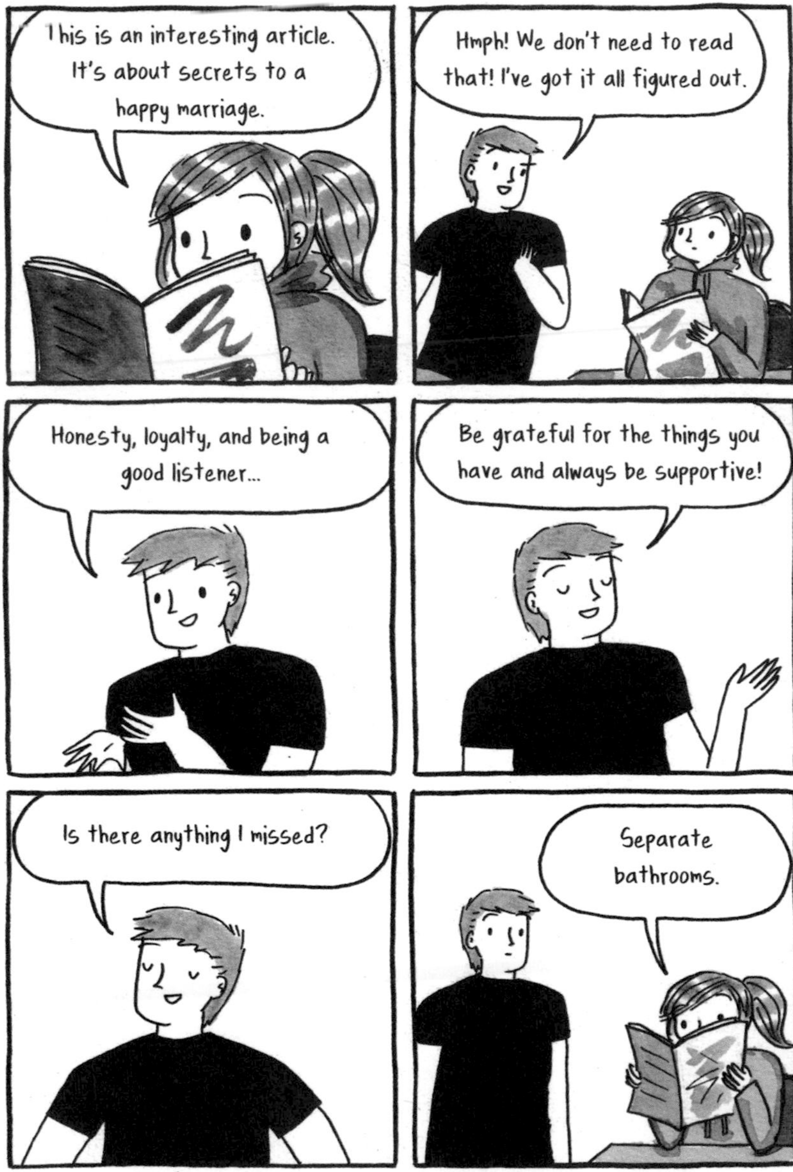
This is an interesting article. It's about secrets to a happy marriage.
Hmph! We don't need to read that! I've got it all figured out.
Honesty, loyalty, and being a good listener...
Be grateful for the things you have and always be supportive!
Is there anything I missed?
Separate bathrooms.

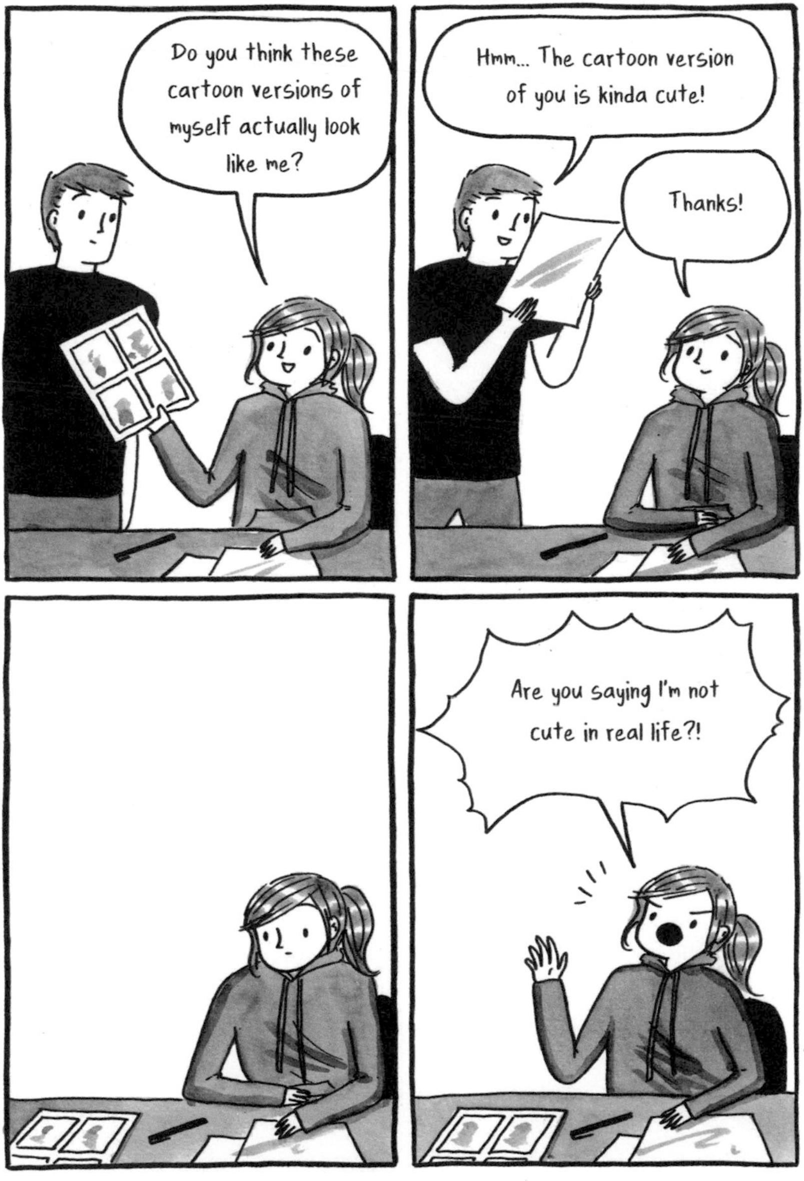
Do you think these cartoon versions of myself actually look like me?
Hmm... The cartoon version of you is kinda cute!
Thanks!
Are you saying I'm not cute in real life?!

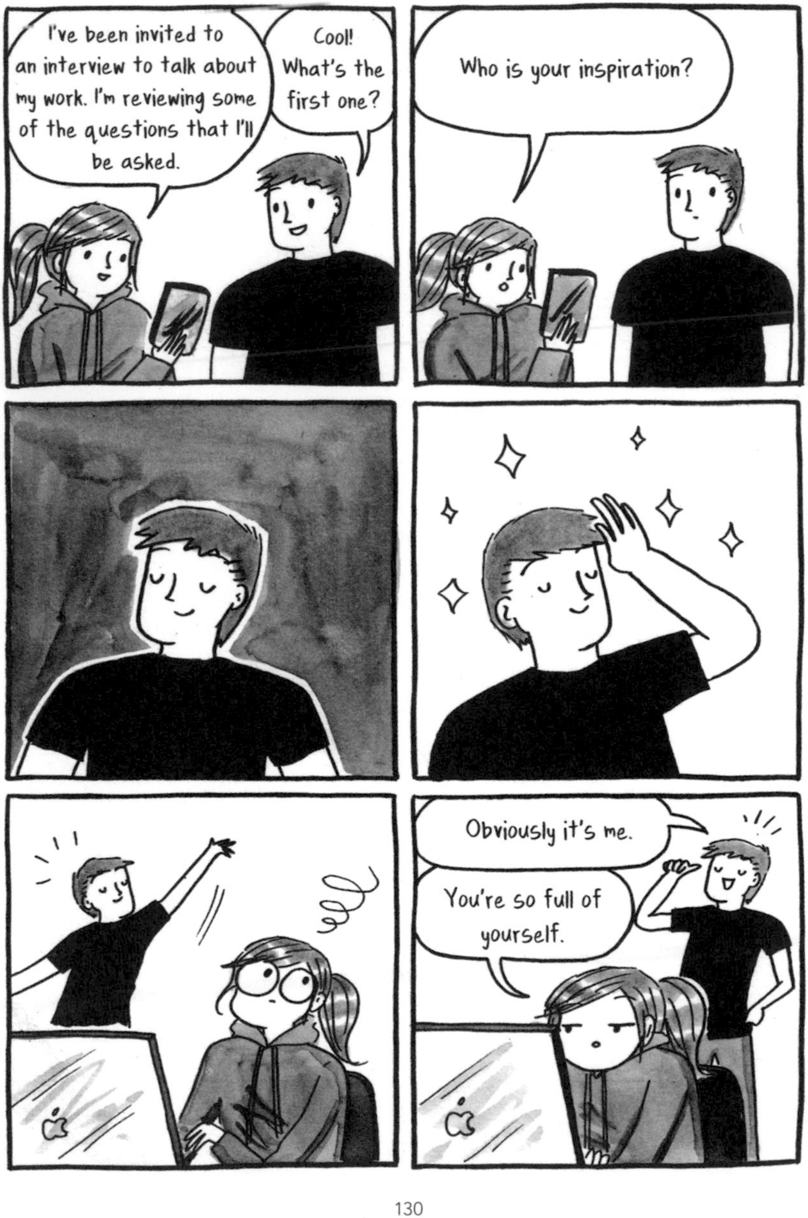
I've been invited to an interview to talk about my work. I'm reviewing some of the questions that I'll be asked.
Cool! What's the first one?
Who is your inspiration?
Obviously it's me.
You're so full of yourself.

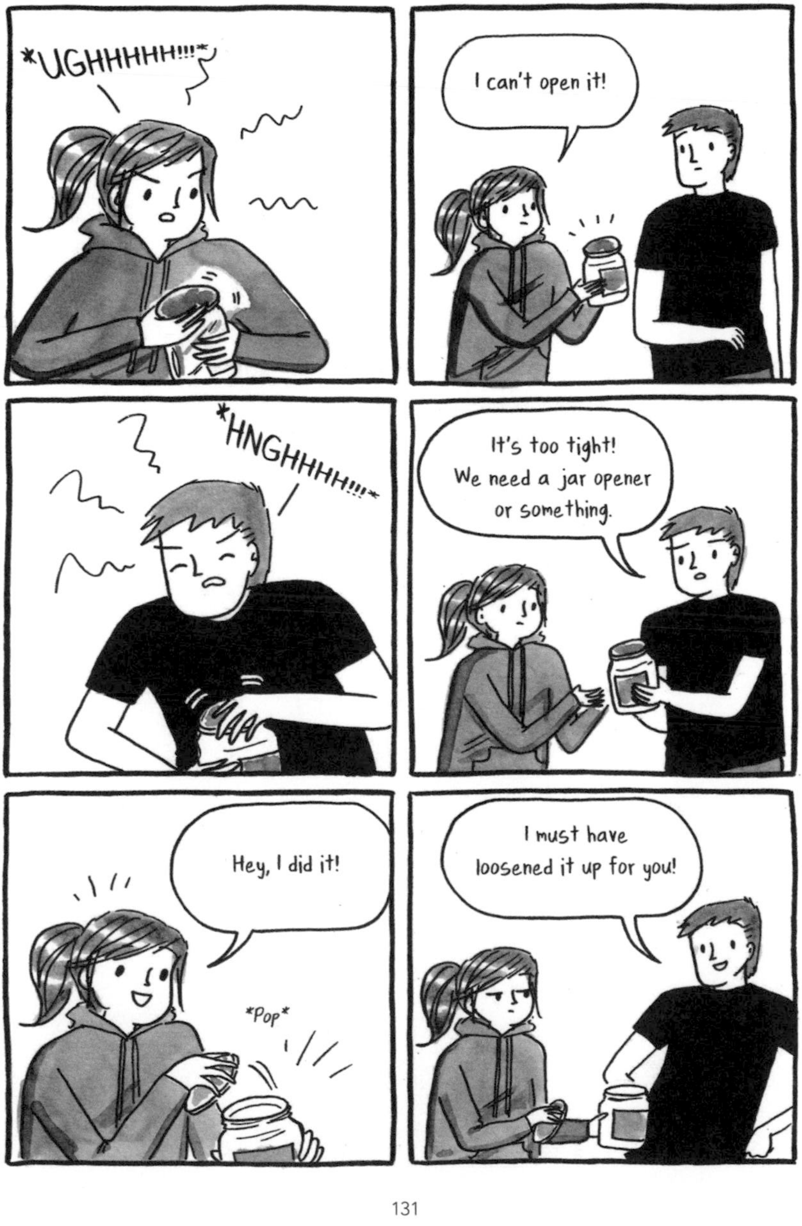
UGHHHHH!!!
I can't open it!
HNGHHHHH!!!
It's too tight! We need a jar opener or something.
Hey, I did it!
Pop
I must have loosened it up for you!

The Thermostat Conundrum

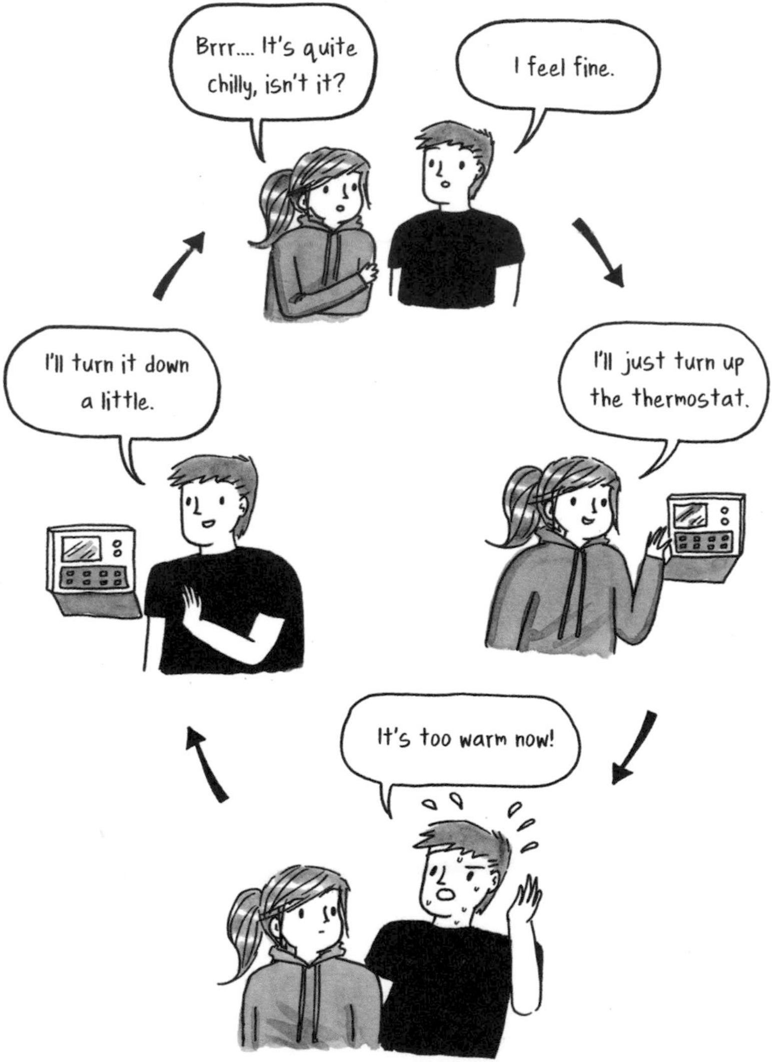

Brrr.... It's quite chilly, isn't it?
I feel fine.
I'll just turn up the thermostat.
It's too warm now!
I'll turn it down a little.

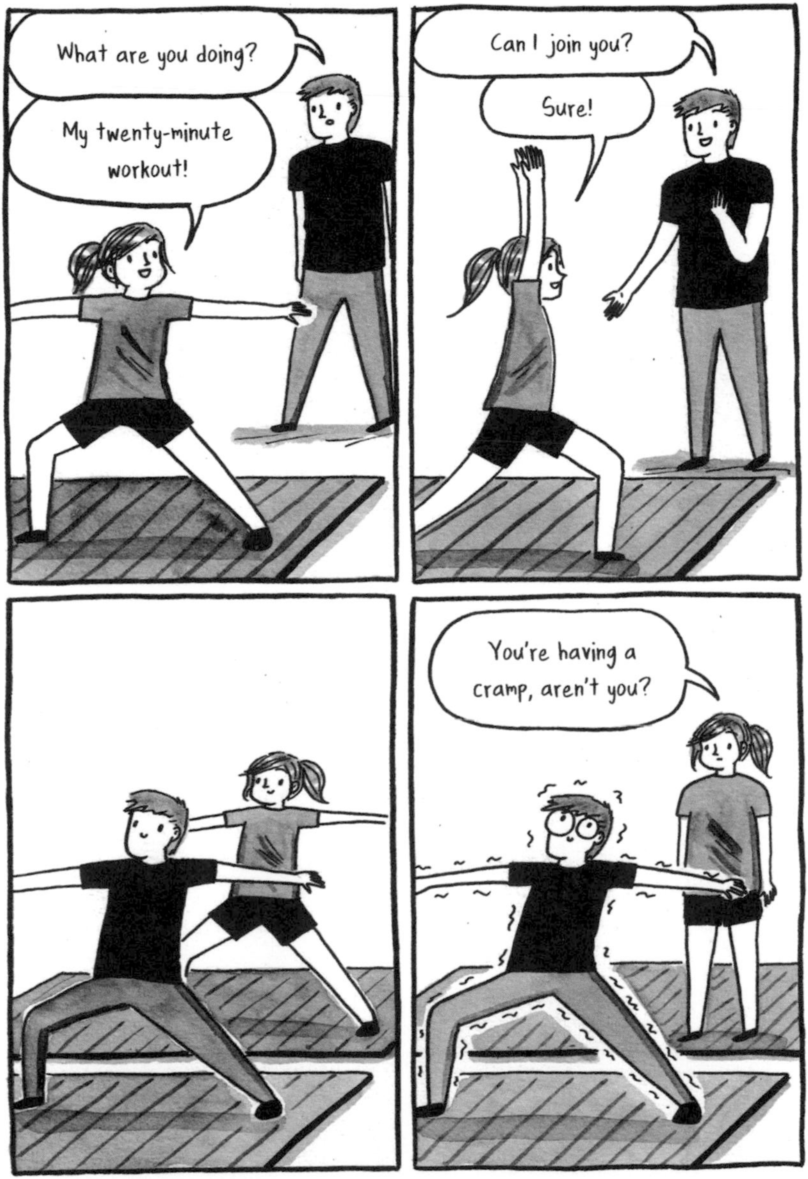
What are you doing?
My twenty-minute workout!
Can I join you?
Sure!
You're having a cramp, aren't you?

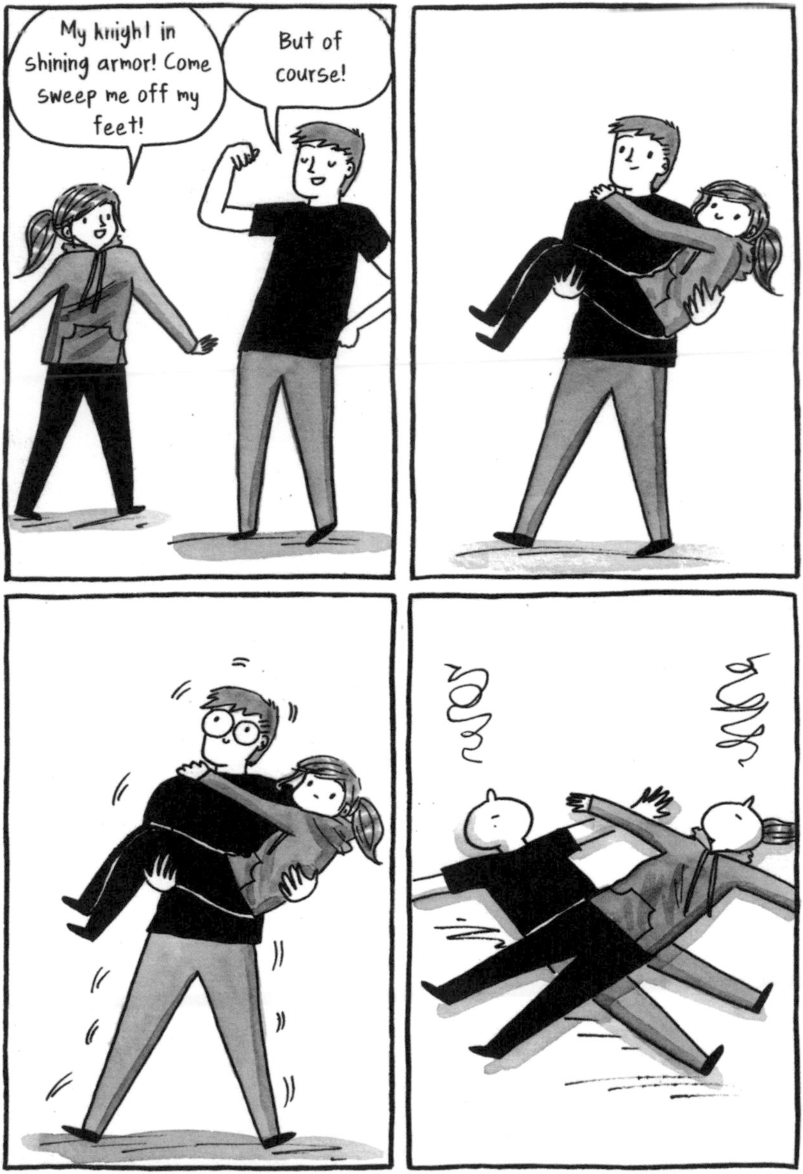
My knight in shining armor! Come sweep me off my feet!
But of course!

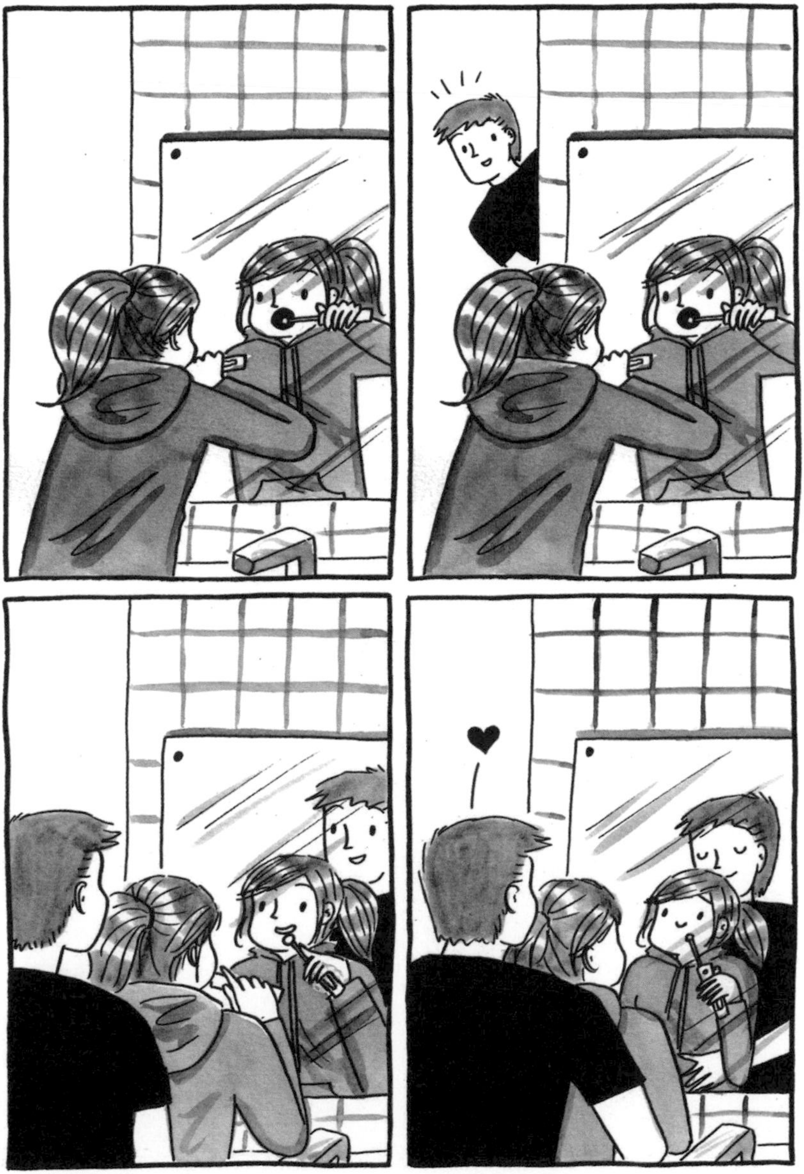

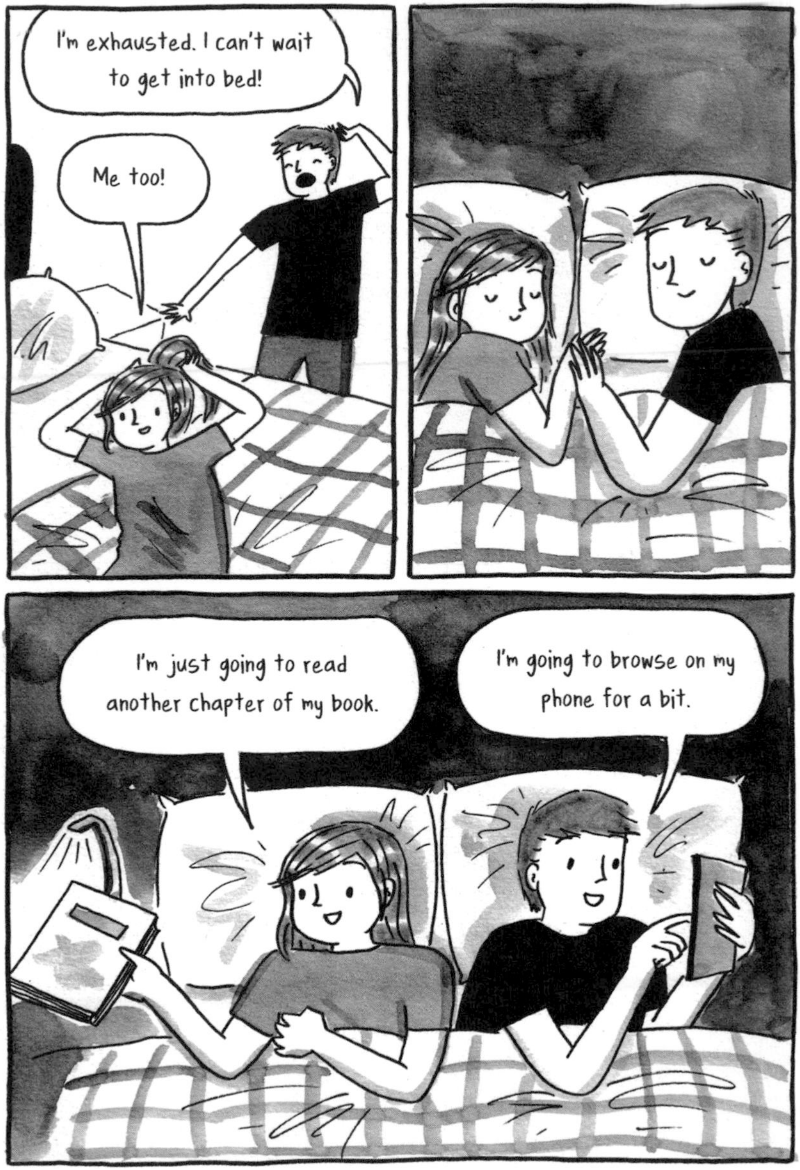
I'm exhausted. I can't wait to get into bed!
Me too!
I'm just going to read another chapter of my book.
I'm going to browse on my phone for a bit.

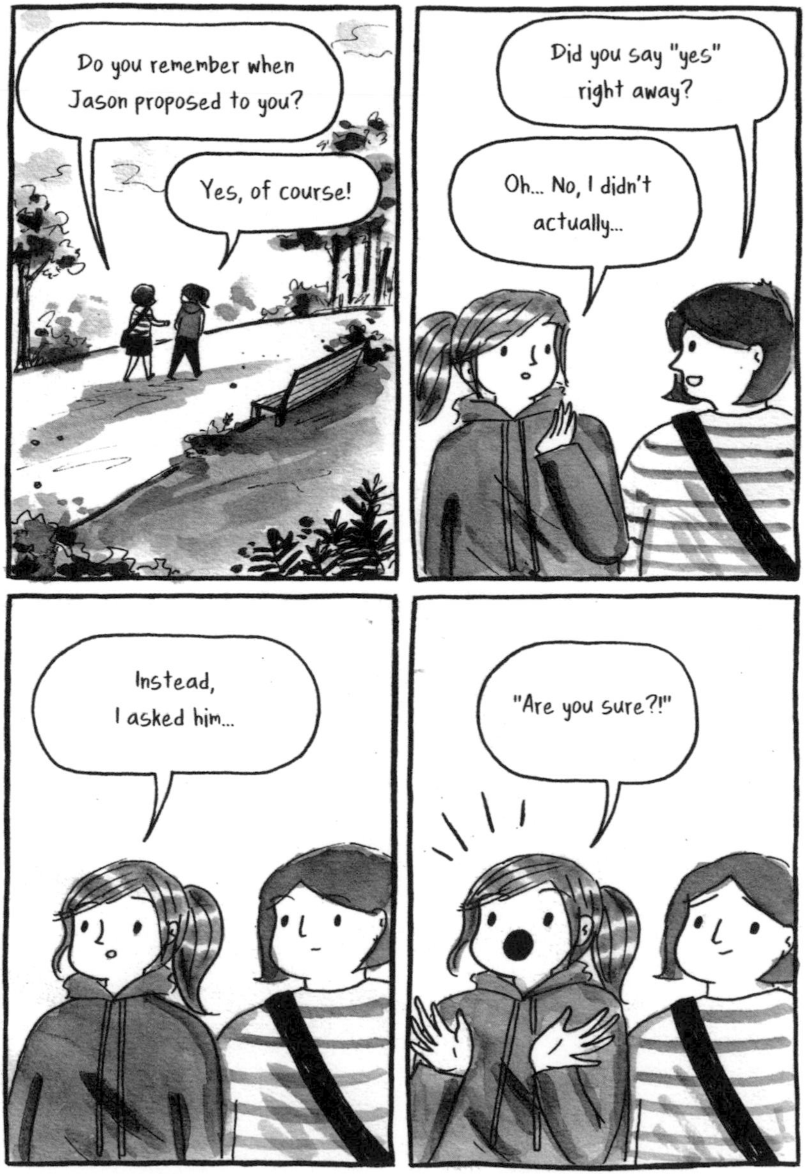
Do you remember when Jason proposed to you?
Yes, of course!
Did you say "yes" right away?
Oh... No, I didn't actually...
Instead, I asked him...
"Are you sure?!"

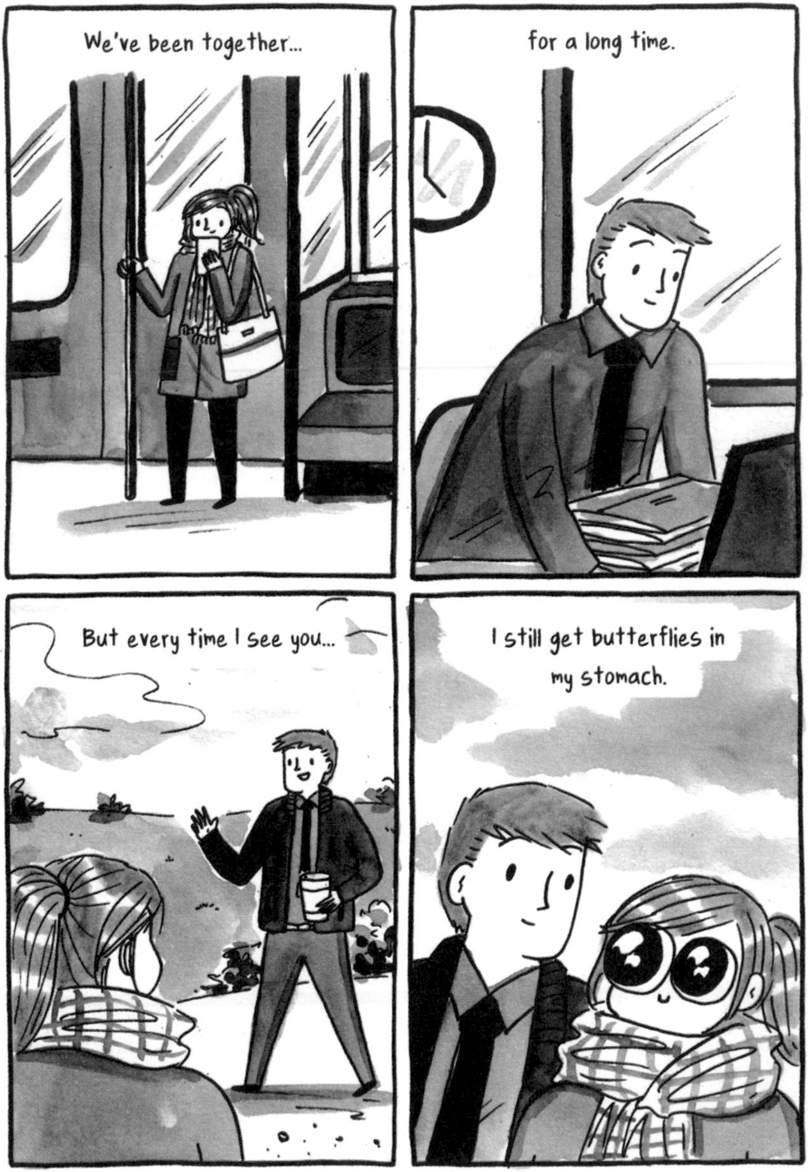
We've been together...
for a long time.
But every time I see you...
I still get butterflies in my stomach.

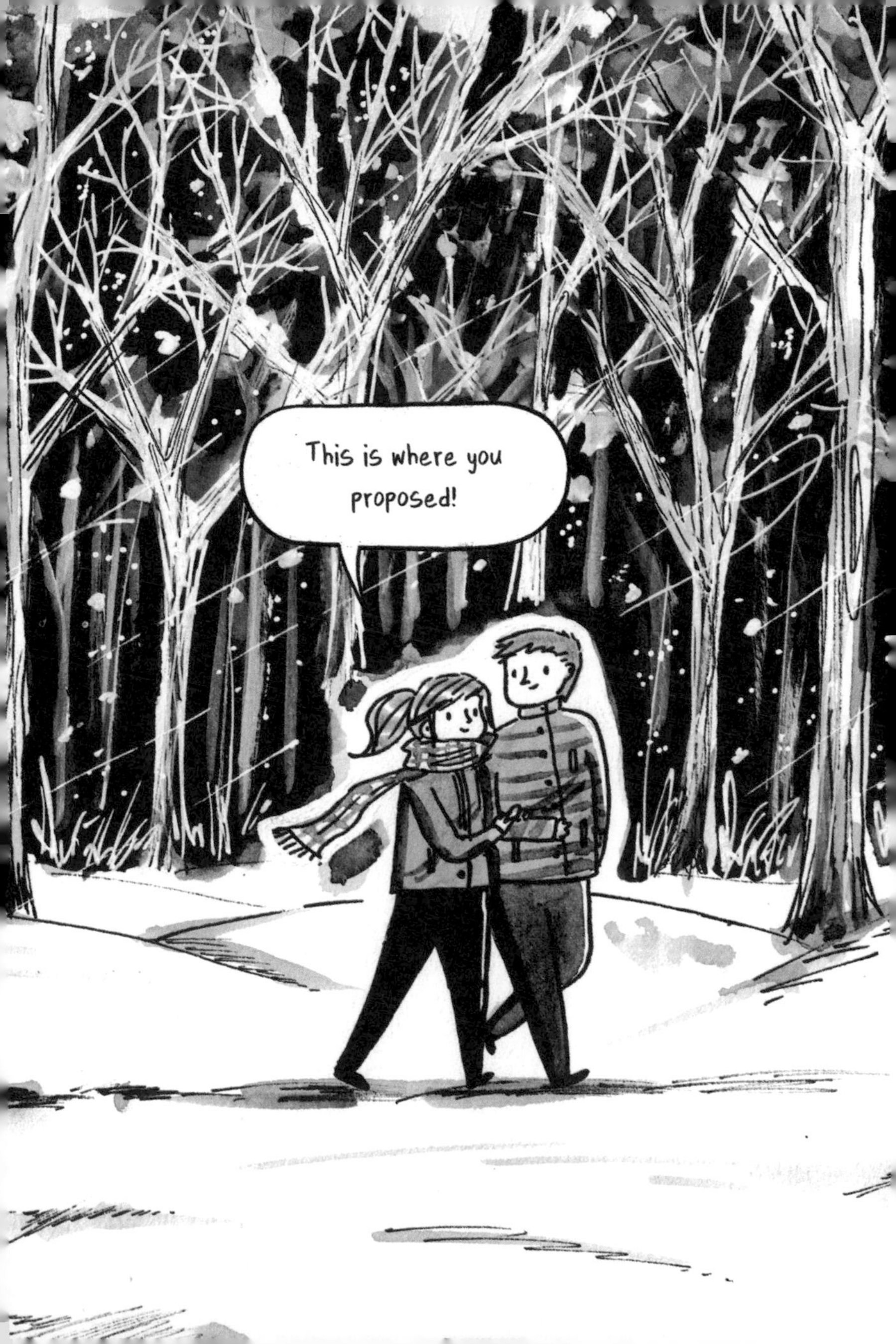
This is where you proposed!

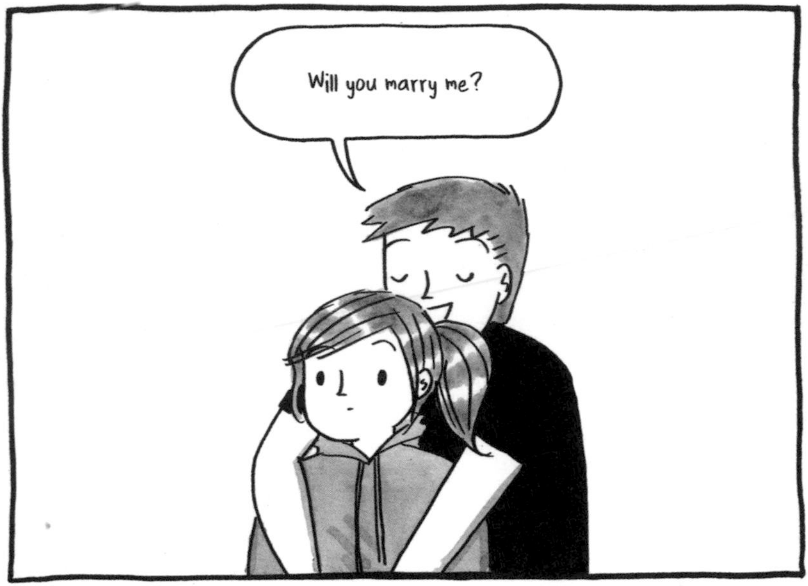
Will you marry me?

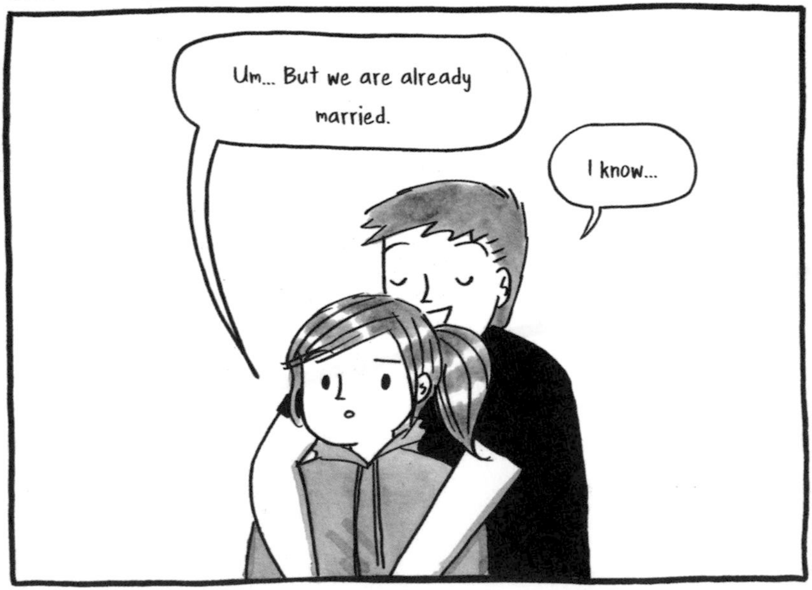
Um... But we are already married.
I know...

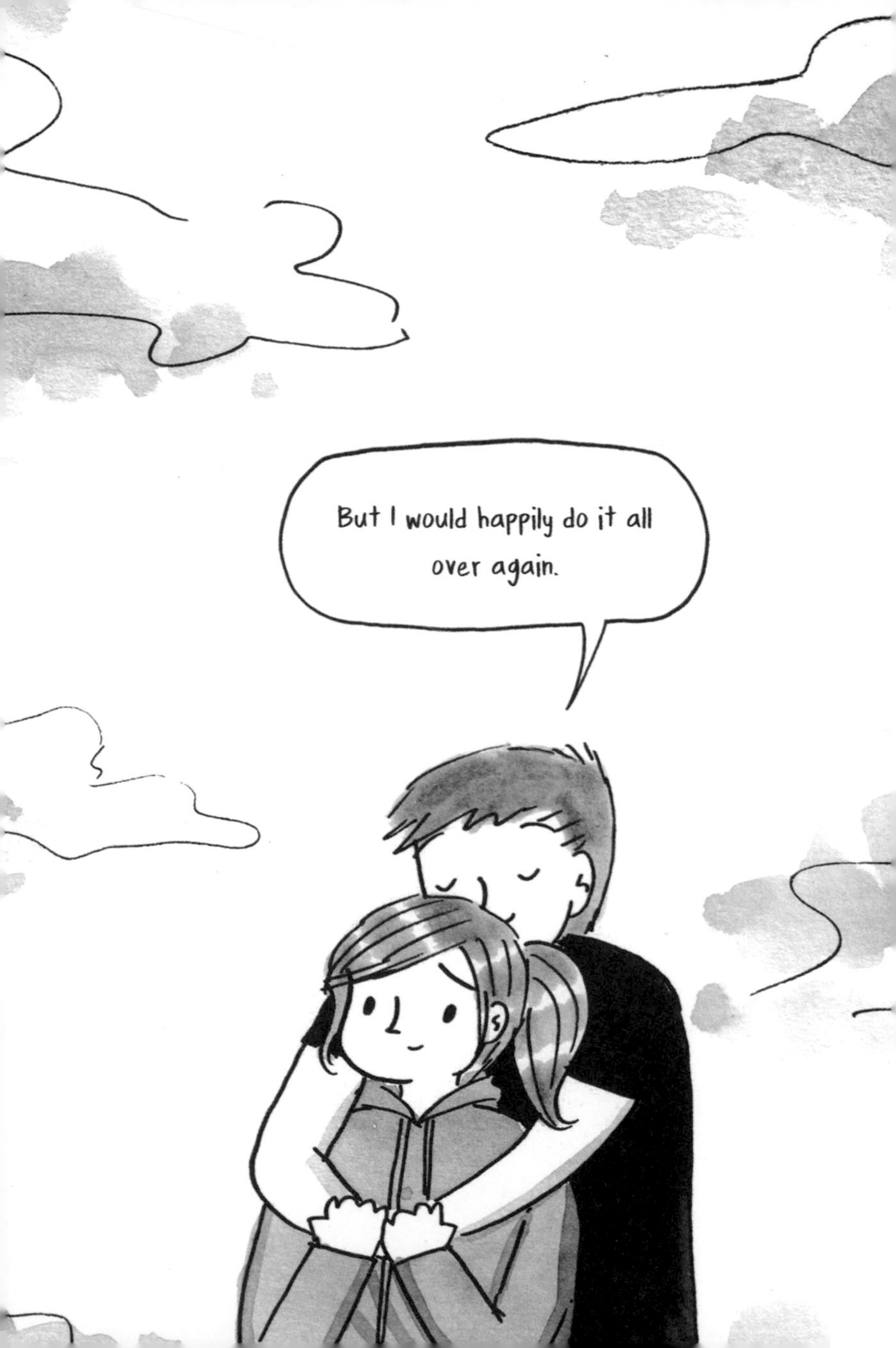
But I would happily do it all over again.

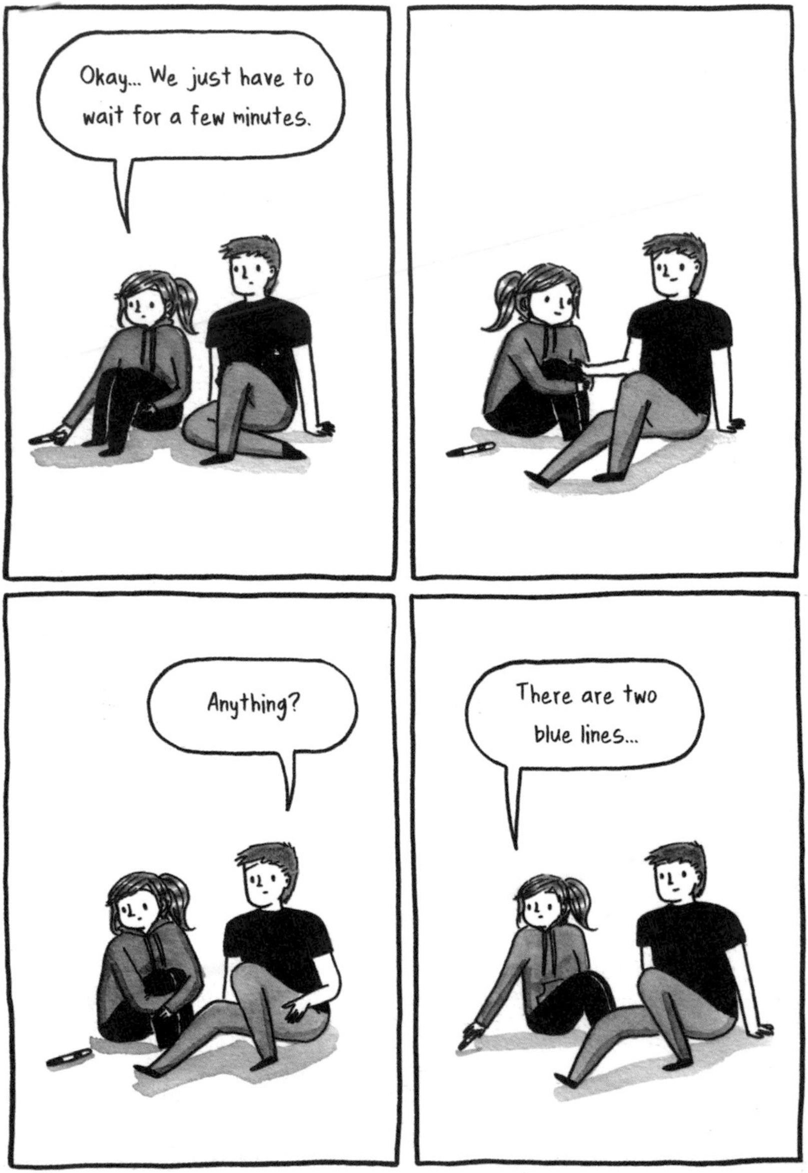
Okay... We just have to wait for a few minutes.
Anything?
There are two blue lines...

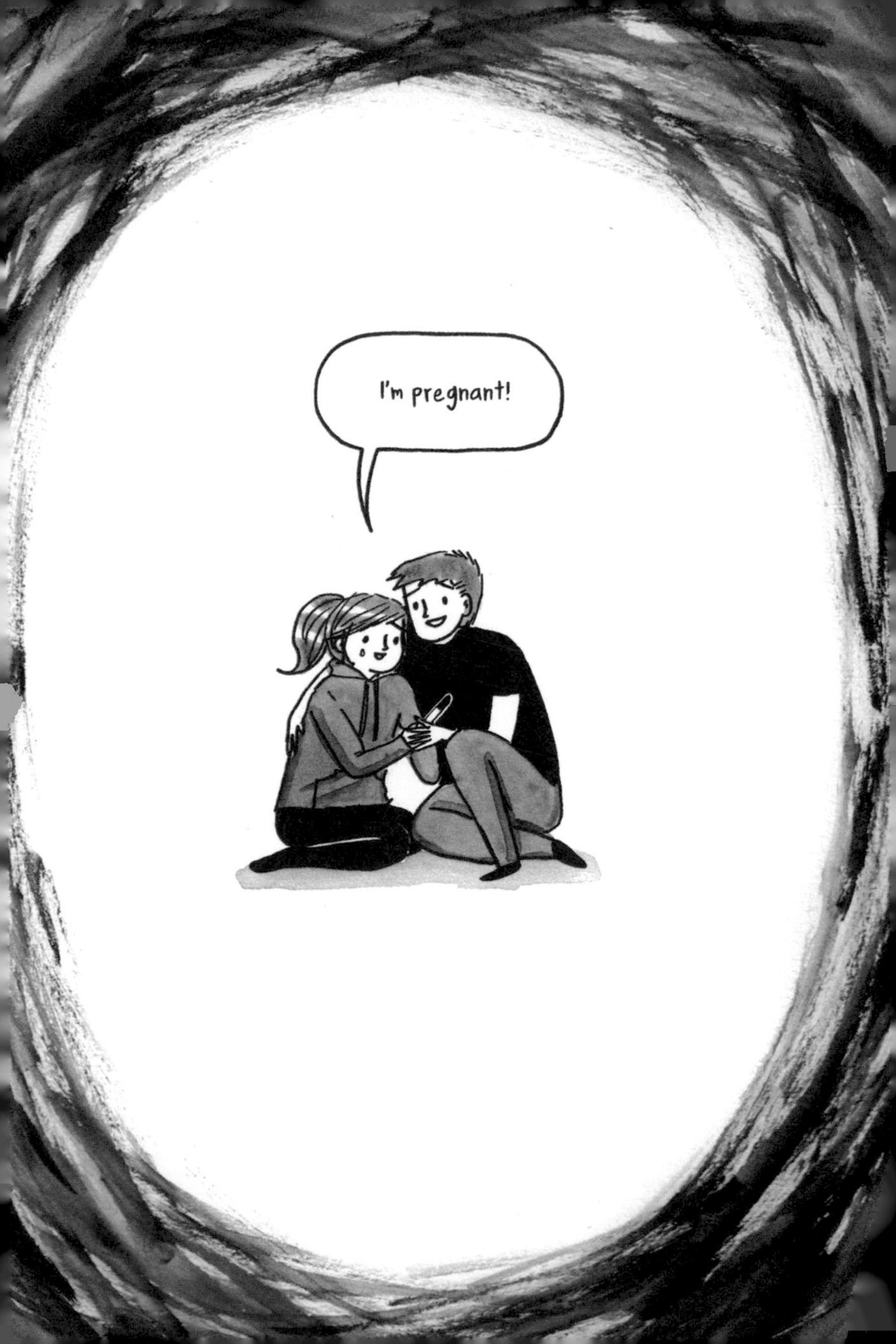
I'm pregnant!

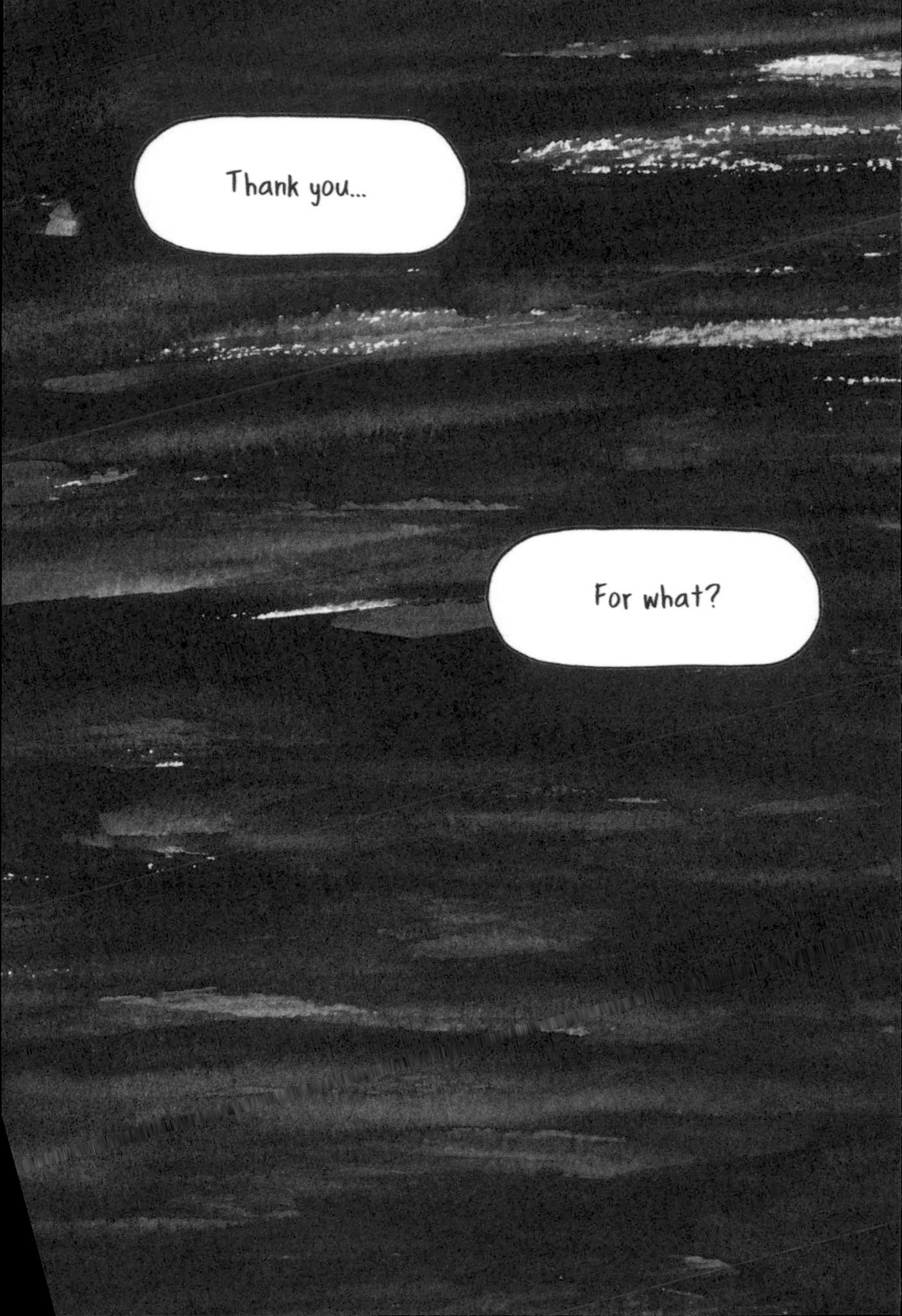
Thank you...
For what?

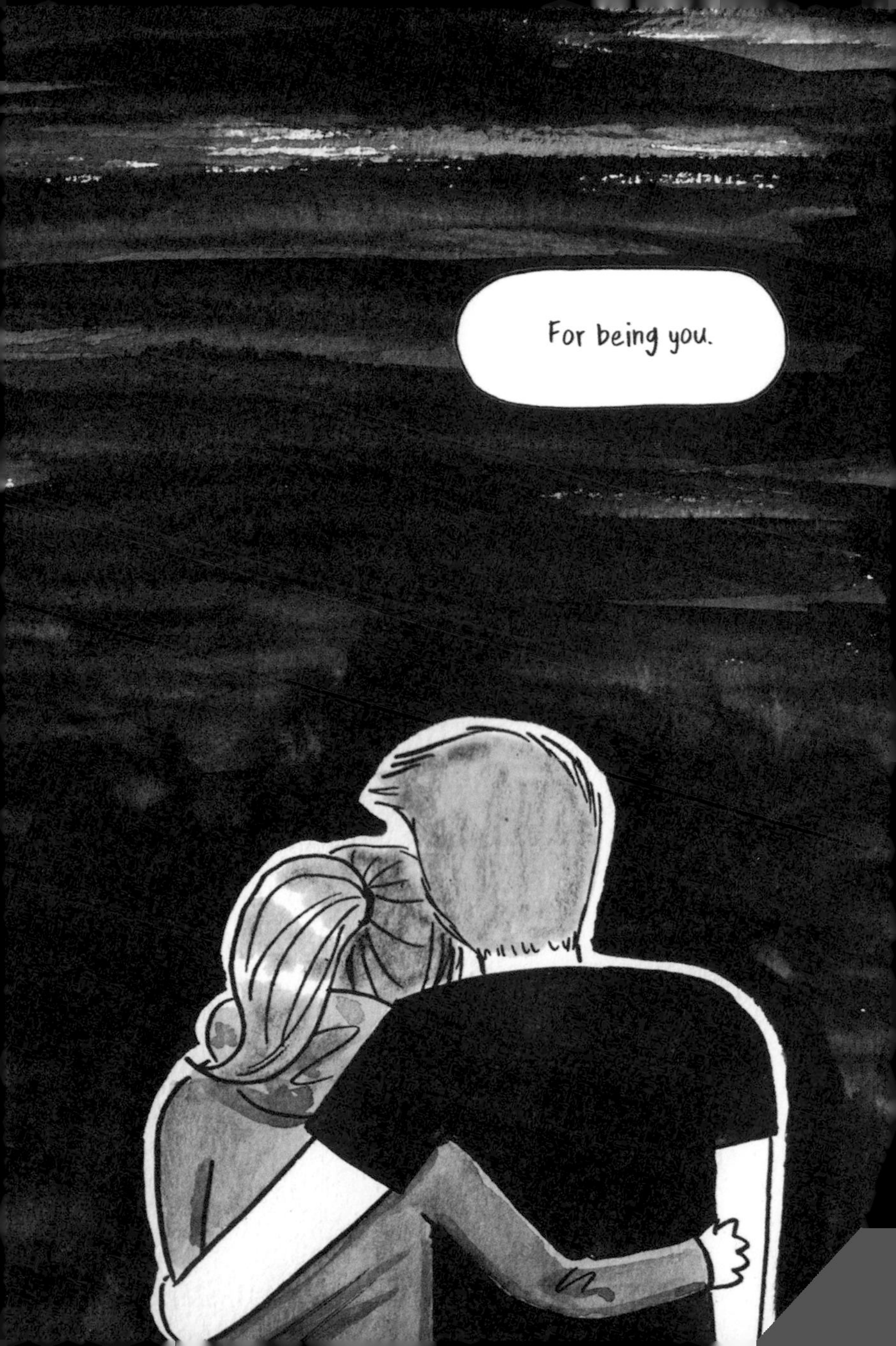
For being you.

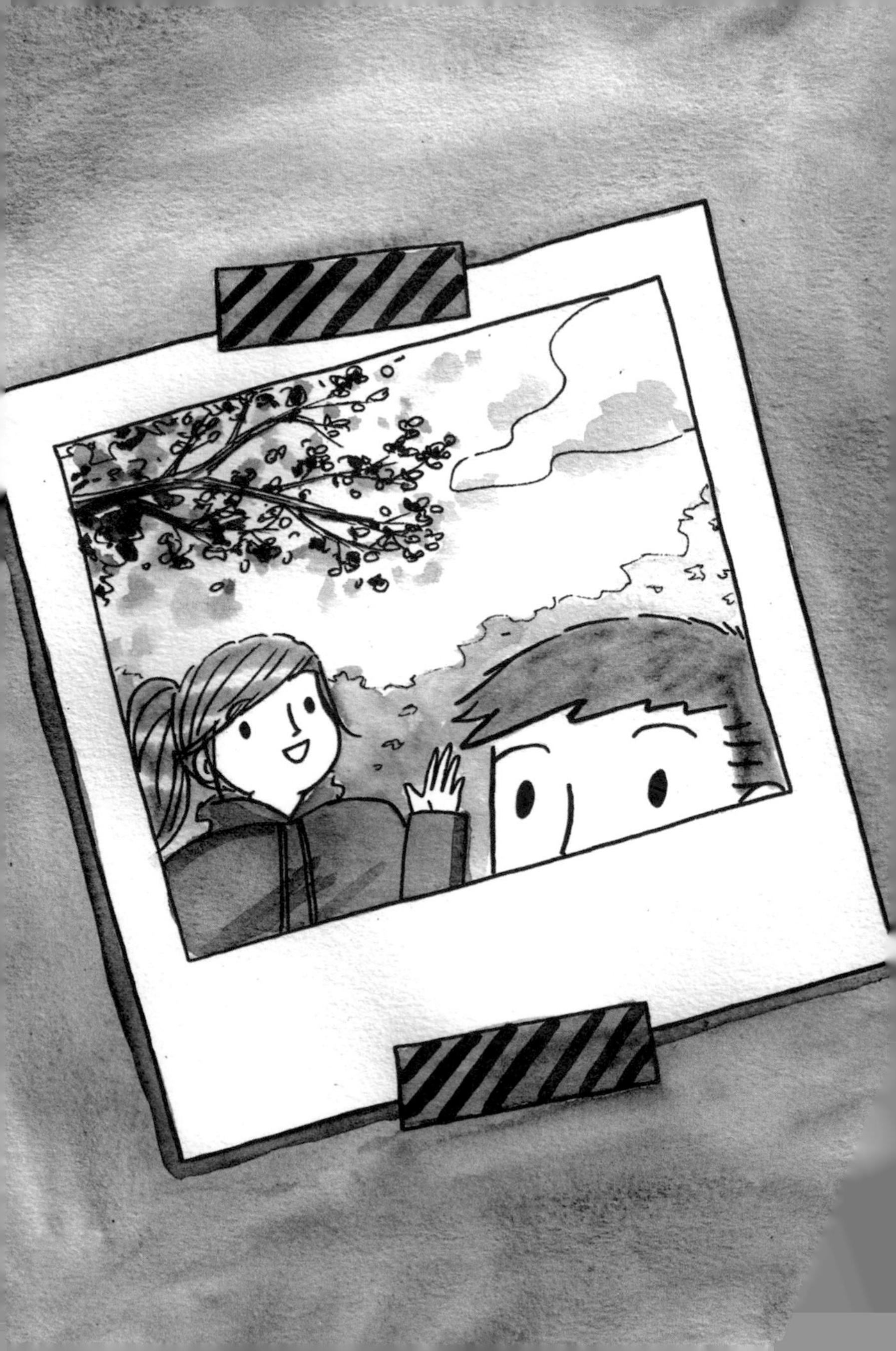

About the Author

Debbie Tung is a cartoonist and illustrator based in Birmingham, England. She draws about everyday life and her love for books and tea. Debbie is also the author of *Book Love* and *Quiet Girl in a Noisy World*, which was listed as a recommended read in *O, The Oprah Magazine*. Her comics have been shared widely by *HuffPost*, *9GAG*, *Bored Panda*, and *Goodreads*, among others.

You can see more of Debbie's work on her website (www.debbietung.com) and social media (@WheresMyBubble).

Andrews McMeel Publishing
a division of Andrews McMeel Universal
1130 Walnut Street, Kansas City, Missouri 64106

www.andrewsmcmeel.com

20 21 22 23 24 SDB 10 9 8 7 6 5 4 3 2 1

ISBN: 978-1-5248-5066-1

Library of Congress Control Number: 2019954189

Editor: Patty Rice
Art Director/Designer: Diane Marsh
Production Editor: Elizabeth A. Garcia
Production Manager: Tamara Haus

Attention: Schools and Businesses
Andrews McMeel books are available at quantity discounts
with bulk purchase for educational, business, or sales
promotional use. For information, please e-mail the
Andrews McMeel Publishing Special Sales Department:
specialsales@amuniversal.com.